*Children Who Kill*

# Children Who Kill

## Profiles of Pre-teen and Teenage Killers

## CAROL ANNE DAVIS

First published in Great Britain in 2003 by
Allison & Busby Limited
Bon Marche Centre
241-251 Ferndale Road
Brixton, London SW9 8BJ
*http://www.allisonandbusby.com*

A catalogue record for this book is available from the British Library

ISBN 0 7490 0610 2

Printed and bound in Ebbw Vale,
by Creative Print & Design

CAROL ANNE DAVIS was born in Dundee, moved to Edinburgh in her twenties and now lives in southern England. She left school at fifteen and was everything from an artist's model to an editorial assistant before going to university. Her Master of the Arts degree included criminology and was followed by a postgraduate diploma in Adult & Community Education.

A full time writer since graduating, her crime novels *Shrouded*, *Safe As Houses*, *Noise Abatement* and *Kiss It Away* have been described as chillingly realistic for their portrayals of dangerous sex and death. She is also the author of a previous true crime book *Women Who Kill: Profiles of Female Serial Killers*.

Carol's website can be found at www.tellitlikeitis.demon.co.uk

*For Ian*

# Contents

# Acknowledgements

I'd like to thank Claire Rayner OBE for talking to me about the dangers of offering violence to children. Claire has published numerous books on medical issues and has been an energetic advocate of children's rights throughout her life.

I also thank Ron Sagar MBE for answering my interview questions in depth and for providing unique details. As a Detective Superintendent, he interviewed Britain's most prolific juvenile killer, Bruce Lee, at least twenty-eight times. With over thirty years experience in criminal investigation, Ron offered much insight into Bruce, a multiply-abused boy who claimed twenty-six lives.

I was similarly fortunate in interviewing Don Hale who fought for seven years to gain the freedom of the wrongly imprisoned Stephen Downing. Stephen was seventeen when he was jailed for a murder he didn't commit - and was forty-four before his conviction was overturned and he was finally freed. As a result of his first class journalism on the case, Don Hale was made both Man Of The Year and Journalist Of The Year in 2000. I'm delighted that he took time out of his busy schedule to contribute to this book.

Thanks also to crime writer David Bell for drawing my attention to an interesting case I hadn't heard of. David is author of the *Staffordshire Murder Casebook*, *Nottinghamshire Murder Casebook* and *Leicestershire Murder Casebook* amongst others.

Most of my interviewees live in England, but my thanks extend overseas to Florida-based Lisa Dumond, a contributing editor to *Black Gate* and many other science fiction magazines. Though hard at work on her latest novel - and busily promoting her existing novel *Darkers* - Lisa helped me track down some vital criminal facts.

I'm also grateful to the organisations which answered my questions and sent me invaluable reports, namely *The Children's Society*, *Children Are Unbeatable*, *Save The Children*, *Kidscape* and *The Howard League For Penal Reform*. Finally, my thanks to The Home Office for providing me with year by year statistics of children who kill.

# Preface

As a child, I was friends with a twelve-year-old boy who attempted to murder a slightly older girl. They'd argued over which television programme to watch and he fetched a knife from the kitchen and thrust it deep into her back. Paul (not his real name) then left the room.

At first the girl thought that Paul had just punched her very hard. She felt ill and lay down on the settee on her stomach. When the pain intensified she looked back and saw the protruding handle of the knife.

The teenager staggered downstairs to alert a neighbour. Thankfully the neighbour left the weapon in situ - if she'd pulled it out, the girl would certainly have died. As it was, the blade had done irreversible damage to one of her lungs and she spent weeks in hospital, initially in intensive care. She later faced reconstructive surgery for the hole left in her back and had to take strong prescrption drugs to help her sleep.

Twelve-year-old Paul now faced an attempted murder charge - but numerous adults came forward to say what a polite and helpful boy he was. He belonged to a youth organisation and they too were very impressed with him. The judge recommended that he see a psychiatrist and the parents said that they'd arrange this, but didn't. His teenage victim was terrified that he'd attack her again.

It's unclear how much the judge knew of Paul's background - but I know that he and his siblings were regularly terrorised by their alcoholic father. He verbally mocked them and beat them with his belt. Paul's mother did nothing to stop these sessions, instead adopting a slightly martyred tone and telling anyone who would listen that her children were very polite to strangers and that she couldn't understand why they glared at her when they were at home.

In fairness, I really liked Paul's parents and spent as much time as possible with them. Both had the capacity to be kind and generous to a child who wasn't their own. Paul's mother cooked me excellent meals and both parents took me with them on family outings, adventures I'd otherwise never have enjoyed. It was only in child-nurturing that they failed, presumably parenting as they had been parented.

Paul's attempted murder charge was just one of numerous instances of violence in my childhood so it quickly faded from my consciousness. I rarely thought of it again until halfway through writing this book. Only then did I realise that Paul's story had the same ingredients as almost every child's story that you'll find here. That is, the child is physically and emotionally abused by an adult or adults, often the very people that created him. In turn, he - or she - goes on to perpetrate violence on someone else.

The children in this book tortured, burnt, battered, strangled or raped their victims - victims aged from two years old to eighty. But these young killers had been tortured, burnt, battered, half strangled or raped before they carried out their pitiless acts.

The first two profiles are historic ones which demonstrate that children who kill aren't a modern phenomenon brought about by horror videos or by single parent families. There are also brief details of other latter day killers in some of the sociological chapters, one of which bears a striking resemblance to the Robert Thompson and Jon Venables case.

The rest of the profiles are contemporary, featuring young killers from Britain and America whose ages range from ten to seventeen. But there are case studies in the later chapters involving younger children including a boy who killed at the age of three.

Several of the murders involve a sexual element, but as many readers find it difficult to understand how young children can become sexual predators, I've incorporated a chapter on youthful sex killers which offers many more case studies. These killers are male but some were sexually molested by their mothers so the chapter also looks at female sex offending, an under-reported crime.

These crimes are horrifying but comparatively rare. Though the media likes to suggest otherwise, there isn't an epidemic of mini-murderers in Britain. To give some examples, in 1995 - 1996 there were 30 people under the age of eighteen convicted of murder in England and Wales. In 1996 - 1997 there were 19 and in 1997 - 1998 there were 13 such deaths. 1998 - 1999 saw 25 and the following year there were 23. These later numbers may rise as some cases are still being dealt with by the police and by the courts.

The numbers rise by approximately twenty convictions per year if we add manslaughter and infanticide to the murder statistics. But children are still far more sinned against than sinning when you consider that one child a week dies in Britain at its parent's hands.

Moreover, the children who commit violent crimes have invariably been victimised by violent adults. A recent study of 200 serious juvenile offenders found that over 90% of them had suffered childhood trauma. 74% of the total sample had been physically, sexually and/or emotionally abused and over 30% had lost a significant person in their life to whom they were emotionally attached.

The following profiles, then, are stories of cruelty and of loss, of children who weren't allowed to experience a happy childhood. But they can also be stories of hope because the power to change future childhoods is within our grasp.

# I
# THE HURTING
## Jesse Harding Pomeroy

Jesse was born to Ruth and Thomas Pomeroy on 29th November 1859. The couple already had a four-year-old son called Charles. They lived in a dilapidated rented house in Boston, USA.

The Pomeroys were an impoverished and argumentative couple from the start. Thomas was an angry, heavy-drinking man who hated his work at the local shipyard. Ruth was more industrious but equally morose, an intelligent women who was worn down by life.

She was also worn down with caring for Jesse as he was a physically weak infant who suffered numerous ailments. A serious illness in his first year left one of his eyes milky white. This clouded-over eye gave the fretful baby a sinister cast.

Thomas said that he couldn't stand the sight of his second son and frequently hit the toddler. In response, little Jesse had skin rashes and terrible headaches and insomnia. He also had lengthy nightmares when he did eventually sleep. Charles too was being regularly beaten by his father and took it out on Jesse, who lived in constant fear.

Mrs Pomeroy was equally badly treated by her increasingly alcoholic spouse. Determined not to be the sole victim, she sometimes lashed out at her unhappy sons. Abuse makes children physically tense and clumsy so Jesse walked increasingly awkwardly, his shoulders hunched.

## Victim becomes victimiser

When a child is constantly hurt like this, he naturally wants revenge but there was no way that Jesse could stand up to his enraged, belt-wielding father. So he turned to victims that couldn't fight back. When he was five years old he caught a neighbourhood kitten and stabbed it with a small knife, enjoying its agonised cries. By the time that a neighbour intervened the animal was bleeding badly and Jesse had apparently gone into a trance. Later Ruth Pomeroy brought home a pair of pet birds to add colour to the household

21

but Jesse waited till she'd gone out then killed them by twisting their necks. He was showing one of the traits of the fledgling serial killer - cruelty to animals. (The other signs include bedwetting into puberty and starting fires.)

When Jesse was six, his father changed employment and became a porter at the local meat market. He now carried carcasses around by day and beat his sons at night.

At school the other little boys played football whilst the increasingly-hunched Jesse sat and watched, nursing his most recent bruises. He fared little better in the classroom as he constantly lapsed into daydreams and the teacher caned him for this. We now know that excessive daydreaming is one of the symptoms an abused child displays in a desperate attempt to escape the painful reality of their lives - but many teachers of the mid nineteenth century believed that children were mischief makers who had to be broken down.

Finding that school offered him no more understanding than his home, Jesse started to play truant, going for long walks by himself or sitting reading novels. He bought some of them with dimes stolen from his mother's purse. His father beat him for this and for playing truant, using a horsewhip on the child's naked back.

Jesse ran away from home to escape further pain but was found by his father each time and punished. There was a strong humiliation element to these sessions, with Thomas Pomeroy making Jesse strip before taking him out to the woodshed and hitting him until he bled.


**The fantasy phase**

Desperate to be the victimiser rather than the victim, Jesse kept searching for small animals to mutilate. But it wasn't enough and he began to fantasise about hurting a human, someone he could verbally taunt during the abuse just as his father always taunted him. He therefore joined in a game in the schoolyard where cowboys were tortured by Indians. Jesse insisted on being one of the torturers and became so elated that his playmates regarded him with distaste. He couldn't forge any camaraderie with these boys excepting the torture games so remained apart from them, lost in his own lonely world.

When he was ten, his mother left his father as she couldn't stand to see

Jesse suffer any more abuse. But by then the damage had been done, and Jesse's sadism was firmly rooted. He looked for sadistic scenes in novels and in boyhood conversations and eagerly thought about the day when a helpless victim would be his to extensively hurt and verbally torment.

Charles was constantly battering Jesse and though Jesse now fought back, he was still on the losing end of these vicious encounters. He needed a smaller boy that he could control.

## The first torture victim

On Boxing Day 1871 Jesse seized his chance. He was now twelve and tall for his age. He found a three-year-old boy called Billy Paine playing unattended and made up a story to get the toddler to follow him. He led Billy into a disused building. Now he could make his sadistic fantasies a reality.

Jesse undressed the uncomprehending child then tied him to a roof beam by his wrists. By now the child was terrified - exactly the response that the boy torturer wanted. He beat the boy's back with a stick again and again. Jesse himself had often been punished in this way by his brutal father but now he was the one in charge and he was going to make the most of it. It's likely that the sadism continued until Jesse orgasmed but this is conjecture as Billy was too young to explain.

Eventually Jesse ran off, leaving the child swinging from the roof beams. A passer-by heard his semi-conscious whimpers, investigated, and cut him free. The three-year-old was too traumatised to explain exactly what had happened to him or to fully describe his captor so Jesse remained at liberty to torture again.

## The second torture victim

Two months later, on 21st February 1872, Jesse met up with a seven-year-old boy called Tracy Hayden and took him to an abandoned outhouse. There he undressed the younger child and gagged him with a handkerchief. Jesse was already learning from experience, having feared discovery when Billy shrieked during his beating. This time he'd only hear his captive's muffled groans.

Jesse tied the seven-year-old's feet together before roping his hands to an overhead beam. He thrashed the boy with a stick just as he had with his previous victim. But this time the violence was even more extreme and Jesse reigned blows upon the child that blackened his eyes and knocked out some of his teeth. He swore and laughed as he attacked his tightly-bound victim and was clearly overwhelmed by a sadistic glee. He also added a particularly terrifying verbal threat, saying that he was about to emasculate the helpless child.

Tracy was found by passers-by and taken to his parents who immediately called the police. The child was able to give them a reasonable description of the 'big boy' who had harmed him, but unfortunately this didn't include the fact that his attacker had a clouded-over eye.

## The third torture victim

Three months later the bloodlust had rekindled in Jesse and he struck again, asking an eight-year-old boy called Robert Maier if he would like to accompany him to the circus. Instead he led the child to a pond and attempted to drown him but the terrified victim managed to struggle free. Jesse then partially knocked the boy out and dragged him to an outhouse where he undressed him and tied him to a post. He whipped the boy with a stick, forcing him to use sexual (and, for the time, shocking) words like *prick*. Jesse masturbated during this taunting and quickly orgasmed. This sexual release apparently drained him of all tension for he released the child, ordered him to dress then let him leave.

## The fourth torture victim

Seven-year-old Johnny Balch was the next neighbourhood boy to be enticed to an abandoned outhouse by the boy torturer. It was July 1872, a mere two months since the last attack, yet Jesse's sadistic frenzy had increased so much that he actually tore off the boy's clothes rather than unbuttoning them. Then he hung him by his wrists from a beam and flogged him with his belt. The abuse was the most ferocious so far, the belt lashing into every part of the helpless child's anatomy. Again, it was Jesse's orgasm that ended the assault. Thereafter he untied the brutalised boy and hurried away. The traumatised Johnny lay on the floor of the building for hours until he was discovered by a horrified stranger. A week after this assault, Ruth moved Jesse and Charles to a different part of Boston which offered cheaper rents.

## The fifth torture victim

Within days of arriving in his new South Boston home, Jesse went out hunting for prey. On 17th August 1872 he found seven-year-old George Pratt near the beach. Jesse took him to a nearby boathouse where he stripped, gagged and bound him with a rope. As usual, he employed his favourite act of thrashing the child all over, only this time he used the buckle end of a belt. Jesse was becoming increasingly crazed during these assaults. He bit George's face and one of his buttocks. This might have been a result of the atavistic urge that surfaces in some sexual sadists or it may have been learned behaviour, as some abusive parents bite their children as a punishment. Thomas Pomeroy might well have fallen on little Jesse in a drunken rage, battering and biting him in turn.

But even this sadistic biting didn't satisfy Jesse's increasing lust for blood. Now he produced a needle and stabbed the boy in the armpits and shoulders. Again, each act was accompanied by verbal taunting and Jesse clearly took great pleasure in telling the child what he was going to do to him next. His childhood experiences had turned him into a remorseless psychopath - yet he was still only twelve years old.

## The sixth torture victim

A fortnight later memories of the previous attacks were no longer enough to sustain him and he struck again. This assault took place on Thursday 5th September, underneath a shadowy railroad bridge. Jesse led six-year-old Harry Austin there, stripped and battered him, the violence escalating by the second as Jesse produced a knife. He cut the screaming child in the back and under his armpits. Then, carrying out the threat he'd used on a previous victim, he tried to emasculate him. The hugely shocked child was found with cuts to his scrotum and numerous bruises. He was lucky to survive.

Jesse maintained an appearance of normality (or what passes for normality in such an isolated and unhappy boy) and his mother saw nothing different about him after these torture sessions. He continued to attend school and go to Sunday school and have interminable fights with his brother Charles.

## The seventh torture victim

The next week, on Wednesday 11th September, Jesse struck up a conversation with seven-year-old Joseph Kennedy on the beach and lured him to a vacant outhouse. There he stripped and flogged the terrified child. Again the violence was increasing for he broke the little boy's nose and dislodged several of his teeth. He laughed wildly as he produced his beloved penknife and slashed the younger boy on the face and thighs. Eventually he untied him, threw him into the salt marshes and ran away. It was clear to the police, and to the public who read about each new assault, that the torturer's blood lust was escalating and that he'd soon kill if he wasn't caught.

## The eighth torture victim

And indeed, on Tuesday 17th September, the next victim almost lost his life. Five-year-old Robert Gould was led to a quiet stretch of the railway by the scheming Jesse. There the youth tore off Robert's clothes and tied him to a pole. He slashed at the child's head with his knife, alternately laughing and swearing. As the blood spurted, he showed a strange, frenzied joy. He held the knife in the air to watch the blood drip from it and was clearly transfixed at the sight.

Seeking yet further sadistic excess, he told the five-year-old that he was going to kill him and was about to cut his throat when railwaymen approached. Jesse ran away, doubtless congratulating himself that he'd once again evaded detection. He was wrong, for his victim had noticed that his torturer had a rare deformity - a milky eye.

## Capture

There was only one boy in the locale with a milky eye - Jesse Pomeroy. He was arrested and every one of his tortured victims identified him. He admitted his crimes to the authorities, saying vaguely that 'something' had made him do it but within hours had retracted his confession and thereafter pleaded his innocence. He was sent to a reform school for boys, most of whom had been convicted of theft. They were terrified to find that the boy torturer now lived amongst them and they tried to keep out of his way.

Unfortunately the masters at the school flogged the children - and this obviously kept Jesse's thoughts focused on such cruelties. He would seek out the punished victims and ask them how often they'd been caned and how it had felt. He would become visibly excited whilst hearing these details and undoubtedly used them as a masturbatory aid.

Ruth Pomeroy possibly knew that she'd failed her youngest child by letting him be beaten for so long by his father. Whatever her motivation, she kept petitioning the reform school to free him, suggesting that he was innocent of the crimes.

The school was impressed by her loyalty and her hardworking nature - and by the fact that Jesse was a model prisoner who did exactly as he was told. Nowadays we know that organised offenders such as Jesse are often model prisoners, being bright enough to work the system for their own ends. But this was an unsophisticated era and they assumed that Jesse's good behaviour in an enclosed environment meant that he wouldn't reoffend in the outside world. As a result, he was released to his mother in March 1874 after serving only seventeen months.


## The first murder

Fourteen-year-old Jesse now returned home. His mother had opened a small dressmaking shop and his brother Charles was selling newspapers from a street stall. Jesse was immediately employed by both. Outwardly he appeared industrious and helpful - but inwardly he harboured the exact same sadism as before.

A week after his release, he opened up his mother's shop in the early morning. A ten-year-old girl called Katie Curran came in to make a purchase and Jesse told her that she'd find what she wanted downstairs. Partway there, the girl realised that she was heading towards a dark cellar - but before she could retrace her steps, Jesse grabbed her from behind and hacked at her neck with his knife.

He carried the child down the rest of the stairs and cut her clothing away from her bleeding body. Then he proceeded to stab her numerous times and mutilate her genitals. Jesse concealed the little corpse in the cellar and returned to serving in the shop.

It seems that this was a crime of opportunity rather than design, for on previous attacks he'd brought his torture kit with him - namely rope for binding the victim, a handkerchief to employ as a gag and a stick or belt to carry out the flagellation. This time the victim wasn't tied or gagged and the only weapon employed was the knife he carried with him at all times.

The police believed that Katie had been kidnapped by a stranger passing through the area, so Jesse remained free to seek further victims. He asked other children to accompany him into the empty store, but was so eager to get them on their own that they took fright and ran away.

**The second murder**

Serial torturers and killers are incredibly single minded, so Jesse continued his search for vulnerable victims. Five weeks later he found four-year-old Horace Miller who had gone to the nearby bakery to buy himself a cake. Jesse made up a story and lured the little boy to the marshes. There he threw him to the wet ground, undressed him below the waist and brandished a knife. Little Horace put out his arms to defend himself and received cuts to both hands. The blood-crazed Jesse stabbed him again and again. The fourteen-year-old also cut his victim's scrotum, knowing that no one was likely to hear his agonised screams. All of Jesse's rage went into his knife-wielding arm as he lunged at the four-year-old for a final time, almost decapitating him.

Hearing or seeing other people on the horizon he raced off, taking his knife with him. Within minutes two marsh walkers found the newly-dead child.

When the constabulary saw that the victim was a young male who had been undressed, stabbed and partially castrated, they thought of a youth who had committed such crimes before - Jesse Pomeroy. They wondered if he'd escaped from his reform school and checked to find that he'd been released. The police immediately went to Jesse's home and arrested him. He denied everything, despite his shoeprints being found in the wet mud beside the body and dried blood being found on his knife.

At the police station, Jesse continued to invent alibis until they took him to the mortuary and showed him Horace's mutilated corpse. For the first time he lost his composure and staggered backwards, admitting that 'something' had made him kill the little boy. He was referring to the compulsion to hurt and kill that every serial killer has.

This compulsion is incredibly strong - but the killer still chooses to give in to it. As such, he should be found responsible for his actions. After all, he can control it, in that he doesn't give in to the compulsion when there are witnesses around. Jesse took his victims to comparatively remote locations and brought along the means to restrain them and muffle their shrieks and pleading. He also made sure that he didn't get their blood on his clothes.

**Seeking scapegoats**

Now that Jesse had been captured, the local people and the press looked for an explanation. They didn't understand the significance of the violence he'd suffered at his father's hands.

Instead they blamed Jesse's sadism on the pulp fiction that he read, with its themes of sailors being brutalised by violent pirates or of Redskins torturing their prisoners. In reality, most of these novels had print runs of over sixty-thousand so if truly corrupting one would have expected them to produce sixty-thousand boy torturers - but there was only one.

**Awaiting trial**

Jesse read ferociously in jail whilst awaiting trial, though presumably the ostensibly-dangerous pulp novels weren't on offer. He spent the rest of his time writing notes to the youth in the next cell, asking him about his school floggings and telling the boy that he couldn't get thoughts of his own childhood beatings out of his head. He also wrote frequently to his mother and to his brother Charles.

His mother sold her dressmaking shop to a neighbour - and to everyone's horror they found Katie Curran's decaying corpse in the cellar. As usual, Jesse alternately admitted and denied having anything to do with the crime.

## The trial

He remained in jail until 8th December 1874 when his trial began. Witness after witness described seeing him leading Horace away. Others had seen Katie entering Ruth Pomeroy's little shop. Even Jesse's own defence lawyer suggested that Jesse was often overpowered by the need to hurt. These were superstitious times so the defence added that Jesse might have been born with evil powers.

Harsh discipline was only mentioned when one of his teachers said that he sometimes whispered to other children in class and that she 'had to' cane him for this. No one made the connection between Jesse being victimised by his father and then going on to victimise other boys. Jesse himself admitted that his sole interest was in hurting young males. The murder of Katie Curran appears to have been one of sexual curiosity and ongoing blood lust rather than intense desire.

The trial took place over three days and the verdict was guilty of first degree murder. The sentence was life imprisonment. Ironically, the local paper suggested the crimes wouldn't have happened if Jesse had received parental discipline.

## Prison

In prison, Jesse was put into solitary confinement, living in a small cell with his meals pushed through a slot in the door. This was best for the other prisoners as he would undoubtedly have tortured them. But it was bad for his own mental health - isolated prisoners often go mad. He was to spent forty-one years in such enforced solitude, with the exception of visits from the prison clergy and, twice a month, from his mother.

His sanity did seem to crumble during these years as he made numerous wildly-improbable escape attempts, some of which suggested a death wish.

On one occasion he used a makeshift tool to bore through his cell and cut into a gas pipe, hoping to blast his way to freedom. He was knocked unconscious by the blast but made a full recovery.

Jesse wrote simple rhymes for the prison magazine during those years. He continued to read everything that he could get his hands on. His mother brought him snacks - and he was pleased to receive them but showed no pleasure at seeing her. They often discussed the letters requesting his freedom that she was still writing to the governors.

It was said that during these years he paid other prisoners to catch rats for him, which he then skinned alive - but these tales are undoubtedly apocryphal. After all, he was kept apart from other prisoners for most of his life. Then, as now, other prisoners and guards would have sold stories to reporters who were hungry for sensational information about high profile criminals. Then, as now, they doubtless made wild stories up.

After forty-one years alone in his cell, Jesse was given leave to go to religious services and take exercise with the other prisoners. He used his infamy and his machismo to inspire respect in them - but they were unafraid as he was becoming physically weak. Twelve more years passed in this way and Jesse didn't make any close friends.

## A change of scene

By the 1920's, humanitarian reformers began to suggest that Jesse be allowed to live out his final months in a less punitive setting. Eventually the governor agreed. At first, like a battery chicken, Jesse Pomeroy resisted this, saying that his entire life was his cell. But over time he clearly rethought the situation and agreed to be moved to Bridgewater, the prison's mental hospital.

In the summer of 1929 he was finally transferred to Bridgewater, having spent more than fifty years in Charlestown prison. By then he was almost seventy and had muscle wastage through spending so many years cooped up in a tiny cell. He was also partially blind and increasingly lame.

He remained surly after his transfer to Bridgewater and none of the staff managed to create a rapport with him. Some said that they never saw him smile. He often threatened to make escape attempts but it was clear that, given his growing number of infirmities, he wouldn't get very far. He continued to protest his innocence until his death - the result of a heart attack - on 29th September 1932 when he was almost seventy-three.


## The rationale

Jesse Pomeroy committed the early tortures and later torture-murders out of an overwhelming sense of bloodlust. Like many people from highly abusive backgrounds, he'd made a strong connection between sexual satisfaction and extreme sadism. These desires would remain throughout his life.

Jesse's strongest stimulus for years (though he'd hated such floggings at the time) had been as a victim of severe beatings accompanied by verbal taunting. Watching a boy writhe and squeal as he flogged him and threatened him was much more exciting than a lover's caress.

Early criminologists suggested that Jesse's crimes were merely acts of violence, that they weren't sex crimes because the victims weren't sexually assaulted or raped. This shows a misunderstanding of sexual sadism. In sadistic attacks, the orgasm isn't triggered by sexual intercourse but by inflicting pain on someone else.

Indeed, many sadists avoid coitus. If penis-based activity *does* take place it is often forced sodomy followed by forced oral sex, both of which further demean or hurt the victim. But as a callow youth Jesse Pomeroy may not have been aware of these optional extras. He orgasmed during the flagellation or the stabbing attacks, after which his sadistic urge was spent.

Jesse's attacks began at twelve, the age when his libido awoke. He was undoubtedly homosexual so chose males as his lust objects. He chose small boys rather than boys his own age as they were easier to lure away from safe locations. They were also easier to restrain and were soon completely in his increasingly murderous power.

# 2
## PALE SHELTER
## William Newton Allnutt

The pre-teen killer profiled in the last chapter came from a violent American home - but several years earlier in Britain, William Newton Allnutt was born into a British household that was equally damaging.

William was born in 1835 to a farmer and his wife. He came into the world to find that he already had five siblings. His mother was deeply distressed at the time of his birth as she'd borne the brunt of her husband's temper for many years. But she was used to raised voices and fists as her father had also been a violent and tyrannical man.

William was a low-weight baby who was often ill. Several of his brothers and sisters were also poorly. Nevertheless his mother went on to have another two children after his birth.

When William was eighteen months old he fell against a ploughshare and the resultant injury was so severe that the doctor warned there might be brain damage. No such mental change was noted during these pre-school years but the abused little boy understandably became an increasingly sad and sullen one.

His father had by now become an alcoholic who kept terrorising his wife and all eight of his children. As a result, William sleepwalked and had terrible nightmares. The household was religious so sometimes these nightmares were filled with religious imagery.

He was an intelligent and articulate child who did well in his schoolwork and achieved a high standard of literacy. But he showed the disturbed behaviour that children from violent households invariably show - everything from fighting to truancy - so his teachers were often upset with him.

When William was nine years old his father became so cruel that he was considered insane. Mrs Allnutt at last found the courage to leave him. She sent all eight children away to boarding school or to stay with friends. (Within a year of their separation, her husband had developed epilepsy and within three years, at the age of thirty-seven, he would die.)

## From frying pan to fire

She now moved in with her father, Samuel Nelme, and his second wife who were both in their seventies. They had a palatial home in the Hackney district of London with its own grounds. Samuel had been a successful merchant in the city so the family were able to afford a live-in maid.

Unfortunately William's ill health continued, and his boarding school decided to send him home. And so the small, pale boy came to live with his mother in his grandfather's deeply religious and all-adult household. It was a cheerless life without his siblings or schoolfriends for company. Samuel Nelme had always been quick to anger - and this anger was now often directed at William when he got up to everyday boyish pranks.

## The fantasy phase

In September 1847 William committed a more serious act, stealing ten sovereigns from his house. His grandfather thrashed him and lectured him endlessly about the importance of honesty.

By now William - like many beaten children - was fantasising about killing his tormentor. If his grandfather died he, William, would be safe for the very first time. The cause of the twelve-year-old's nightmares would be over and he would be able to relax during the day with his mother. He would have a childhood at last.

William had been taught all his life that people should use violence to get their own way. After all, he'd regularly watched his father hit him, his mother and his siblings. And now he was living in a second household where the man of the house solved disputes with a weapon or with his fists.

Deciding to kill his grandfather, William somehow acquired a pistol. The next time they were walking in the garden he lagged behind and aimed the weapon at his grandfather's head. The bullet missed and William immediately dropped the gun into the bushes. He blamed the incident on a passerby, though no such man could be found.

William continued to suffer at his grandfather's hands. The old man found the twelve-year-old boy untruthful - but William was presumably afraid to tell the truth in case it led to further verbal or physical abuse.

## Killing time

One day his grandfather struck him so hard that he went flying and hit his head on a table. The pain was terrible. Worse, his grandfather said that he would almost kill him next time. The underweight and undersized boy was no match for the well built adult and may well have feared for his life.

He watched the household's rats being poisoned by arsenic and realised he could use this to get rid of his batterer. He added the white powder to the sugar bowl, knowing that his grandfather craved sweet foods.

Over the ensuing week, every adult in the household became increasingly ill, vomiting violently. Samuel Nelme was the worst affected as he added sugar to so many of his drinks and meals. For the next six days his stomach and bowels voided their contents over and over. The doctor who was summoned found him writhing in bed and suspected he was suffering from English cholera. Ironically, each time he felt slightly better his daughter would give him some sweetened gruel to tempt his appetite. After six days spent in increasing agony, he died.

## Suspicion

An autopsy showed that Samuel Nelme had ingested arsenic on several occasions. The police were called in to question the family and his mother admitted that her son had asked her about how arsenic worked. More damningly, he'd told the maidservant that he thought his grandfather would die very soon.

William refused to admit that he'd put arsenic in the sugar so was initially arrested for stealing his grandfather's watch. But whilst in Newgate Jail he was visited by a Chaplain who suggested he admit his guilt to save his soul.

The twelve-year-old then wrote a letter to his mother saying that he deserved to be 'sent to Hell.' The child clearly had no inkling that the violence he'd suffered for so many years had, in turn, made him violent. Instead he said that he wished he'd listened to his mother's religious teachings and that 'Satan got so much power' over him that he'd killed the elderly man.

On 15th December 1847 he was tried before a jury at the Old Bailey. The counsel offered an insanity defence and four doctors testified that William's head injuries and a hereditary taint had driven him to madness. His mother testified that the boy heard voices telling him to steal.

But the judge said that the child was sane and found him guilty of murder. At this, the twelve-year-old almost collapsed and the wardens had to hold him up. The judge sentenced him to death but the sentence was almost immediately lifted, after which William Allnutt disappears from the record books. He may have been transported or given life imprisonment as young prisoners were treated very harshly in those unenlightened times.

# 3
# SUBSTITUTE
## Cheryl Pierson & Sean Pica

Cheryl was born on 14th May 1969 to Cathleen and James Pierson. The couple already had a three-year-old son called Jimmy. The family lived on Long Island, New York.

James was an electrician who worked hard to give his family a good standard of living. He said that no wife of his would ever work so Cathleen spent her time shopping and chatting to the neighbours. She also had most of the responsibility for Cheryl as James said he didn't know what to say to little girls. A very macho man, he was happiest with his male friends or when taking his son to Little League.

He provided the family with a beautiful home and often bought them all expensive presents - but he was equally generous with his punches and slaps.

## Tyrannical

James Pierson's own father had been a very controlling man, and now James copied his parenting methods. Cheryl and Jimmy weren't allowed to speak at mealtimes and had to eat a little bit of everything on their plate in turn or he'd get enraged and slap them across the face. They also weren't allowed to sip from their glasses until they'd finished the food. This control extended to every facet of their lives with the children being warned that they must keep their bedroom doors open at all times.

At six foot two and strongly built, James Pierson was often a frightening figure to his children and his wife - and they all had the bruises to prove it. But rather than removing the children from the home, Cathleen merely told them to try to keep out of their father's way. Cathleen herself had frequently watched her mother beat her brother with a stick so she was used to violence in the home.

Cheryl grew up into a pretty, very feminine little girl who Cathleen loved to dress up in fairytale dresses with ribbons and bows. At school she was only an average student, but academia wasn't particularly important as she wanted to be a hairdresser or a beautician when she grew up. She was good at school sports and was very pleased when her father attended her games.

When Cheryl was eight the couple had another daughter, JoAnn. Cathleen showed Cheryl how to care for the new baby and Cheryl revelled in this, acting like a little mother. She was already becoming the peacemaker of the family, a child old before her time who always tried to make things right.

The neighbours felt sorry for the little girl who was always being shouted at and slapped by her dad, so they often invited her and her equally bullied siblings over. One neighbour even dared to tackle James Pierson for the way he treated his offspring but James angrily told him to 'fuck off'.


## Cheryl's mother becomes ill

When Cheryl was nine Cathleen suddenly became very ill. She was hospitalised for weeks and subjected to numerous tests. James was frantic. In his own way he really loved his wife - and very controlling individuals are often terrified of being left alone. He visited her in hospital every day and kept demanding that the doctors get quicker test results.

Eventually Cathleen was diagnosed as having kidney failure and sent home to await a transplant. She was so ill that she mainly slept on the living room couch, so James started going into the marital bedroom to watch TV. He called Cheryl in to lie on the bed next to him as televised sport was something they both enjoyed. They'd take in cans of soda and crisps and Cheryl would curl up with her head on his chest. Sometimes both father and daughter would fall asleep.

At other times he'd wrestle her playfully or tickle her or lift her over his head. Cheryl was pleased that at last her daddy wasn't ignoring her. But she'd later claim that this touching became increasingly inappropriate.


## Kidney transplants

Cheryl's mother Cathleen remained ill for the next six years, apart from the periods following her first and then her second kidney transplant. When a relative asked her why her kidneys had declined so rapidly, she said it was because her husband was beating her. She also told a friend that she wanted to leave him because he was always shouting at the children and criticising them. Cheryl had by now matured into an attractive thirteen-year-old but she still had to act like a little child in the presence of her dad. Observers noted that James would call her over to him and make her hug him and act in a generally flirtatious or unduly deferential way.

## Incest is suspected

Cathleen now told a neighbour that she wanted Cheryl out of the marital bedroom, that she thought her husband might be touching the thirteen-year-old. The neighbour suggested to Cheryl that she should watch TV in her own room. But when Cheryl did so her father turned mean and said 'Am I not good enough to watch television with any more?' He also picked fights with the increasingly nauseous and swollen Cathleen so Cheryl went back into the marital bedroom to keep the peace.

James became increasingly jealous of Cheryl, punching her in the mouth when he discovered that she'd written a boy at school a Valentine card. He also punched her in the face for putting a pretty sash around her waist to brighten up her school uniform. Unfortunately it's quite usual for authoritarian parents to try to control a teenager's sexuality in this way. He started listening in to her phone calls, just as he'd once listened in to her mother's phone calls - and she often had to end phone conversations with female friends because her father wanted her to take a nap with him.

## James is hurt

When Cheryl was fourteen, her father badly damaged his legs in a work-related fall and it was feared he'd never walk again. Cheryl now had to take care of him and Cathleen and be a surrogate mother to six-year-old JoAnn.

Frightened and in pain, James became even more difficult to live with and his need for control increased. He told his son Jimmy what type of haircut to get, what to wear and what occupation he should be following. Jimmy turned eighteen and left, vowing never to return. But he continued to see his dying mother, though both hid these meetings from his father. Cheryl also saw her brother occasionally and admitted that she missed him a lot.

## I'll be watching you

James now installed an elaborate security system so that he could see into every room and corridor of the bungalow. He also hid a gun - including one submachine gun - in every room.

Cheryl tried harder and harder to please her dad. Visitors to the house noted that he'd punch her and pull her hair in supposed play, but that his actions clearly hurt her. The abuse would end when Cheryl hugged him and said 'Daddy, I love you.' He'd then rub her chest or entwine his fingers through her hair. Various people saw Cheryl lying on top of her father - and one relative was perturbed to find them lying like this, fully dressed, under a sheet on the marital bed.

One of Cheryl's schoolfriends told a school counsellor that she thought Cheryl was being abused by her dad - but the counsellor said that Cheryl would have to come and see her. Like all abused children, Cheryl would have feared both her father's revenge and her own public humiliation, so she didn't approach the counsellor. (At least a dozen adults strongly suspected that Cheryl was being abused by her father - but this young girl was the only one who had the courage to go to the authorities.)

Cheryl's world remained very small. She wasn't allowed to date or to wear nail varnish or makeup. If she went to see a film with a friend, her father would follow her and sit a few rows behind.

## Stunted development

Unable to grow up, Cheryl remained immature. Friends noticed that she often looked frightened. Her father constantly warned her not to talk to boys at school - and if she went over to a friend's house to get her hair cut, he would time her so that she didn't stay out too long. Cheryl was virtually running the Pierson household but James still found fault with her and a visitor was shocked to hear him refer to his daughter as 'a little cunt.'

## Motherless

In February 1985 Cathleen finally died. Now Cheryl and JoAnn were left alone with their grieving father. Cheryl had to do all the cooking and cleaning every night when she came home from class though kindly neighbours sometimes helped by supplying the family with meals. But love at last entered her life when one of the boys at her school, Rob Cuccio, comforted her over the loss of her mum.

## Rob Cuccio

Rob was the son of a retired detective and a bank clerkess. They were a religious family who taught catechism at church.

James Pierson was very unhappy at the prospect of Cheryl dating Rob. He made up lots of reasons why the young lovers shouldn't see each other and finally insisted they sat in his lounge watching TV with him and JoAnn. After a while, Rob found this so awkward that he finished with Cheryl, but he missed her and started seeing her again.

One day as they prepared to eat icecream, James told Cheryl to give each of them a napkin. Cheryl gave Rob a napkin then gave her father one - and her father was so enraged at being served second that he punched her in the face. Shocked and frightened, Rob walked out. It's likely that Cheryl begged him not to say anything. She'd definitely begged other adults not to intervene after she'd been hit by her dad.

## Wishing he was dead

Like numerous abused children, Cheryl had begun to fantasise about killing her dad. Mostly, such revenge fantasies remain just that. They give the abused person a sense of control over what's happening which temporarily makes them feel better. The killing remains at a fantasy level, for the abuser is such a terrifying figure that the child doesn't have the nerve to physically fight back.

Unfortunately, the talk at school turned to a local murder that had been carried out for cash. Cheryl wondered aloud why anyone would murder a stranger for a fee - and one of her classmates, Sean Pica, said that he would kill if the price was right.

## Sean Pica

Sean was born on 18th February 1969 to Benjamin and JoAnn Pica in New York. His father was a policeman and his mother a nurse. The couple already had a two-year-old son called Joe. Three years after Sean was born they had a third son called Vincent and the family was complete. JoAnn took the boys to church every week and also taught catechism to a group of youngsters in her home.

The marriage was an increasingly unhappy one and when Sean was seven his father left. He came back within months when nine-year-old Joe was diagnosed with leukaemia. Joe recovered and counselling failed to resurrect the marriage so Benjamin left again. He and JoAnn were divorced in Sean's tenth year.

Benjamin kept in touch with the children - and they got on well with his new wife - but JoAnn continued to constantly criticise him to her three sons. Sean found this very difficult as he still loved his dad.

In fairness, JoAnn had to work incredibly hard to support her brood. She sometimes spent all night giving private nursing care then went straight on to her daytime nursing job at the hospital. It too was demanding as she worked in Intensive Care.

## Sean's second father

The following year, Sean's mother met a new man called Jim. Three months later she married him, saying that she felt guilty about having sex outside wedlock as her religion didn't allow for this. She told Sean that Jim, a hospital laboratory technician, was really his father now.

At first Sean was happy to have this new father figure in his life. Jim took the boys to games and took an interest in their hobbies. They also enjoyed family barbecues.

But Jim changed when he was drunk. He beat JoAnn and threw the family's beloved labrador against the wall. Sean definitely witnessed this violence - and may also have suffered it. People in his Boy Scouts group noticed that he was troubled, that he had something on his mind.

Three years into the marriage, Jim said he was going out to watch a softball game - but he never returned. JoAnn, who tended to make light of family problems, was very embarrassed by his desertion. She now criticised both Benjamin and Jim to young Sean.

Sean clearly wanted a father figure, and became close to one of the Scout leaders. He also became a surrogate father to a much younger mentally handicapped boy, helping him to earn his badges in the Scouts.

Sean entered his teens, a sensitive and gentle boy who was always willing to help others. He worried about his mother but still enjoyed spending time with his biological father. He excelled in carpentry.

Sean's older brother, Joe, went into the Navy and Sean really missed him. On the upside, he made a good friend called Michael and started to spend more time with the lively teenager.

## Peer pressure

But Michael was much more streetwise than Sean. He burgled local houses and used the money he stole to experiment with cocaine. In time, Sean accompanied him on these trips and acted as look-out. He too tried cocaine and found it made him feel invincible.

Michael stole a gun during one robbery and Sean found that holding it made him feel omnipotent. The slender boy couldn't right his mother's failed marriages or bring in money to support the family - but with a gun in his hand he felt powerful for perhaps the first time in his life.

## The murder plot

Now, as his classmates talked about murder for cash, Sean said that he'd kill Cheryl's abusive father for a thousand dollars. Later he, Rob and Cheryl talked together about the best way to do it and decided that Sean would stab James to death. Sean would throw a brick through the window of the house across the street to attract James's attention then lunge at him with a knife. This first plan was clearly nonsensical for James Pierson was a muscular six foot two whilst Sean was a scrawny kid.

Sean threw the brick but James didn't come out to investigate so

43

they talked some more and decided to kill him with one of his own guns.

So Rob and Cheryl took Sean to Cheryl's house and showed him James's many weapons - but then they realised that the gun would be traced back to the Pierson household. After further talk they agreed that Sean would have to acquire his own gun.

For the next few weeks, Sean said that he'd kill the man that night or the next day - but he always found an excuse not to do it. Rob kept asking him why nothing had happened and Cheryl begged him to act soon. Sean felt sorry for the pretty teenage cheerleader who often arrived at school with black and blue marks on her. He wanted to protect Cheryl and he wanted Rob to stop pressuring him. So when Michael gave him his rifle to look after, he went to a wooded area for target practice. Later he loaded it with five bullets and went to kill James Pierson, a man he'd never met.

**The murder**

On 5th February 1986 Sean left his house in the early morning and made his way to the Pierson's bungalow. He hid behind a tree and nervously watched their front door. At 6.20am it opened and James left the house and walked towards his truck. Sean raised the .22 rifle and shot him in the back of the head. James fell to the ground - but he was still moving. Overwhelmed with hatred, Sean raced up and fired another four shots into the dying man.

The corpse lay there until Cheryl let the dog out. She saw her father lying on the path and ran to get a neighbour. At first everyone assumed he'd slipped on the ice - but when the police turned the body over, they saw all the blood and the expended bullet casings scattered around.

Cheryl alternated between calmness and tears, which soon turned to nightmares. She believed in life after death, so feared that her father's ghost might visit her. She said in the speech she wrote for his funeral that she believed one day she'd see him again.

Sean went on to school as if nothing had happened and Rob gave him some of the thousand dollars he'd taken from James Pierson's safe. Sean bought some jewellery for his new girlfriend, who he'd only been seeing for a week. Everyone thought that Sean was the same as usual and had no idea that he'd just become a killer. But soon afterwards he started to run a very high fever and took to his bed.

## Arrest

Meanwhile the police were looking for the killer. They heard that James Pierson was planning to cut his son Jimmy out of his will, so they started to lean on the teenager as a likely suspect. He finally told the police that it was Cheryl who'd wanted their physically-abusive father dead. Cheryl had asked Jimmy to arrange a contract killing, but Jimmy had said that she should just endure the physical abuse as he had then get out when she was eighteen.

The police went on to talk to Rob, who eventually admitted everything. They then arrested Cheryl and Sean. Sean's girlfriend said that she'd stand by him and he soon bought her an engagement ring.

For the first time in her life, Cheryl told adults - the police - about the fact that her father had been having sex with her. The police believed her but James's mother and sister did not. They said that he might have touched her inappropriately in play but that he would never have had full intercourse.

Cheryl added that she was carrying her father's baby and that he knew this and had been trying to arrange an abortion for her. But she soon had a miscarriage - and tests on the foetus proved that the baby was Rob's.

## The trial

There was further damaging evidence against Cheryl at the trial when her ten-year-old sister JoAnn - now living with James's mother who didn't believe the allegations of abuse - wrote a letter to the jury. She said that she'd often seen Cheryl lying on top of her father, but hadn't seen her father reciprocate.

Incest experts were quick to point out that sexually abused children are encouraged by their abusers to be highly seductive. In other words, it was likely that Cheryl was doing what her father insisted of her. And JoAnn had previously told a neighbour that 'Daddy slept with Cheryl last night' and the neighbour testified to this at the trial.

Cathleen's friends also came forward to say that James was always hitting the children and pulling their hair and punching them. They'd seen him touching

Cheryl's bottom and he'd asked a neighbour 'doesn't she have a nice pair of tits?'

A neighbour reported that Cathleen's stepfather had seen James and Cheryl in bed together under the sheets, with Cheryl lying on top of her father. A regular babysitter at the house said that James would grab her and that it was clear he held women in low regard.

Cheryl herself said that her father had made her masturbate him after her mother became ill - but that after her mother died the abuse had increased to include intercourse. She said that she'd wanted to kill him because she feared he was about to start abusing JoAnn. Cheryl was often out at cheer-leading practice and her father had started to wrestle with JoAnn the way he had with her.

An alternative explanation was that Cheryl knew she was expecting Rob's baby and was terrified. After all, her father hit her for virtually nothing, so what would he do when he knew she was with child?

But an expert on child sexual abuse testified that she'd spent time with Cheryl since her arrest and that the teenager did fit the profile of an incest survivor. She said she came to her conclusion by looking at Cheryl's physical state, the testimony of witnesses, photographs of the family, the profile of James Pierson and Cheryl's account of what had taken place.

And the judge noted that most of the witnesses in court had suspected that Cheryl was being abused by her father - but only her teenage friend had actually done the right thing by telling a responsible adult. That is, she'd told her guidance teacher but the teacher hadn't done anything.

## The sentence

Ultimately, the judge believed Cheryl's account of what had happened and said that she'd been subjected to repeated acts of intercourse by her father. She collapsed on the floor before the sentence was read out and had to be revived and helped into a chair. The judge said that she must serve six months in jail then remain on probation for five years.

There was much less to debate at Sean's trial. The prosecution said that he was a cold-blooded killer who had shot James Pierson for financial gain. They also alleged that he was a drug addict. Sean's defence said that if the motive had been financial he'd have asked for much more cash. They offered psychological reports which said that Sean had believed he was the only person who could help Cheryl, who was clearly in a very bad way. They also admitted that Sean had a lot of pent up rage against father figures, as his mother had constantly criticised both of his fathers and generally had a poor opinion of men. By now, Sean's mother and her latest boyfriend were arguing a lot - and Sean's remaining brother would later leave his mother's house to live with his dad.

Sean was found guilty of manslaughter and given the sentence of twenty-four years in jail with the proviso that he serve at least eight of them. Rob, whose testimony had been vital, was put on probation for five years.

## A new start

Cheryl didn't cope well in jail, losing a lot of weight and generally feeling ill. She was desperate to spend time with those relatives who were still supportive. Ironically, the many rules she faced in prison - that she could only wear certain clothes and was forbidden perfume and makeup - were identical to those she'd faced at home.

Fourteen weeks later she was freed and immediately became engaged to Rob. In October 1988 they married in church.

## Update

Rob and Cheryl went on to have a child. When a journalist made enquiries six years later, the family were still together. Sean Pica fared less well - his girlfriend soon broke off their engagement and during his first year in prison he got into an altercation with another prisoner and was moved to a different jail, a move which made it much more difficult for his family to visit him. Photographs show that he changed a great deal in prison, turning from a cute, beatle-haired youth into a shaven-headed and sad-faced young man.

# 4
# I AM, I SAID
## Peter George Dinsdale (aka Bruce Lee)

Peter was born on 31st July 1960 to single mother Doreen Dinsdale. He was born with a partially paralysed and withered right hand and leg. His mother, who lived in Manchester, England, was a prostitute. His father is unknown.

Within weeks of his birth, Doreen was back on the game and he was shut away and ignored whilst she entertained her clients. A year later she gave birth to a daughter, Sharon. Both children ended up in local authority care.

Peter first went into an orphanage at age three or four when his mother deserted him. The authorities could see that he hadn't been adequately nourished and was very unkempt, small for his age and exceptionally thin. His hair was raggedly cut and was a dirty blonde shade, his eyes were sad and his expression haunted. He had received so little attention that his diction and speech were poorly developed for his years. His IQ would variously test at between 68 and 75, in the educationally subnormal range.

The neglected boy stayed in the orphanage for a year or so then the authorities tried to reunite him with his mum. The reunion was a failure. She alternately ordered him about or told him to hide away as she didn't want her clients to know that she had 'a crippled kid.' At nights she'd walk the streets and he'd do the same, perhaps hoping to find her. Ill clad and underfed, he mentally retreated into his own little world. The recognised signs of neglect include constant hunger, emaciation, a lack of social relationships and increasingly destructive tendencies. Peter had all of them.

Returned to the orphanage within weeks, Peter became increasingly withdrawn. A second attempt was made to unite him with his mother when he was six, but this too failed abysmally. Doreen's increasing dependence on alcohol and her own unhappy childhood rendered her incapable of loving and nurturing her bewildered son. Social workers could see that the little boy was becoming increasingly anti-social and disturbed.

Peter's mother presumably thought of herself as bad and projected that badness onto her offspring. Over time the constant cruelty and neglect began to change the child's way of viewing himself and the world.

## A punitive philosophy

Dorothy Rowe (writing in her book *The Successful Self*) has explained how a child's mindset is changed by abuse. At first the child recognises that the parent who hits or mocks him is bad. But that is too terrifying a notion to live with, for it means that he is totally at the mercy of a bad person. So he changes his viewpoint to believe that the parent is good and he is bad and deserves to be hurt. This gives him back the illusion of control. But if the violence recurs again and again, the juvenile redefines the hurt so that he still believes he is bad - *but determines that when he grows up he will punish others who are equally bad.*

The increasingly punitive-minded Peter attended a school for handicapped children but he felt different to his schoolmates. They went back to loving homes each night whereas he returned to the functional briskness of council care. Here he was sexually abused by persons unknown, probably older male inmates. He'd later say that they used him sexually from the time he was small. Sadly, the abuse of such handicapped children is commonplace. In a study of over 40,000 disabled American children, 31% of them had been maltreated, often in the first five years of life.

## Intellect

With so much abuse to contend with, Peter found it hard to concentrate in school and though he learned to read and write, his spelling was very poor and he used language badly. The lack of nourishment and lack of stimuli that he'd received as a baby and a toddler may well have affected his growing brain. That said, he liked human biology and maths classes and enjoyed his trips to school on the bus.

Peter had by now been diagnosed as epileptic, but his anti-epilepsy medication kept the convulsions at bay. Unfortunately his partial paralysis meant that he limped with his right leg and held his right hand high and crooked across his chest, which made him look intellectually challenged. As a result, the local boys called him Daft Peter and often laughed at him.

But though Peter would never become scholarly, he was blessed with a native cunning. He'd found that when he shared his secrets with others they told someone else - so he learned the art of silence. The outside world was so untrustworthy that he preferred to live inside his own head.

During these formative years, Peter saw a bonfire for the first time and found it excited him. By nine he had become obsessed with fire.

## First serious arson attack

When Peter was nine he lit a fire in a shopping arcade, causing £17,000 worth of damage. No one suspected the small disabled boy. Peter watched till the flames got out of hand then hurried away. He continued to play with matches and seek out bonfires and had dreams about people burning in flames that he'd created, but it was another four years before he killed for the first time. His first murder victim - and several of his later murder victims - were physically handicapped. He'd fallen out with them at school, or simply felt jealous that they had pleasant homes to go to, so determined to exact a terrible revenge...

## Not so happy families

The local authorities were still trying to forge a relationship between Peter and his mother, so sometimes sent him home for trial weekends. When he was eleven his mother married. From then on these weekends included a stepfather called Lee who he described as 'alright.' Often when he went home for the weekend, his mother and stepfather would be partying and he'd be expected to entertain himself as best he could. Trying to join in, the eleven-year-old went around the house finishing off all the beer cans, something he'd first done as an undernourished toddler. As a result he soon built up a remarkable tolerance for alcohol and could drink without getting drunk. At night he couldn't sleep and would wander about the house or the darkened streets. The location of these streets would vary because his mother moved from Manchester to Hull and had several addresses within each city - but the lack of care he received didn't vary. Peter simply didn't have a childhood.

**The first murder**

In June 1973 the twelve-year-old was living with his mother in Hull and tensions were high. In the middle of the night, he left the house and went walking around the town. Soon he made his way to the home of a six-year-old epileptic handicapped boy who travelled on the school bus with him. Peter entered the house by an open window and set the property on fire.

Both parents and their children suffered from severe smoke inhalation and the parents sustained injuries as they helped their able-bodied children escape by jumping from an upstairs window. But, despite Herculean efforts, they were unable to reach their handicapped child and he died.

It took firefighters two hours to bring the blaze under control, after which they carried out the six-year-old victim in a body bag. Twelve-year-old Peter was now a murderer.

**Sexual identity**

On the streets, with his paraffin and his matches, he was in charge - but at school and in his local authority home Peter was still an obvious target for older boys who wanted sexual satisfaction. One man went to jail for having sex with the adolescent boy. In time, Peter would become more predatory and would persuade younger boys to 'muck about' (as he put it) with him. Though aware that these were homosexual acts, he told anyone who asked that he wasn't gay.

**The second murder**

Four months after killing the six-year-old boy, Peter was ready to set another fire. The date was 12th October 1973. This time he chose the house of an elderly recluse who lived in squalor. He entered the home by a window in the early morning and saw the man sleeping in his chair. Peter lit a fire then raced out of the door. The seventy-two-year-old man, a semi-invalid, died from smoke inhalation. He had refused the help of social services and bravely maintained his independence, only to be killed by a deeply disturbed child.

## The third murder

Less than a fortnight later the teenage Peter crept into a pigeon loft, possibly planning to torture or steal the birds. The pigeon fancier found Peter lurking there and hit him. Peter ran off, shouting that he would kill the man.

A few days later he strangled most of the pigeons. Then he crept into the owner's house and poured paraffin on the thirty-four-year-old as he slept. His victim, clothes on fire, raced into the street and collapsed. He mumbled something about 'why would anyone do that?' to a neighbour then lapsed into unconsciousness, spending the next seven days in hospital in a coma before he died. The blaze was assumed to have started when some clothes drying by the fireplace went up in flames. Yet again, no one suspected an arson attack.

## The fourth murder

Either Peter didn't start a fire for the following fourteen months, or he did but didn't give the police details. All that's known is that on 23rd December 1974 he entered the house of an eighty-two-year-old female. He went into her bedroom and saw her lying in bed. He lit a fire in the corner of the room and the unfortunate woman burnt to death. It's unlikely that he knew her. He simply hated what she stood for - someone with a home and a family. The unwanted boy loved fire and despised the people it destroyed.

## The fifth murder

Another eighteen months elapsed before he started another lethal fire. It was June 1976 when he went to a house which included a seven-year-old spastic girl who went to the same special school as he did. Peter entered by an unlocked back door and heard someone moving about upstairs - the girl's grandmother who was putting the child's one-year-old brother to bed. Peter quickly started a fire in a downstairs cupboard and left.

The grandmother came downstairs and found the rooms filled with smoke. She managed to get the seven-year-old girl to safety and her five-year-old brother made his own way out of the burning building. But, despite heroic attempts to save him, the one-year-old boy perished in the flames. Peter had done his work well, using paraffin as an accelerant, and the house was burnt to a shell. The grandmother assumed the five-year-old had been playing with matches, though his parents later explained they didn't keep matches in the house. This fire too was seen as an unfortunate accident rather than an arson-related death.

## Cause for concern

No one knew about Peter's arson attacks but they could see that his behaviour was deteriorating rapidly. That year, 1976, the local authority sent him for psychiatric tests suspecting increasing mental illness. But the analysis showed that his disturbance was a result of his dreadful childhood and his physical handicap. In other words, he had behavioural problems rather than mental ones.

Peter had by now been physically and emotionally abused for sixteen years and was increasingly out of control. He'd been told what to do so often in his formative years that he couldn't stand authority. He'd quarrel with anyone who tried to direct him in any way.

## The sixth murder

On 2nd January 1977 Peter entered a house by the back door. He knew the woman and her children who lived there, and he had fallen out with the children's father. The man had struck him and now Peter was intent on revenge. He started a fire beside the couch, having seen a cot in the room. Peter fled as soon as the flames took hold, burning a six-month-old baby girl to death in the inferno. Unusually, he was seen with other onlookers watching this particular fire. He would later say that he was sorry about this death as he liked babies - but he clearly wasn't sorry enough to stop his arson attacks.

## Eleven men die

Three days after killing the baby, Peter killed again. By sheer chance, his next eleven victims were at the other end of the age scale, ranging from seventy-two to ninety-five. They had survived the rigours of war and illness, only to die at a teenager's whim.

Peter felt the familiar tingle in his hands that said it was time to commit arson. Putting his paraffin bottle and his matches under his coat, he hurried into the night. He stole a bicycle and cycled along till he saw a large building. Unknown to him, it was an old folks home.

He broke a window, climbed into the home, found some kindling and soon had the huge house ablaze. Once again he felt powerful. Eleven men died and several of the rescuers were burnt. Peter allegedly heard some of them shouting 'God help me' - but no one saved them from the flames.

## A foster mother

By now he'd been sent to stay with one of the area's best foster mothers. She found him to be a very quiet teenager who had no friends. She had no idea that he was walking the streets looking for buildings full of victims that he could burn. Peter was happier with her than he'd been for a long time - but it was too little, too late.

Though still physically weak, he fantasised about being important and strong. He started to watch Kung Fu films over and over. He was particularly impressed with Bruce Lee, who could defeat several opponents effortlessly. In real life, Peter was called a cripple by his mother and mocked by some of the local children for his epilepsy, but in his dreams he had a sweet revenge. He lay there night after night imagining whose house he would torch next, how strongly the fire would burn - and how shocked his victims would be when their happy family dwellings went up in flames.

He began to take long walks along the old railway lines, thinking about his crimes. He soon felt depressed again and started to read a Bible that he found at his foster mother's house. It said that 'man cannot serve two masters' so he decided that his master would be fire.

## Two more deaths

Three months later, in April 1977, he set light to a family home, killing a girl of thirteen and a boy of seven. It's believed that he killed such victims because they represented family happiness, something the rejected boy could never have. Ironically, the seven-year-old boy had reached a window and definite safety - but he went back into the smoke filled rooms to rescue the thirteen-year-old and both perished in the fire.

## Four more deaths

In January 1978 Peter was feeling low and bored so went out with his beloved paraffin can. He chose a house at random and poured accelerant into it then lit a piece of paper. The resultant inferno killed a young woman and her three children, who were aged five, four and sixteen months. Peter didn't know who he'd killed untill afterwards when he saw it on the news. Hearing that he'd incinerated four people in this attack seemed to shake him, and he again started to read his Bible, a book he turned to intermittently.

This fire was typical of Peter's arson attacks in that it occurred in winter. Most of his fires were set in October, December and January between 1973 and 1979. Only three occurred outside these months, taking place in April and June.

The timing of these attacks presumably ties in with the depression that preceded them. Even those of us who have homes and life plans my tend to feel depressed in December and January. For a youth with no home, no education and no friends, the winters must have been incredibly bleak. But the anticipation of setting a fire gave him renewed purpose - and it was followed by the excitement of hearing the fire engines racing to the scene. Afterwards, Peter would hear people talking about the fire and about the victims and would feel a secret satisfaction in knowing that he'd caused such a destructive blaze. Most of us take pleasure in creativity, but he'd turned this value system on its head and taken pleasure in destroying buildings and their contents. And though he seldom said so, he clearly took pleasure in destroying the people that were inside.

He later said that he 'didn't think' about the potential victims of his fires - but after the first deaths were reported he must have known that his fires killed the occupants. If he'd really wanted to cause fire without death, he could have targeted abandoned buildings. Instead, he torched family dwellings and a residential home.

Aware that he was often at a loose end, the authorities put him on a Community Action course. This involved painting, gardening and looking after children. He was to repeat this course and seemed to enjoy parts of it, later telling the police that he liked babies and was sorry when they died in his fires.

Peter had at least two relationships with females during these teenage years and had both their names - Barbara and Yvonne - tattooed on himself. Name tattoos are often a sign of insecurity, for people in secure relationships don't feel the need to make such obvious public statements about their love.

## What's in a name?

Peter continued to be obsessed by the Kung Fu film star Bruce Lee, and in the summer of 1979 he changed his name by deed poll to that of the actor. Or, to be more precise, he changed it to Bruce George Peter Lee, reversing his Christian and middle birth names to form two middle names. This involved consulting a solicitor so it was a remarkable action for a youth with such a low IQ. The police would later tell this author that Peter had no one to help him contact the solicitor, that he did it on his own. Bruce Lee was the name under which he would later be charged when he went to court so from now on he is referred to by that name.

## No place like home

By this time Bruce was too old for council and foster care and ended up drifting from one place to another. Sometimes he'd stay at his mother's house, though he'd be there alone if she was out drinking. At other times he'd sleep rough on the streets and on other occasions he'd rent a room in a Salvation Army Hostel where he kept himself to himself.

To pay his way, Bruce found a labouring job at the local meat market where he was paid seven pounds a day for penning pigs. He also claimed unemployment benefit. For kicks, he hung around the public lavatories and had sex with other boys. Presumably he was now taking the predatory role for one of his sexual partners, fifteen-year-old Charlie Hastie, always asked him for money afterwards. Sometimes Charlie took a pound from Bruce forcefully and Bruce was enraged. Charlie had two younger brothers and all three of them were well known for their wildness in the neighbourhood. Eventually Bruce decided to kill them with his beloved fire.

## A final three deaths

In December 1979 he crept up to the doorway of their house in Hull and put paraffin-soaked paper and rags through the letterbox and lit it. The three brothers - aged 15, 12 and 8 - all died in the flames and their mother was badly burnt. (Their father escaped injury as he was in prison at the time of the arson attack and their three sisters escaped as they were staying with friends.) As usual, Bruce disappeared unseen into the night. He spent the next few days alternately sleeping rough and hanging around men's toilets in the hope of some sexual activity. At other times he played the one-arm bandits in a gaming parlour in a bid to stay out of the cold.

## A red herring

Originally the police had thought that a poison pen writer was responsible for the Hastie fire, for a year earlier the Hasties had received an anonymous note written on a cornflake packet. It said that the Hasties were 'a family of fucking rubbish' and warned that if they didn't move house 'then we'll bastard well bomb you.' But further enquiries revealed that the letter writer was a pensioner who had been stoned and mocked by the Hastie children. She was a regular at her local Methodist church who had written the swear words because she thought it was the only language that they would understand - then had been terrified that she'd be sent to prison when she heard a year later that the house had indeed been set on fire.

## An unlikely suspect

Shortly afterwards the police were faced with an equally unlikely suspect. In January 1980, the innocuous looking Bruce Lee was questioned by the police about so-called indecent acts with other men. He admitted having sex with Charlie Hastie and also admitted that Charlie had taken money from him. He didn't say that he'd been enraged by this - in fact the police were impressed at how calm the thin, pale young man actually was.

The enquiry dragged on, and in June of that year the police invited Bruce back in to talk about his relationship with Charlie Hastie. Detective Superintendent Ron Sagar began to interview the surprisingly likeable young man. Earlier that day Bruce had been drinking but now the police had given him cups of tea and fish & chips so he was sober and relaxed.

Acting on a hunch, Sagar said to Bruce that he believed he'd started the fire at the Hastie house. Bruce's features became serious but his voice was expressionless as he said 'I didn't mean to kill them.' He went on to give full details of the accelerant he'd used, how he'd applied it and even what he'd worn that night. He seemed very proud of his actions, saying that the authorities tended not to assume house fires were arson and that he'd covered his tracks well. After taking many more details, the police took him to the cells for the night.


## A murder charge

The next day, Ron Sagar spoke to Bruce again and got him a solicitor. A few hours later he charged him with Charlie Hastie's murder. Bruce looked the detective square in the face but didn't say anything.

The following day Sagar and another detective visited him in prison and said they believed that he'd set previous fires. At first Bruce denied this but after a little more conversation he continued 'Do you know somat? You are the only bloke I know who shows any interest in me. You said before that in my life I've never had a chance. You are right.'

Sagar agreed that Bruce had 'been kicked from pillar to post' and then asked him if he had a grudge against various people. The youth replied that he did and added 'My mum never cared a shit about me. No one ever has.' At other times he swore that he just liked setting fires and hadn't wanted to murder anyone. He was clearly reinventing history, either to gain favour with the police or to feel better about himself.

The boy seemed grateful for the few kindnesses the police had shown him and admitted that he'd expected to be beaten up. He talked some more about his life then the detectives suggested he might have set further fires. At this stage, Bruce's eyes became tearful and he admitted that he'd killed a baby in a fire in West Dock Avenue. He also talked about killing a handicapped boy he went to school with in another house fire, a boy he claimed to have liked.

Promising to come back and see him tomorrow, the police left. They checked and found that a fire had occurred in West Dock Avenue in which a six-month-old baby girl had died and that another fire had killed a handicapped boy. Moreover, a woman who had been burned in a separate fire told the police that she and Bruce Lee didn't like each other and that he'd been seen in the area shortly before her home became an inferno. Everything that Bruce said was checking out.

Detective Superintendent Sagar and Sergeant Martin went back to Leeds Prison the following afternoon and Bruce said that his solicitor had told him not to speak to the police but that he would anyway because 'it's on my mind, not his.' He then spoke of setting the fire that killed a fellow school pupil, of setting the fire which killed Charlie Hastie and his two brothers, of torching the old folks home at Hessle in which eleven men died. He then asked if he could have a Bible to read, and Ron Sagar duly got him one.

## A change of scene

On 30th June the police asked Bruce if he was willing to show them the houses he'd set on fire. Sagar privately thought that Bruce might have made the whole thing up to get attention. Deep down he hoped that the undernourished and ill-educated youth wasn't guilty of the crimes.

Bruce seemed to enjoy the ride in the car and pointed out the scenes of his arson attacks. He was able to give full details of the fires he'd started - what his mood had been like at the time, which windows he'd broken or door he'd entered by, what accelerant he'd used.

Though responsible for twenty-six deaths, he was still only twenty. But he had far more insight into his problems than most serial killers, admitting that he'd caused such mayhem because no one had ever shown him love and his mother had failed to provide him with even a basic home.

## Orgasms by arson

Some arsonists fall into distinct groups. That is, they set fires for a revenge motive or because of some pathological compulsion (a form of mental illness) or because they are fire fetishists so it excites them sexually. Bruce could claim all three motives. Fire had become all things to this alienated boy. It rid him of his enemies, it calmed the restlessness in his psyche and it gave him sexual pleasure. (Though it's untrue that this was his sole form of sexual release.) A legal report produced in December 1980 on his offending would say that he was likely to 'continue to be sexually aroused by thoughts or acts of fire setting particularly in relation to killing people by fire.'

Bruce had the typical background of a pyromaniac. That is, he was abused during his childhood and was poorly parented. He also showed the common pyromaniac traits of sexual sadism and paranoia. He told the police that when he had the urge to start a fire it was very hard to ignore it. He even admitted that he'd felt like setting fire to his cell whilst he was awaiting trial. He added that he'd like to burn his mother for what she'd done to him - that is, for failing to provide him with love or a decent home. His mother would later take part in a documentary admitting that she was 'back on the game' within weeks of his birth.

## Friendless

Detective Superintendent Ron Sagar continued to feel sorry for Bruce Lee as a result of his sad childhood. He visited him in prison to make sure that none of the other prisoners were beating him up. By now Bruce had been on remand in prison for several weeks without a single visitor.

Ron Sagar also spoke to the prison doctor who confirmed that Bruce was immature and indifferent. But he was also streetwise as a result of his very tough life. Other professionals who spent time with him confirmed that he was perceptive and alert.

## The trial

Bruce Lee's trial, on 28th January 1981, only lasted for a few hours. He was charged with twenty-six counts of manslaughter and ten counts of arson. The victims were aged from six months to ninety-five years old. It was noted that he had a grudge against four of the victims, though the grudges were trivial. (That is, they seemed trivial to someone who was thinking rationally - not to a rage-filled youth who'd been mocked and rejected all his life.)

Bruce's defence was one of diminished responsibility though he pleaded guilty to each of the charges. He was sentenced to be detained indefinitely in Park Lane Special Hospital near Liverpool under the Mental Health Act.

## Change of heart

Bruce had initially wanted to go to such a hospital - but in time he changed his mind and decided he'd rather be in prison or have his freedom. This decision may have been prompted by newspaper reports which cast doubt on his convictions, suggesting that a physically handicapped boy could not have climbed into houses to set these fires. But Bruce had shown Ron Sagar how he held the petrol can - and he clearly wasn't without dexterity as he could even ride a bicycle. He'd also held down a job at the local cattle market for a while.

Most of the fires had originally been viewed as accidents, caused by gas leaks, lit cigarettes and so on, and a newspaper suggested the fires were still nothing to do with Bruce Lee. But several of the victims had attended the same special school as Bruce and several others had had arguments with him. There were too many such factors for it all to be coincidence.

Whatever his prompting or motivation, Bruce withdrew his confession. He now said that he didn't like fire or watching fires. (But he'd been seen in the crowd watching one fire and was shooed away from the door of another house shortly before a fire started inside.) He also admitted that he'd changed his mind many times about everything, but that he now wanted to go to prison rather than stay in the special hospital. Bruce's legal counsel explained that it was difficult to take instruction from the youth as he kept changing his mind.

Meanwhile a newspaper made allegations that Detective Superintendent Ron Sagar had influenced Bruce to confess to the fires in order that the police could clear their books. But this made no sense as most of the fires that Bruce had confessed to weren't being treated as arson. Instead, they had been viewed as acts of negligence or as accidents.

That said, there have been many miscarriages of justice where educationally-subnormal or otherwise vulnerable youths have been questioned at length without a responsible adult or a solicitor present. (Two such cases are outlined in a later chapter, Watch Me Bleed.) But Ron Sagar had given Bruce tea and food and had spaced out the interviews. And Bruce would later write to Ron, wishing him well.

After a judgement about the case, the Lord Justice said that the police had behaved admirably and that certain sectors of the media owed Ron Sagar an apology. A full account is given in Ron Sagar's own impressively detailed book *Hull, Hell And Fire: The Extraordinary Story Of Bruce Lee*. The book shows the full complexity of the case and also delineates the courage that Ron Sagar showed in taking on a powerful media in a determined effort to clear his name.


## A fair cop

In March 2002 this author travelled to Yorkshire to interview Ron Sagar. The former Detective Chief Superintendent is a man with a lifetime's worth of crime-fighting experience having spent thirty years as an operational detective in Britain before becoming a Criminal Investigation Adviser in Southern Africa. Though he and his wife have since returned to Yorkshire, they still make regular trips to Africa in their efforts to help the country's poor.

Ron Sagar is equally aware of the poverty of Bruce Lee's life. He interviewed the youth on at least twenty-eight occasions, both in police custody and in prison. Ron provided many of the details in this profile, details which aren't readily available as so little truth - and so much fiction - has been written about this case.

Asked about his first impressions of Bruce, former Detective Chief Superintendent Sagar said that he was 'insignificant - you wouldn't notice him walking into a room.' He could see that the young man was 'an obvious loner' yet he wasn't totally reclusive as he was clearly searching for a friend. Ron Sagar quickly became a friendly figure to Bruce because of his non-macho approach to interviews. He simply refuses to engage in verbal battles.

'I never fall out with offenders or potential offenders,' he explains. This likeable manner would later work in his favour when he was libelled in a newspaper - many prisoners phoned up to say that he'd always treated them well and that they'd be happy to give him a reference.

Ron didn't think that Bruce looked at all dangerous. His only previous conviction was for carrying an offensive weapon, but this could have been solely for self-protection as he was sometimes living rough on the streets. 'It may even have been an appeal for attention,' Ron says.

When Bruce first started to confess to fire after fire, Sagar wondered if the boy was simply fantasising. At one stage he even thought he'd caught the youth out in a lie. Bruce had said he'd poured a circle of paraffin through a letterbox - but later he'd mentioned that there was a net curtain over the inside of the door. Ron figured that the curtain would have made it impossible to pour the paraffin as neatly as Bruce described - but when policemen checked on the door they found that the curtain only covered the upper glass panel. Bruce was right once more.

Nevertheless, the police hoped that Bruce would plead not guilty to the crimes so that the entire story would have to be laid out in court. Instead, Bruce pleaded guilty to each charge of manslaughter. He was so calm and so clearly spoken when answering the charges that he appeared to have a very high IQ. He always seemed to be careful about his answers in a legal situation and remained alert.

During my interview, Ron Sagar was able to squash many of the myths involved in the case. For starters, Bruce didn't say that he was only happy when he could hear people roasting. (Though he did admit to getting a kick from some of the fires.) Instead, he seemed sad about some of the deaths, including the second major fire he'd started. He told a doctor that it 'killed me, mate. I didn't mean to do it' then added 'I don't like speaking about that one.'

Another myth is that he could only orgasm if he started a fire. He did obtain sexual pleasure from some of the arson attacks and this was noted in a legal document. But it wasn't his sole source of satisfaction - he had relationships with various men in public toilets. It's clear that he wasn't acting as a rent boy as at least one of the boys (Charles Hastie) had demanded money from him.

Bruce also told a female senior medical officer that he had had relationships with females but that he had no children because he used contraception.

He said that he'd never cohabitated with a female because he liked 'keeping by myself.' But he'd had relationships with a few females and had two girl-friend's names tattooed on him. He at first denied to her that he'd had any homosexual experiences, but later admitted it, explaining that it had started when he was in a children's home.

A third myth about the case is that the police were running an investigation for a serial arsonist called The Holocaust Man. There was no such investigation because the police weren't looking for a serial arsonist. Most of the fires had been wrongly attributed to electric faults, dropped cigarettes and so on.

Former Detective Chief Superintendent Sagar was also able to refute a fourth story that went the rounds, namely that he found a singed piece of paper at the Hastie fire which contained the address of the Salvation Army Hostel where Bruce had been living, went there and found a can of petrol under his bed. These stories may have been invented by writers looking for a sensational angle or by amateur crime writers trying to fill in the gaps of Bruce Lee's life and arrest.

Bruce himself lied to his prison doctor and his exaggerations may have led to some of the myths. For example, he told his doctor that he was spending £20 a day on alcohol. In the seventies, this was a formidable amount of cash to spend on drink - and Ron Sagar says it's unlikely to be accurate. Bruce was more moderate when discussing his smoking, saying that he bought forty cigarettes a week.

Bruce also told the doctor that he'd been paid to start some of the fires and was given between £300 and £500 for such arson attacks but he refused to elaborate on this. These allegations might have been true or could have been invented to boost his ego, but they weren't brought about by organic brain dysfunction because an EEG showed that Bruce's brain wave was only mildly abnormal. Instead, he was diagnosed as having a psychopathic personality disorder and written up as 'a highly dangerous repetitive arsonist who derives pleasure from this behaviour.'

Asked by this author why there was occasionally a year between Bruce lighting a serious fire, Ron Sagar explained that it's possible he started smaller fires which didn't make the newspapers and which he subsequently forgot about. Or he might have set fires which failed to ignite.

Ron has maintained compassion for Bruce, though he's aware that this isn't a view shared by the general public. (This author has encountered the same attitude when delineating the horror of most killer's childhoods. For some reason, the public doesn't believe that it's possible to have sympathy for the childhood yet hate the murderous actions that can spring from such a violent start.) Ron says that Bruce 'still crosses my mind - with a touch of sympathy for him as a mere human being.' At the time of his arrest, the youth clearly wanted to bond with someone for he befriended Ron Sagar and subsequently related to a female doctor who interviewed him as a motherly figure. When she asked how he got on with his birth mother he admitted he 'never did - she did stick up for me sometimes. She was adapted (sic) to booze, an alcoholic.' Bruce also bonded with his solicitor.

Asked if he'd met many offenders as disadvantaged as Bruce, Ron Sagar says 'many people have had rough upbringings - but Bruce was disadvantaged in all three ways, mentally, physically and socially.' This made him a particularly unfortunate case.

So does Bruce fit the profile of a typical arsonist? 'Yes, he's tending towards the classic profile. The arsonist is often a loner. Bruce fits the upbringing and personality type, the feeling of resentment towards his fellow human beings.' So is this type of arson attack unique to developed countries like Britain and the USA? Ron Sagar says not, that 'it could happen anywhere.'

Sadly, he knows of many other criminals who started offending as young as Bruce. 'Eight or nine-year-olds were arrested with monotonous regularity in the early sixties and presumably in earlier decades, and paraded before the juvenile court.' He goes on to paint a picture of unthinking adults and traumatised children that many of us are very familiar with.

'These children would be described as difficult - but no one seemed interested in looking into their background to find out *why* they were difficult. They were thrown into approved schools and didn't see a relative for many months. Nobody thought that the poor little devils would be homesick.' These kids would try to toughen up in order to survive - and as a result they'd probably end up in borstal. An adult prison would be next.

Bruce's life was as hopeless as many of these kids. Indeed, he'd had so little encouragement from society that he simply couldn't envisage his future. His prison doctor would write 'Asked about future plans, he has none.'

That said, Ron was pleased at how much better nourished and cared for Bruce looked when he visited him in prison after his arrest. For the first time he had the security of a roof over his head and three meals a day. He was later moved to the secure hospital in Liverpool where he still resides. 'He's better off since his arrival there than at any time in his life,' Ron says.

Bruce also has friends of sorts for the first time. Ron says that the former arsonist 'enjoys his reputation and likes rubbing shoulders with the more notorious inmates.' Some of these inmates leave, of course, so he has to make other friends. He sometimes talks about his 'defence team', a term he seems to have picked up from another offender or from television. In truth, there isn't one.

He still resents being told what to do (who doesn't?) and acted strangely when first imprisoned, having shouting spells for no apparent reason. But he seems calmer now and has access to a snooker table and a TV.

Ron has understandably chosen not to keep in touch with Bruce, preferring to maintain a professional distance. But he was pleased to get a letter from him in 1990 via his solicitor. Bruce had heard that Ron was going to Africa to work and told him to take care.

It's interesting that a boy as brutalised as Bruce Lee would worry about a detective, albeit a caring and insightful one. But it seems that Bruce could be two very different personalities at different times, an uncaring arsonist who wanted to seek revenge on society and a desperately uncared for child who simply wanted love.

Bruce once told Ron Sagar of his earliest memory, possibly stemming from an age before he could walk. 'I was crawling about floor (sic) looking for anything left in beer bottles and cans at me home once. My mum always had men in for a drink and that and I used to get the slops they left. I was only little then.'

It's unlikely that any psychiatrist will risk setting such a confirmed arsonist free in the future, especially now that Bruce has spent almost his entire forty-two years in some form of institution - that is, in orphanages and then a secure hospital. It's a sad indictment of society, but this special hospital has provided Bruce with the closest he's ever had to a secure home.

# 5

## DARE TO BE DIFFERENT
### Luke Woodham

Luke was born on 5th February 1981 to John and Mary Anne Woodham who lived in Pearl, Mississippi. John was an accountant and Mary Anne a kindergarten teacher. The couple already had a son, John junior, who was eight years old. Mary Anne was thirty-four and John senior was forty-two by the time baby Luke came on the scene but she was able to take him to work with her, which made it easier to cope.

It also suited Mary Anne as she was an over-protective mum obsessed with her sons' diet, neatness and bath times. She was also very protective towards the children she taught at her work, constantly asking them if anything was wrong at home. Ironically she didn't seem to notice that her older son resented the sudden arrival of his baby brother and often nipped Luke as he lay in his crib.

Mary Anne also seemed not to notice when her husband started to work longer and longer hours. When he did come home he'd find her still obsessing over the children. There seemed no place for him in her very full life. He pointed out that the house was a mess and she retorted that she'd been busy working and shopping. Their voices rose until the neighbours could hear and decided to keep their own children away. Little Luke listened to these increasingly common screaming matches and was terrified.

Mary Anne was religious and took both children to the Baptist church but it's not known how the increasingly timid Luke fared at Sunday school. He did his best to please his mother at home though, saying his prayers at meal times and last thing at night.

Luke became very clumsy and Mary Anne frequently shouted at him for knocking over her ornaments or his teacup. Perhaps realising that she needed some space, she tried taking him to a friend's house but he'd been so used to an aggressive atmosphere that he immediately managed to create one, breaking the other children's toys.

By now his dad was staying away more and more often and Luke doubtless blamed himself for his absence. His older brother was able to visit schoolmates to escape from his mother's nagging but Luke had nowhere to go because he was too young to be independent and hadn't any friends. So the pre-school Luke adopted various pets and made them into his confidantes instead. He'd go out into the yard and speak to his cats and dogs in order to keep out of his angry and over-critical mother's way.

Not that his mum was always so negative. At other times she was very loving towards Luke and gave the impression that he was all that mattered. But it wasn't the healthiest type of love - friends thought that she acted as if she owned the little boy.

By the time Luke was four or five, his mother had had enough of simply being a wife and mum. She decided she wanted more fun in her life and started going out with her friends most evenings. This meant that John junior, now in his early teens, was left to babysit Luke. Unfortunately John still had no feelings for his brother and tended to trip him over or tease him mercilessly.

## School days

Unsurprisingly, Luke was school-phobic by his first day at school. He'd had so few good experiences of life that he suspected everyone was out to get him. And as his older mother had given him an old fashioned haircut he really did stand out in a negative way from the crowd. Mary Anne also insisted that Luke wear shorts all year round so he was teased in winter when the other boys wore trousers to school. Before long the trendier boys were pushing and shoving him and calling him names.

Luke hadn't been in junior school for long when his father got the sack. Now his dad was at home all day and his parent's fights intensified. Mary Anne insisted on bringing both children into the room to hear these arguments, telling them to listen to what their father had done now. Sometimes Luke's dad would take him out to the park but at other times he hid away in his study for the entire day. Luke did what he could to cheer up both parents but by now the marriage had crumbled irrecoverably.

When Luke was seven his father finally walked out. Luke had loved his dad and he was devastated. He turned even more to his animals for succour as they didn't let him down in the way that other people did. Mary Anne was also thrown by the desertion and began to party even more determinedly. She also worried about how she'd pay the bills. John junior understandably stayed at a friend's house as often as he could because he hated the tension in the household. This meant that Luke was left on his own most evenings with his pets.

Even when Mary Anne was home, the evenings were not a success. She wanted Luke - still only eight or nine - to talk to her like an adult. But Luke was so tired of her criticism that he preferred to keep his feelings to himself. He possibly also resented the fact that he could only see his mother when *she* felt like it - he was clearly second best to her friends. So he'd answer in monosyllables and she'd shout at him some more and further alienate him. He'd end up watching TV with her in complete silence or escaping to the privacy of his room.

Not that his room was as private as he'd have liked it to be. His mother often checked up on him and took away some of his pocket money if his bedroom wasn't immaculate. If she found one of his toys or games out of place she'd throw it out and refuse to let him fetch it from the trash.

Desperately lonely and bored, Luke often took a large packet of crisps up to his room with him. It was one of his few pleasures, given that he knew he'd be picked on again by his schoolmates the following day. At other times his mother gave him fattening snacks to cheer him up then criticised his expanding girth. As his size increased he became even more clumsy at recreational sports. His eyesight was also worsening and his mother got him heavy-rimmed glasses which further contributed to his already old fashioned look.

Every area of Luke's life was going wrong. Mary Anne now worried so much about cash that she refused to allow him to leave scraps of food on his plate. Once he threw some leftovers in the bin and she pulled them out and made him eat them. Like many such parents, she seemed unable to put herself in her son's place, to recognise that he needed love and respect. His life consisted of church with his mother and of being home alone or with her there, nagging at him. He had no friends and no fun and was old before his time.

A photograph taken of him at age ten shows how unreasonably he was expected to dress. His hair is cut so short that it looks like he has the receding hairline of a fifty-year-old. He's peering through the previously-described glasses and wearing a white jacket, shirt and tie. The fact that he's several stones overweight adds to this impression of someone who is prematurely aged - and his tension is evident from the set of his mouth. It's as if Mary Anne has subconsciously tried to turn him into the husband that she'd permanently lost. In the photograph he has his hand on her shoulder but she's half turned away from him, her older son on her other side, smiling at something that the camera can't see.


## Never good enough

Mary Anne was very interested in Luke's education but she showed it in an unhelpful way, going to the school if she thought that his grades weren't good enough. If he got a B, she criticised him for not getting an A. With his IQ of 115, Luke was reasonably bright but was no genius.

Parents who put academic pressure on their children often find that the child's grades slip - and Luke was no exception. Learning, which could have been an escape from the physical bullying of his schoolmates, had become a chore.

Mary Anne would nag Luke about his studies at night and would check his homework before taking him to school in the morning. She also nagged him about his diet, the state of his bedroom and his gardening chores. By now he was silently fighting back, saying that he'd cut the lawn then only cutting a little strip down the centre of the grass. Suburban gardening standards being high, the source of conflicts were endless, a creatively trimmed lawn starting the equivalent of World War Three. Neighbours were used to the shouting, but on at least one occasion they heard terrified screams coming from the house and informed the social services. But Mary Anne opened the door and insisted everything was fine so the authorities went away.

In fairness, her own life was increasingly under stress. Her part time teaching salary was too small to support herself and her sons so she'd switched to a full-time job as a receptionist. This meant starting work early, so she had to take her sons to school even earlier. This was also difficult for Luke as it meant he was at school - a place he feared and hated - for well over an hour before his first class. To help pass the time, he would sit in the corridor reading a book and eating yet more snacks.


## Low years in high school

By the time he went to Pearl High School, Luke was almost two stone overweight, desperately shy and very different. Many of the children loved and revered sports but he hated games. Other children found their place in the hierarchy by being cool, but with his round face, short hair and old-fashioned clothes Luke simply didn't fit the bill. The other teens often tripped him up as he walked along the corridor before start of class - and if he sat down outside the classroom in order to become a smaller target, they'd step on him. They called him Fatso and Snotball and made every day a physical and mental hell.

The hell would start when his mother took him right up to the school doors and insisted he kiss her on the cheek. The cooler kids would line up to watch and roar with laughter. The misery continued when he went into an extended daydream (something that abused children do to shut out the misery of their lives) and was picked on by the teachers for not paying attention. He tried ignoring them, tried answering back and at one stage even got into a physical fight with one of the name callers. But it made no difference and the cruelty went on. Luke tried to find solace in food but the bullies stamped on his snacks until they were inedible.

Luke tried playing truant from school but his mum found out and yelled at him then grounded him. Not that the grounding made much difference as Luke had nowhere special to go. Desperate for a peer group - even a long dead one - he started to read the work of existential philosophers, identifying with the works of Nietzsche and Dostoievsky. Doubtless he identified with Dostoievsky's Underground Man.

Luke was himself becoming an emotionally underground man. For years he'd tried to win his father's and his mother's love and had tried to act happy at school and at Sunday school. But now the years of cruelty were taking their toll. At age fourteen he wrote in his diary that he had been 'always beaten, always hated.' He also wrote that his brother sometimes punched him - and everyone could see that he was often pushed and stepped on in school.

## Three's a crowd

But when he was fifteen, life briefly improved when a new girl arrived at his school. Christine Menefree was pretty and kind and soon befriended him. She encouraged him to grow his hair longer so that he looked more modern. The teens both loved animals so they had something to talk about.

Luke asked Christine out and she said yes. To his horror, his mother stipulated she had to drive them to the cinema. She was also waiting for them in her car when they left. On another occasion she insisted on coming with him to Christine's house and mocked the fact that the young couple sat close to each other. She was still treating him like a child.

Unfortunately, Luke was becoming as regimented as his mum and demanded that Christine be home at certain times to take his phone calls. Within a few weeks she'd had enough and finished with him.

## Suicidal

All of Luke's feelings of love now transmogrified into hatred - and into self-hatred. He told Christine's friends that he was going to use his father's old rifle to take his own life. They took the threat seriously and successfully talked him out of it but Luke's hatred didn't go away. Instead, he made up enraged posters for his room that said 'America is dead' and 'Fucked Forever.' It's unclear what his mother made of these communications during her tidiness inspection sprees.

## A friend at last

But again Luke's spirits lifted slightly when he heard of a fantasy role-playing game at school that had openings for new players. Grant Boyette, the leader of the game, was from a deeply religious family so believed in Satan. He told friends he prayed to him for influence. Some of the older boys were also religious and prayed to God. They found Grant's belief system unacceptable so they drifted away from the group - at which stage Luke was allowed to join in.

The group was called The Kroth and it involved mock fights to the death between characters representing good and evil. It gave the teens a focus for their meetings and a chance to talk about their various embryonic philosophies. Grant, for some reason known only to himself, admired Hitler and always took the most malignant roles. But Luke found the youth, who was two years older than him, unusual and enigmatic and the two soon became close.

Luke had been suffering from insomnia and intense loneliness since

Christine finished with him so was very glad of Grant's esoteric company. Grant would come to his house and the teenagers would listen to heavy metal music. They also read voraciously and, like most people who haven't acquired any power, were particularly interested in a book of spells. He and Grant ostensibly put a spell on someone - and that person's friend died in a road accident. This was enough to make the impressionable Luke believe that Grant had special powers.

In this Luke was gullible - but he was bright enough to recognise that he was living in a world which values sporting achievement and fashion sense over creativity and intellect. If he'd bided his time until he became an adult, he could have left home and put his various insights to good use. He might simply have been a late developer - for many children who do badly at school go on to live successful and fulfilling lifes. But, like most children raised in hypercritical and over-protective households, Luke didn't have the confidence to believe that he could live on his own. His home, unpleasant as it was, was the only refuge from the school bullies that he'd ever known.

## A part time job

By early 1997 the unpleasantness at home had reached a peak and his mother said that she could no longer give him any pocket money. Perhaps she was hoping that he'd no longer buy the music that he loved to play in his bedroom - but Luke proved unexpectedly resourceful and found himself a weekend job at a pizza place. He liked it so much that he thought he might work there full time after he left school and the management encouraged him as he was punctual, hardworking and unfailingly polite.

## The fantasy deepens

But the weekend job simply wasn't enough to put the troubled teenager's world to rights. He still had to go to school five days a week to be spat upon and mocked and hit. He still had to deal with his mother criticising his weight, his grades, his room, his friends, his very being. His new friends noticed that she was always picking on him and they hated the atmosphere in the house. By now Mary Anne had started going out with male friends and couldn't find time to go shopping so there was sometimes very little food in the house. Bereft of love, Luke found it difficult to sleep at nights. He also suffered from depression and crying jags. He had his friend Grant, of course, but Grant was only his friend as long as Luke didn't question a word he said.

In his real life Luke would admit that he felt like 'a total reject' but in his daytime fantasies he was an imposing master. In these fantasies he hit back at the people who had hurt him and he watched them cower and fall.

## Animal cruelty

He decided that he had to harden himself against society so that it couldn't hurt him any more. He and Grant began to talk of how it would feel to really harm another creature. Sickeningly, they turned their attentions to Sparkle, Luke's Shih Tzu dog.

Luke held the animal in place and Grant beat it with a stick, hurting its legs so much that it could barely walk afterwards. A neighbour witnessed the abuse but doesn't appear to have contacted the authorities. Luke's older brother later saw that the animal was limping and said that he should take it to the vet for treatment. Knowing that a professional would notice the animal's bruises, Luke decided to kill the dog instead.

He and Grant took the animal to the nearest forest and beat her then encased her in several bin bags. Then they put the semi conscious creature into a heavier bag and set the bag on fire. The dog was still alive so Luke added more fuel, at which stage the desperate creature managed to escape from the bag. Luke then broke the animal's bones with a club and set it on fire yet again. He clubbed the little dog for a final time, taking an almost clinical interest in the fact that it had lost control of its bladder and its bowels. Then he threw the satchel with the dead or dying creature into the lake and both youths laughed.

Back home, John junior asked where Sparkle was and Luke said that the dog must have run away. He clearly felt no remorse for his incredible cruelty, writing a week later that he and Grant had 'been beating the bitch awhile... I'll never forget the howl she made. It sounded almost human.' It may be pertinent that he referred to the animal by gender rather than by breed.

Sadly, Luke's treatment of the dog isn't unusual for an abused child. Abused children often start off by loving animals but, as the abuse continues, they

show violence towards their pets and towards wild creat
this is simply a desire to pass the pain onto something el
instances the target is a more specific one. For example, m
killers have admitted torturing their abusive parent's favou
in childhood as a way of getting revenge.

Indeed, it's well documented that three of the warning signs that a child
will become violent towards adults are cruelty to animals, fire-raising and
bedwetting. Luke had now demonstrated the first two by setting his dog on
fire. And this wasn't his first attempt at fire-starting, for he told a friend that
he loved to set fires.

Mary Anne hardly noticed that the dog had gone. By now she was dating
various men so was often preoccupied. Luke and his role-playing friends sat
around at his house and talked about killing their various enemies. To their
schoolmates - and to Luke's mother - they were inadequates but in their
heads they ruled the world. And rulers can do whatever they like.


## Matricide

Alternatively over-protective and hypercritical, and raising her son without a
father, Mary Anne fit the classic profile of the mother who is killed by her
own male offspring. Clearly unaware of the danger she was facing, she kept
telling Luke that he'd never amount to anything. He also got the impression
that she blamed him for his father leaving and for the fact that her older son
kept out of her way. For years Luke had tried to either please her or avoid
her but now he'd run out of feelings and just didn't care about seeking her
approval any more.

He may have told some of his role-playing group that he wanted his mother dead - but the game was about killing off people in fantasy land so it's
unclear how seriously they took him. But Luke was in deadly earnest and the
fifty-year-old was about to die.

On 1st October 1997 he set his alarm for 5am, got up and fetched a knife
from the kitchen drawer. Noticing his baseball bat in a corner, he grabbed
that too.

Sixteen-year-old Luke had planned to kill his mother whilst she slept, but
to his shock he found her dressed and preparing to go jogging. He chased
her into her bedroom where she tried to hold the door shut - but he had

of rage on his side and forced his way in. He then slammed the bat against the furniture, terrorising her further. For perhaps the first time ever he had control of what he did.

What followed would be an act of overkill, the actions of someone who really hates their victim. Luke brought the bat down on his mother's face, breaking her jaw. Then he forced a pillow over her face with one hand and stabbed at her body seven times with his other arm. He also slashed at her a further eleven times so that blood spattered the bed, walls and carpet, one of the knife wounds entering her brain. Some of the slash wounds were to her hands as she tried to defend herself - and Luke was stabbing so hard that the knife sometimes slipped and cut his own palms. Apparently thinking rationally, he went into the kitchen after the killing and bandaged his own wounds.

He then wrote a letter somewhat like a Last Will And Testament, leaving his few possessions to his role-playing friends. He did so because he knew that he was about to massacre his school colleagues and believed that he would be shot dead by the police. He wrote very honestly of what had happened to him saying 'Throughout my life I was ridiculed. Always beaten, always hated. Can you, society, truly blame me for what I do? Yes, you will, the ratings wouldn't be high enough if you didn't, and it wouldn't make good gossip for all the old ladies.' There were several pages to this effect. Ironically, the media would indeed go on to blame the matricide on the fact that Luke played fantasy games and others in the Bible Belt would suggest that 'the Devil' had taken over the abused boy's mind.

Luke now phoned his friend Grant and spoke in a three-way call to another friend, though we'll probably never know exactly what all three said. He sounded depressed and slightly tearful - but obviously determined to continue in his murderous plans.

**School slaughterhouse**

Further bloodshed on his mind, Luke took his dead mother's car and drove erratically to Pearl High School. He parked, entered the building and gave his notebooks to another pupil. Then he walked along the corridor holding his father's rifle until he found the girl he had dated a few times, Christine. He shot her twice, one bullet entering her shoulder and the other fatally entering her neck. The girl she'd been talking to, Lydia Dew, tried to move and he shot her several times in the torso. Both girls died at the scene. Witnesses said that Luke's face was blank and that he moved in a slow shuffle. It's unclear why he shot Lydia because she and her sister had always been kind to him. (Christine had also been kind to him, but ever since she'd ended their relationship he'd borne an unfair grudge.)

Luke continued to fire, hitting one girl in the shoulder and another girl in the stomach. He wounded a male student in the legs and another in the hip. He seemed to know what he was doing during this shooting spree as he apologised to one male he had no quarrel with and who he'd shot by mistake. Other children were also hit in the lower legs and in the upper body before Luke left the school and tried to make his escape. But the car got stuck in mud and he was tackled by an armed teacher and taken into custody. He said to the teacher 'the world has wronged me', his tone as deferential towards adults as it had always been.

## Arrest

Rumours soon went around that Luke had killed the students because one of them - Christine - had finished with him. It was only when the police asked Luke how he'd cut his hands that he told them that he'd stabbed and 'probably' killed his mother. The police were surprised by this but they shouldn't have been - spree killers often kill one or both parents before going on to shoot further victims at their school or place of work.

Fifteen-year-old Kipland Kinkel, profiled later in this book, killed both his mother and father before massacring fellow school pupils. The exact same pattern can be seen with adult males. For example, Michael Ryan killed his mother before shooting fourteen pedestrians in what became known as the Hungerford Massacre.

The police raced to Luke's house and found his mother's blood-spattered body lying on her bed with a pillow over her head. They noticed that the house was dust-covered and looked unlived in. The only family photograph on display was the one Luke hated in which he looks many years older than he actually was.

Meanwhile most of Pearl was talking about the cold blooded killer whilst refusing to recognise the abuses that had driven him to commit the killings.

77

The abuses aren't an excuse, but they are an explanation. One parent was more insightful, however, and is quoted in a book about the case - *Child's Prey* - as saying 'he was a student whose intellect was not appreciated, his family life was not going well and he'd reached a breaking point.' In fact, these are understatements - his intelligence was mocked, his unfashionable looks earned him endless kicks and vicious name-calling and he had no family life at all.

For some reason, many people find it hard to empathise with children who suffer in this way. Yet they'd be sympathetic towards an adult. If an adult was physically assaulted just once by another adult and told that they were worthless they'd have victim support and recourse to the law. But when Luke was kicked and spat on endlessly at school it was dismissed as child's play. When community members heard his mother screaming at him, they merely kept their own offspring away. Even when he was seen beating his beloved dog, a sure sign that something was seriously wrong, no one intervened.

As usually happens, various special interest groups tried to hijack the case to publicise their own cause. A religious teenager suggested that if there had been school prayers then the murders wouldn't have happened. This was nonsense - a huge percentage of the students had been to the school's Bible class before class started and Luke had been sent to church at least once a week for his entire life. Belief in a deity is absolutely no protection against being murdered - people have been killed in churches and on their way to church.

Other groups tried to blame the role-playing game, refusing to recognise that it was the personalities of some of the players that was suspect. Some of these youths came to the game with hatred in their hearts - but there were various sociological reasons for that hatred. The media preferred to leave that particular stone unturned.

But Luke wasn't the only teenager about to end up in the dock. Having listened to various stories about The Kroth, the police now arrested several members of the role-playing game and charged them with conspiracy to commit murder. Later all were released without charge, with the exception of Grant Boyette who was eventually charged with conspiring to impede a public official, and given five years probation plus a month in a boot camp.

## Two trials

Luke's first trial was for matricide and it was held in the first week of June 1998. It held no surprises. After all, Luke had admitted to killing his mother, telling police that he wanted to do it and giving them some examples of his problems at home. He cried when the prosecution said that he was hateful. A psychologist for the defence testified that he had a borderline personality disorder. Borderline personalities tend to suffer from low self-esteem and act impulsively. The disorder often goes hand in hand with depression so Luke certainly fits the bill. But it was clear that he'd known exactly what he was doing and was not insane.

His second trial later that month was for the school massacre. Again, the guilty verdict was a foregone conclusion. There were numerous witnesses to the fact that he'd shot dead two girls and wounded seven other students who'd been unfortunate enough to be in his line of fire. He cried again and apologised to the sister of Lydia, one of the girls he had killed.

As usual he was alone, for none of his remaining family showed up to support him. (His father had visited him once for a few minutes in prison.) Like many abused children he spent most of the day in a fugue state. But he did show rage when being doubted by the prosecution, saying 'Y'all don't know what I went through. You've never been in my shoes.'

By now his shoes had taken him along the religious path, for a pastor had encouraged him to have a religious conversion and he'd later say 'God has forgiven me.'

The teenager - by now aged seventeen - was sentenced to the maximum penalty that the state allows, life imprisonment, and will become eligible for parole when he is sixty-five. He is locked up in the notorious Parchman prison in Mississippi where he tries to survive by spending as much time as possible on his own, writing poetry. He also writes to his new penpals for he gets dozens of letters each week from teenagers who say — alarmingly - that they completely identify with him.

# 6

# WAITING FOR A GIRL LIKE YOU
## Cindy Lee Collier & Shirley Katherine Wolf

Cindy was born on 18th April 1968 to nineteen-year-old Linda and twenty-two-year-old David Collier. She came into the world to find that she already had two half-brothers, Keith and Jeff. These brothers were the product of Linda's previous marriage - an attempt to escape an unhappy home life - at age sixteen.

Cindy was a seriously underweight baby who was born with legs that were out of joint. As a result she spent her first two years in a metal brace. She was often ill, possibly picking up on the stress within her impoverished and haphazard home. Her father was unemployed and had a troubled history and the couple argued constantly.

When Cindy was four, Linda presented her with another little brother - and when Cindy was five, her father walked out on the family for good.


## Violent men

Linda, who had learning difficulties, found it hard to cope. She soon got involved with another man. And another. She frequently left for work leaving her latest man in the house with the four kids. Joan Merriman, who wrote a book about the case, says that these men were 'of various temperaments and moralities... each one leaving his telltale mark on the children.' Sometimes these marks were left literally as the men wielded their power over the helpless kids.

Cindy was a pretty little girl, who was very attractive to some of these men. Others enjoyed ordering the children about, knowing that all four were at their mercy. Violence or the threat of it filled many of their days.

By the time Cindy was seven, she was being sexually abused on a regular basis by a ten-year-old relative. (It's a safe bet that this relative had also been abused, as abused children become sexualised very early.) This abuse continued as the years went by.

The frequently-beaten child had little quality time with caring adults and nothing to look forward to. She increasingly hated school, where she was one of the more impoverished students. As a result, she started to play truant, staying away from school and home for as long as she could. When she was home she tended to be protective towards her mother and to make excuses for the fact that Linda sometimes stayed in the pub until closing time.

Cindy turned twelve and began to fight back, getting into increasingly violent arguments with other pupils. One playground fight was so brutal that the police were called and she was charged with assault and battery. She was given community service, but was soon in trouble again for stealing. This time she was sent briefly to Juvenile Hall.

Cindy started to run away. Teenagers often do this to escape a desperately unhappy home - yet the public and police often misconstrue the motive as being 'just for fun' and react punitively. As a result, Cindy got even more custodial time. Photos taken of her at age thirteen show a bright-eyed girl whose smile no longer meets her eyes, is fixed.


## A suicide attempt

By now her health was even more precarious as the relative who was sexually abusing her had given her a venereal disease. Her menstrual cramps were almost unendurable and she sometimes bled for twenty days in a row. She was so unhappy that she attempted to take her own life - and would threaten to do so again.

When she was fourteen she stole her mother's car and took off, living on the streets. She lost weight and soon had a serious hygiene problem. After four weeks she contacted the police and asked them to take her home.

The authorities decided to put her in a group home, where she'd later claim she was raped. (Such homes are magnets for paedophiles.) After a few weeks she was moved into foster care but within hours she'd absconded again. She was desperate to be a free spirit - but understandably didn't have the peace of mind to truly be free. Meanwhile her brothers were being questioned by the police about acts of vandalism and theft and drugs.

Like many unhappy teenagers, Cindy began to overeat. By the time she was fifteen she weighed ten stone. Superficially she looked old beyond her years and hard and angry - but people who looked closer could see that she was still a desperately vulnerable child. She was also an increasingly dangerous child as the years of sexual and physical abuse had taken their toll and she told herself she no longer cared who she hurt. In fact, she'd started to enjoy hurting those who'd had more privileged childhoods. She also swore and lied and insulted the various authority figures who she came into contact with, surviving by cutting herself off from emotional pain.

Cindy soon gained a reputation for being mean to other inmates in the group home. Even the boys were afraid of her. She'd now grown to five foot nine and could pack a powerful punch.

On 14th June 1983, Cindy went to visit a friend who was living in a group home, and met up with another resident called Shirley Wolf. Shirley was still missing her mother and her brothers and even wanted to see her dad. The teenagers talked and decided to flee together, determined to have a big adventure. As they walked and hitched they exchanged life stories, finding that both had suffered a lifetime's worth of violence and sexual abuse. Within hours *they* would become the violent ones, killing an innocent victim in a prolonged and brutal attack...


## Shirley Wolf

Shirley's life had been even worse than Cindy's. She was born on 17th April 1969 to Katherine and Lou Wolf, the couple's first baby. Katherine had been physically and sexually abused by relatives during her childhood and Lou had been physically battered by his father - and had watched his father batter his mother - then was put into a care home where he was beaten by a priest. (Despite these brutal experiences, he had a religious tattoo on his left arm.) Lou, a carpenter, now controlled his young wife, who initially adored him and was used to being controlled.

But control freaks tend to control their children too, so by the time Shirley was a toddler her life was becoming a less happy one. Her father - who was over six foot tall and powerfully built - hit her for any imagined misdemeanours whilst Katherine looked the other way. On other occasions Katherine also lashed out. She'd given Shirley two brothers in quick succession so was coping with three pre-school children and a husband who ruled the household with an iron fist.

Not that life was all bad. Lou would sometimes bring home presents for the children. He'd stroke Shirley's silky brown hair and look into her dark brown eyes and tell her that she was his little princess.

## Incest

One night, when Shirley was three, the little princess awoke to find her father in her room. He took her from her bed and rubbed her body against his until he ejaculated. Then he awoke his wife and told her he'd had a dream in which he'd imagined he was having adult-to-adult sex. He said that he'd woken to find that he was really touching little Shirley. Would Katherine go and clean the child up?

Katherine's relatives had pretended not to notice when *she* was sexually abused - and it now seems that she emulated this not-seeing. She picked up the frozen, watchful child, stripped off her semen-soaked pyjamas and dressed her in clean clothes.

## School days

By the time Shirley was ready to start school, the family had moved to New York. The years of violence and abuse had already taken their toll and she was old before her time, her little face often vacant. She was desperate to please her teacher - or any adult in the vicinity - but clearly found it hard to approach the other kids. The school told her parents that the five-year-old needed counselling. The couple nodded - but didn't follow through.

## Another brother

When Shirley was six, her mother presented her with another baby brother. By now Shirley's brothers were emulating their parent's violence and were constantly battering each other. Months later Lou fell from a window ledge at work and shattered his legs. He had operation after operation but remained in pain and was often wheelchair-bound. At other times he managed to walk on crutches - but he couldn't return to his carpentry work so the family now lived on social security.

Lou's temper worsened after the accident and he began to imagine slights. Other adults in the vicinity gave him a wide berth, especially when he began to appear outside holding a submachine gun. Katherine would chainsmoke, nervously sensing the build up of his latest rage. He beat Shirley if she scuffed her shoes or spilt a drink or did any of a million other normal childish things. He even beat her if she didn't get top grades in school.

There was a strong humiliation aspect to these punishments, for he would pull down her pants before lashing into her with his belt. She also had to watch and listen as her three brothers suffered similar assaults, and often saw him punching and slapping her mum.

## Alienated

Hurt and frightened, Shirley found it increasingly difficult to make friends at school. The other children had the usual childish concerns of whether they'd win at sports, get good grades, be given that much-wanted toy for Christmas. In contrast, Shirley had to cope with being stripped and beaten by her father - and assaulted by her increasingly hysterical mother who was determined to have some power. Katherine had even threatened her daughter with a knife. Shirley never knew exactly what she'd return home to, but it was usually ugly and frightening - for example, her father often shaved her brothers' heads as a punishment.

## Statutory rape

When Shirley was nine the family left the urban excitement of Brooklyn and moved to rural California. Lou started fixing up the house and sent his wife on a long errand to get carpentry materials. He ordered her brothers to leave the house then told Shirley to take off her clothes and show him how much she loved him. Moments later, he took her virginity.

The thin, frightened child continued to have intercourse forced on her by her father during the next few years. The other schoolchildren and teachers noticed that she had a rancid scent that she was clearly ashamed of. Her childish body was being made to accept demands that it couldn't handle, and she must have been in terrible pain.

The physical abuse also continued unabated. Lou got one of his friends to erect a wooden pillory in his backyard. He would put Shirley or one of her brothers into this makeshift stocks so that their head and arms were held in situ. Then he'd yank down their lower garments and beat their bare buttocks with a cord or with his belt. Neighbours heard the children screaming - but as Lou was an imposing figure on a very short fuse they elected not to intervene.

## Child porn

Lou increasingly bought Shirley unsuitably sexy outfits and makeup which she wore to school. At other times he made her pose nude for his camera. He even made sexual passes at her only friend.

The school strongly suspected sexual abuse - and they knew that there was physical abuse because Lou Wolf had told them he believed in severe physical punishment. But when Child Protection Services approached the family they were met with blank faces and a wall of silence. Shirley believed that her mother knew nothing of the sexual abuse so thought that she was protecting her. And Katherine was still trying to pretend that nothing was wrong. Moreover, Shirley had been beaten severely for simply getting her clothes dusty. Surely her father would kill her if she told strangers that he was having full sex with her every time Katherine left the house?

## Changes

At last, as she turned twelve, Shirley began to pass on the violence that she'd suffered. She started vicious fights in the playground, fights that were terrifying to observers. She told another group of girls about being sexually abused and they could see her pain and her hate. She started to menstruate and her father immediately put her on the pill.

One day he attacked his wife more brutally than usual, then slammed out of the house. Shirley rushed to her mother's side where a fearful Katherine admitted that she couldn't take any more and feared for her life. Taking on the role of the adult, Shirley now comforted her mother by saying she'd tell of the abuse so that her father would be locked away for a very long time.

Katherine phoned the local police - who had long suspected that Shirley was being sexually abused - and Shirley made a statement. Katherine added that for years she'd been 'worried that something funny was going on.' (Yet she had gone away for days at a time to visit her family, leaving Shirley - who pleaded with her not to go - alone with Lou.)

Lou was brought in for questioning and immediately went in for some serious victim-blaming, saying that from the age of three his daughter had been a sex maniac who led him on.

The police searched his home and found numerous child pornography mags and articles which tried to legitimise incestuous sex within the family. Katherine admitted that her husband's demands were relentless and that she was so worn out that she'd persuaded a friend to sleep with him.


**Shirley is ostracised**

In the months leading up to his trial, Lou was ordered to keep away from Shirley. But Katherine missed him and soon wanted him back home. She realised that he'd be able to live with her again if Shirley was living elsewhere.

To the child's consternation, her mother now put her in a foster home. Shirley had never been able to make friends with other children - yet now she was living with lots of them, all strangers. She desperately wanted to be back with her brothers and her mum.

Katherine said that everything might go back to normal if Shirley withdrew the charges. Shirley did just that. As a result, Lou only got three months in jail after pleading no contest to child abuse.

Shirley's mood deteriorated further and she continued to be sent from one foster home to the next. Her self-esteem was so low that she was convinced her foster parents couldn't love her so she went all out to make herself unlovable. She refused to speak and got into vicious fights with the neighbourhood children. She ran away and was soon returned to residential care.

By now, like many sexually abused children, she was very promiscuous. By age thirteen she was writing in her diary about boys she'd slept with and wondering if she was pregnant. Thankfully the answer was no.

Shirley was bored and lost. The days stretched ahead with very little to look forward to until her room-mate introduced her to Cindy Collier, who wanted someone to run away with. Shirley volunteered to run away with her and the two girls sloped off into the night.

The next day they tinted their hair and hung around by an outdoor pool and traded their desperately unhappy life stories. Within hours, fourteen-year-old Shirley was thinking of Cindy (who'd turned fifteen just two months before) as her best friend. Both girls had hitched lifts before, but now talked about how brilliant it would be to have a car of their own. They could go wherever they wanted, keep moving around the country. They could sleep in the car and seek shelter there whenever they wished. Each perhaps talking tough in front of the other, they decided that they'd steal themselves a vehicle - but that they'd have to kill the owner first.

## The killing

The teenagers made their way to a nearby housing estate and started knocking on doors asking for glasses of water and to use the telephone. An elderly man pandered to both these requests but didn't have a car and they duly left. Other residents turned them away as they looked so shifty and unkempt. The next person to let them in was an eighty-five-year-old woman called Anna Brackett. She gave them water to drink and all three chatted amicably for an hour.

Anna Brackett was a shy, sweet woman who loved to go dancing with her beloved friend Jim. He was terminally ill in hospital and she missed him and told the girls all about him. They told her anecdotes about their own lives and she told them about her children and grandchildren. They asked about her car and she told them she had an old brown Dodge.

Then Mrs Brackett answered her phone and explained that it was her son, who was coming round to take her out in twenty minutes. The girls looked at each other, each wondering if the other still wanted to carry out their cruel plan.

Cindy told Shirley to 'do it' - and it seems that Shirley was happy to oblige. She knocked the small woman to the floor and threw herself to the ground where she attempted to manually strangle her, an act which was clearly going to take some time. As the octogenarian gurgled and fought, Cindy raced into the kitchen for a weapon, finding a little potato-peeling knife. She dashed back and handed it to Shirley. Fearing that the neighbours were hearing the commotion and might ring at any moment, Cindy also ripped the phone from the wall.

Shirley proceeded to stab the old lady but she was surprisingly strong and managed to shake Shirley off and get to her knees. Cindy now added to the violence, grabbing a broom and battering it into the helpless woman's face. She collapsed again and Shirley rained further knife blows into her blouse-clad frame, the blade puncturing her back almost thirty times. The woman was still making noises so they stuffed a cloth into her mouth.

During the stabbing the knife blade had buckled so Cindy fetched a second one with an eight inch blade and Shirley cut Anna Bracket's throat. By now she was probably unconscious as the knife had done tremendous damage to one of her lungs and to her spleen. But she was still breathing so they cut her throat again. Blood oozed from the woman's nose and mouth where the force of one of the blows had forced her dentures out. At last she lay silent and still.

## Aftermath

Pleased that she was dead, the teenagers grabbed a bunch of keys and ran to Mrs Brackett's car - but they'd brought the wrong keys and couldn't get it to start. Flustered, they raced up the road and started hitchhiking. They were high on adrenalin and immediately talked about killing someone else. The male driver who gave them a lift worried about their safety and had no idea that he should have been fearing for his own.

By hitching and walking, the teenagers soon got back to Cindy's house, where both girls spent the night. They told Cindy's mum that they'd heard about an old woman being killed and clearly wanted to discuss the death in some detail. They also avidly watched the news.

## Arrest

Cindy's friends had seen her with Shirley in the vicinity of the murder - and local residents told the police that girls of the exact same description had asked to use their phones. Cindy had already done time in Juvenile Hall so the police knew just where to find her. They separated the teenagers to question them and Shirley almost immediately told the truth. She even showed the police her diary where she'd written that the killing 'was lots of fun.'

Cindy denied everything - but couldn't explain Shirley's bloodstained clothing or the fact that they had Anna Brackett's keys.

## Folie a deux

At the police station it soon became clear that neither girl would have killed alone. Cindy liked to control other people, so she'd been in her element telling Shirley what to do. Shirley, in turn, was a follower who admitted that she'd have chickened out if she was on her own. Shirley had carried out the actual stabbing whilst Cindy directed, though she'd joined in to hit the woman with a broom.

When asked for a motive, the girls said that they'd needed to steal a car and couldn't let the car owner live or else she'd identify them. To rational people, it seemed an incredibly flimsy reason to kill a stranger - but these teenagers had been shown over and over again that life was cheap. Unsurprisingly, given the level of abuse they'd both suffered, neither girl valued her own life. Both girls were seen as a suicide risk and Cindy actually vowed that she'd attempt suicide again.

## Reality bites

The teenagers were returned to Juvenile Hall to await their trial. There, Shirley took her shower, went to bed and went to sleep. Cindy was showering when a care worker noticed some home-made tattoos on the girl's skin. Gently, she wiped them off - and at this unexpected kindness Cindy started crying as if she was never going to stop. Back in her cell, she curled into the foetal position and went into shock. Shirley had more of a delayed reaction to taking a life, having such a bad nightmare later that week that her screams echoed through the hall.

## The trial

There was little doubt even before the trial that the girls would be found guilty. Several of Mrs Brackett's neighbours testified that Cindy and Shirley had come to their door. Mrs Brackett's own son had seen them hitchhiking away from the murder scene as he drove towards his mother's house. And within minutes of being questioned by the police, Shirley had admitted that they'd killed. Meanwhile, forensics showed that Anna Brackett's blood was on Shirley's clothing and Cindy's fingerprints were on the telephone which she'd ripped from the wall.

At the trial, details of the girls' horrendous childhoods were heard. Shirley at first pleaded not guilty by reason of insanity, then she revoked this plea, then she tried to reinstate it. Meanwhile Lou Wolf told reporters that social workers were to blame for his daughter's confused state of mind.

At visiting time, Lou would hold his daughter's hands and kiss them whilst his wife stared blankly ahead. At other times Shirley played with his hair or lay with her head in his lap. She was doing what she'd been taught to do to win her father's approval - or to at least avoid the worst excesses of his rage.

Cindy also reverted to type, trying to be brave whenever her mother visited. Cindy hugged her mother and was very protective towards her, blocking out the fact that her mother had failed to protect her throughout her life. (In fairness, her mother came from an impoverished family, had learning difficulties and had married at aged sixteen. She was a child raising children and simply didn't know how to do this properly. All four of her children would end up in jail by early adulthood.)

Shirley yet again withdrew the allegations of child abuse against her father - thought witness after witness testified that Lou Wolf had behaved inappropriately towards her and towards other young girls. And Lou Wolf read out a statement which said he hoped God would remember the people who had said negative things about him. The press continued to say such negative things about him that he soon left the neighbourhood with his wife.

After due consideration, the judge sentenced the girls to incarceration until the age of twenty-seven. Both were sent to Ventura, run by the California Youth Authority.

## Update

For the first few years, both teenagers had a difficult time behind bars. Shirley's parents soon stopped visiting and she had few other visitors. She remained violent and turned increasingly to drugs.

Cindy's mother visited her in the youth authority jail whenever she could. Cindy was fiercely loyal to her mother - and this made it impossible for her to tell the truth about her childhood in group therapy. She too continued to get into fights.

When Shirley was eighteen she stabbed a supervisor in the face and hand. She was given an additional nine years and transferred to the much tougher California Institute For Women, an adult prison. Whilst awaiting this transfer she broke a deputy's wrist and was given another sixteen months. She'd had enough of being the victim and was determined to make herself the toughest inmate in the prison.

At around the same time, Cindy started to confide in a caring parole officer that she wanted the equivalent of her high school diploma. She worked hard and passed then went on to take further qualifications. By her twentieth year she'd passed several college courses. She went on to study law, tutored by law school attorneys, and was released on parole in 1992.

Shirley remained troubled and tried to break out of the prison grounds by driving a truck through the security fence. She failed and was sent to a maximum security prison. Here the distressed young woman got satanism, then she got religion. She eventually found comfort in another inmate's arms. A beautiful young woman with a flair for creative writing and art, she was scheduled for release in 1994. Thereafter she disappears from the record books.

# 7

## SAVE ME
### Robert Thompson & Jon Venables

Robert was born on 23rd August 1982 to Ann and Robert Thompson. The couple already had four sons aged nine, seven, five and four. The seven of them lived in a modest terraced house in Liverpool where Robert worked as an electrician whilst Ann stayed at home.

It was not the happiest of homes. Robert Thompson senior was a heavy drinker who often beat Ann. She, in turn, would hit the children. She'd often been beaten with a belt during her own childhood and had married on her eighteenth birthday to escape her violent home. But there were some relaxing times, such as when the couple bought a caravan and took two-year-old Robert and his older brothers on weekend trips to Wales.

When Robert was a month shy of his second birthday, his parents provided him with yet another baby brother. He was initially protective towards this younger child.

Robert was a polite and timid little boy who liked to watch cartoons and play with the neighbourhood children. He was very concerned about his depressed and exhausted mother and did all that he could to give her support. But life was difficult for him, as he was now being hit by his elder brothers as well as by his mum and dad. His mother's weight ballooned to eighteen stone and his father pointed out a house that he said was a home for disobedient children. He threatened to leave them all there.

Social workers became involved when one of the children, aged four, was found with a cigarette burn and bite marks. Another child would later have bite marks on him too. It was clear that there were multiple acts of violence going on in the household though no one was ever charged.

Then, when Robert was six, his father left to live with an older woman, a friend of the family. A week later the Thompsons' home burned down and they were rehoused in a hostel for the next two months.

## Robert's brothers find safer homes

Ann turned to drink and soon spent much of her time at the pub. She'd later admit that she put a bottle of whisky under her pillow most nights and that she'd start drinking from it when she awoke in the morning. Later in the day she'd go to the local pub. Some of the men there called her a slag and said that she should be at home with her large family. She'd shout at them and hit them if they persisted in their remarks.

Robert's oldest brother, a teenager, was unfairly left in charge. Unable to cope, he hit his siblings frequently and tied them up or locked them in the pigeon shed.

The six unparented boys became increasingly lost and unkempt. One of Robert's brothers took him out on stealing binges. Another brother became an arsonist. One brother was investigated for molesting younger children but this couldn't be proved so no charges were brought.

In 1990, when Robert was eight, one of his older brothers was taken into care. Within months a second of his brothers went into care and eventually a third brother followed suit.

## Yet another brother

Ann now entered into a new relationship and had another baby. She stopped drinking, but still had little cash as the family were all on welfare. Ann was too busy with the new baby to take the younger children to school so Robert continued to play truant. He also began to steal things for his baby half-brother and for his mum.

He'd just turned ten when Ann allegedly hit one of his older brothers with a cane. It was the last straw for the boy as he'd been trying to look after the family and get the others to school each morning. He asked to go into care and didn't see much of his siblings after that.

In January 1993, Robert took his eight-year-old brother to the canal, kicked him and punched him and left him there. The child made his way to the nearby Strand shopping centre in a very distressed state. He told his teacher that his brothers all hit him, but that Robert hit him the most.

At this stage one of Robert's older brothers tried to commit suicide by taking an overdose of paracetamol. Another brother would later attempt suicide, just as his mother Ann had done in the early days of her marriage. The boys had their stomachs pumped out in hospital and they both survived.

Robert himself was clearly in distress. His nails were bitten away and he constantly sucked his thumb. At ten years old, he still sat on his mother's lap and rocked back and forwards. By now he was often staying out until after midnight, wandering the streets and lighting fires on the railway to keep warm.

Robert kept asking other children to join him on the darkened streets - or keep him company when he played truant during the day - but none of them dared. Sometimes he'd give his eight-year-old brother a pound to stay with him, but his brother (an intelligent child who still enjoyed school) often told the teacher. So Robert was very pleased when a new boy called Jon Venables joined his class and soon agreed to truant with him.

## Jon Venables

Jon was born on 13th August 1982 to Neil and Susan Venables. The couple already had a three-year-old son who'd had an operation for a cleft palate and who would later be diagnosed with learning difficulties.

The family lived in Liverpool, an area of high unemployment, so Neil often couldn't find the work he was trained for, driving forklift trucks. Neil and Susan both had a history of serious depression and Susan's own childhood had been very strict.

When Jon was one year old, his parents gave him a sister. All five of them lived in a nice terraced house with a little front lawn. But Susan felt lonely and isolated at home on her own during the day and her eldest child's constant screaming drove her mad.

## Divorce and para-suicide

The couple had an increasingly unhappy marriage and they divorced when Jon was three. At this stage Susan went back to her mother for three years, then she moved in with Neil. Later she got a council house of her own but she still spent much of her time at Neil's home. He, in turn, lived with his father, before getting his own place and finally moving back to his father's house after his father died. Unsurprisingly, all of these changes caused the three children stress.

Susan found it particularly hard to cope - and social service reports would later allude to 'two traumatic incidents.' Reporting on these, author Blake Morrison says that they seem to have been suicide attempts.

By now, Jon's older brother was attending a school for children with special needs. His younger sister was diagnosed with the same learning disorder and, in time, she also would attend the same school.

At five, Jon went to an ordinary school - but he was teased by the other children who wrongly called his siblings retarded. He started to ask if he could attend a special school too.

## Violence and foster care

By the time Jon was six his older brother was becoming frustrated by the number of things he couldn't do and was having tantrums. Social workers arranged for him to go to foster carers for one weekend each month to give his mother a break. Susan kept a nice home and Jon was well fed and clothed, but she was very controlling towards him. She hit the children, especially at night when they didn't want to go to sleep. Jon found it particularly hard to sleep and had lots of cuddly animals to 'guard' him in bed. He often felt tired, bit his nails and had bad dreams. But he did what he could to please his mother, reading quietly in a corner when at home or attending church where he joined the choir.

The Venables worked out a joint custody arrangement so that Susan had the children from Monday to Wednesday and Neil had them from Thursday to Sunday. When one parent couldn't cope, they'd send the children to the other's house.

By the time Jon was ten, he was so disturbed that his concerned teacher kept a journal of his behaviour. The child would rock back and forwards in his chair, bang his head against the wall and cut himself with scissors. He threw things at other school boys and stuck pencils in the neighbourhood children. Finally he tried to choke another boy with a ruler - and it took two adults to set the victim free.

## School suspension

Jon was suspended and in autumn 1991 was moved to a new Church Of England school where he met Robert Thompson. The boys very quickly became friends. Jon hadn't played truant before - but Robert soon convinced him of how much fun it was and Jon's attendance deteriorated significantly.

Jon continued to bully younger children and many of them feared him because of his quick temper. He also remained self-destructive, throwing himself about the playground and often disrupting the class. An experienced teacher noted that the child was clearly desperate for attention - after all, most of the attention at home was going to his siblings as they had special needs. The teachers could see that he wasn't a bad boy, that his antics were a desperate plea for help.

## Video

But there were happier times, when the family settled down to watch videos together. And Neil rented adult-certificated videos to watch by himself after the children had gone to bed. Jon sometimes got up early and watched the video so it's possible he saw at least part of an adult film that Neil rented called Child's Play 3. The story revolves around a toddler-sized doll called Chucky which is possessed by the soul of a serial killer. It's basic shock-horror, the strapline being 'Don't fuck with the Chuck.'

Chucky eventually dies - with blue paint on his face - on the train ride in a funfair. To most children it would just have been a scary story, but to a boy as disturbed as Jon, it might have meant more...

## Abduction

On 12th February 1993, the two boys slipped out of school and eventually made their way to The Strand, a large indoor shopping centre. There, they stole a little pot of blue modelling paint and a packet of batteries.

Jon started to entice away a two-year-old boy but his mother called him back. He tried and failed to attract another little boy's attention. Then they saw a third toddler, James Bulger, hurrying from a butcher's shop whilst his mother queued inside.

Jon beckoned to James, who happily followed him and took his hand. The trio were filmed by the security cameras. James was a month short of his third birthday, a happy and trusting child.

Jon and Robert now took the toddler on a two and a half mile journey during which he understandably became increasingly tired and distressed, asking for his mum. But the ten-year-olds, probably egging each other on, felt no empathy for him. (In their own lives, they hadn't been shown much empathy.) They let him fall on his head, leaving a bad graze, and they both swung him by his arms.

Numerous people saw the three of them but just assumed it was two brothers taking their younger sibling home. One woman offered to take the toddler to the police station at which Robert looked ready to run away - but Jon told Robert to take James's hand again and said that they would take him to the police by themselves.

## Sexual exploration?

At last Jon and Robert reached an isolated part of the railway. The exact sequence of events will probably never be known, but at one stage they stripped the toddler below the waist. Jon admitted to taking James's shoes off but said that Robert had taken off his trousers and underpants. He said that the child was unconscious at this time.

Jon would later say that Robert touched the toddler's private parts. It's very likely that Robert had been sexually abused himself - and children who have been molested often feel compelled to repeat the abuse. What's certain is that the toddler's foreskin was retracted and his lower clothes had been removed.

## The killing

This possible sexual exploration was preceded or succeeded by escalating violence. They threw the blue modelling paint and at least one of the batteries at the toddler, who continued to cry.

Jon and Robert had a childish view of how easy it was to silence a Chucky-sized child. Robert said 'Stay down, you divvie' and both boys were clearly shocked when the toddler kept getting up.

They threw stones and bricks and hit him with a heavy metal bar, fracturing his skull in several places. They kicked him and stamped on him. Blake Morrison said that the violence probably lasted for five minutes. They also put some of the batteries in his mouth in what was possibly a naive attempt to bring him back to life. Leastways, his mouth was damaged and Jon later told his father that they'd put the batteries there.

The children placed the body over the freight line, presumably to make the injuries look like a train accident. Blood was coming out of the unconscious toddler's mouth and they didn't like to look at it, so they put bricks over his face. Shortly after this, James died. Cause of death was fractures to the skull. Later a freight train cut the little corpse in half, the driver thinking that he'd run over a large doll.

## Aftermath

After killing the toddler, Robert and Jon went on to the local video shop. They were filthy, and Jon had some of the modelling paint on his jacket, but they acted normally. At ten years old they couldn't fully comprehend the enormity of what they'd done. They'd been on the railway from approximately 5.30pm to 6.45pm and Susan had been looking for them for much of this time.

She saw the boys entering the video shop and she hurried after them, grabbed Jon by his hair and started hitting him. She grabbed Robert by the wrist - and witnesses said she had him on the floor - and dragged him out of the shop, at which point he started to cry so she let him go. Susan then dragged Jon to the nearby police station for a telling off. The policeman shouted at Jon and he cried some more.

Susan took Jon home and started hitting him again. He fell on the floor but she kept hitting him. His father shouted at him too. Then Susan sent him straight to bed saying that he couldn't have his evening meal.

Meanwhile, Robert went home and told his mother that Jon's mother had hit him in the face - so Ann went to the police station to complain about this alleged assault, saying that Susan was an alcoholic. The policeman couldn't see any mark on Robert's face so the two Thompsons went home. But it meant that, within hours of James's death, both juvenile killers were briefly in the police station in a distressed and dishevelled state.

At this stage the toddler was only reported as missing and it was hoped that he'd be found alive. The police were searching the centre's shops in case he'd fallen asleep in one of them and were also looking for a known paedophile who'd been in The Strand shopping centre that day. They had no reason to suspect two sad-faced, frightened little boys.

## Arrest

The footage taken in the Strand was soon shown on television and a friend of the Venables phoned in to say that it looked like Jon. The abductors were known to have stolen blue paint - and the phone caller said that Jon had had blue paint on his jacket. He was arrested at his mother's house. When Susan saw the police she thought they'd come to give him an additional telling off for playing truant. The police already knew that Jon had truanted with Robert so Robert was arrested too.

The boys were taken to different police stations and interviewed separately. At first both boys denied being in the shopping centre but by Robert's second interview he admitted to being there but said that Jon had taken the child.

For his first four interviews, Jon continued to deny going to The Strand. Then the police told him, truthfully, that Robert had admitted they were there. He became hysterical - and journalists who heard the tapes have said they never want to hear a child in such distress again.

Jon was visibly distressed during much of the twelve hours of interviews that spanned three days. Robert cried less often, but his body language showed that he was also very anxious. Robert had been teased for years for 'acting girlish' and for sucking his thumb, so he was now trying to act tough.

Having admitted taking the toddler (whom they called 'the baby') they said that they'd left him by the canal. But eventually Jon sobbed 'I did kill him.' Robert continued to protest his innocence but his shoe print was found on James's face so it's clear that he kicked the child.

Jon said that it had been his idea to take the toddler - but that it had been Robert's idea to kill him. Jon said that he had only thrown stones at James, not bricks like Robert had, but he admitted to stamping on him. Robert said that Jon had hit the child with a metal plate and had kicked him - and James's blood was indeed found on Jon's shoes.

At other times it was clear that the gravity of the situation hadn't registered with the ten-year-olds. They were happy when offered a bar of chocolate or a Chinese takeaway and often asked if they could go home. Their lawyers said that they were more like eight-year-olds than ten-year-olds. Robert was more worried about his mother than about himself, wondering if she could have a glass of water and a headache powder and asking if she could see a nurse.

## A sexual motive?

The police were convinced there was a sexual motive to the crime - and the fact that James had been stripped below the waist does tend to confirm this. Both children found it very difficult to talk about sex.

Yet they were clearly preoccupied with it. When questioned about 'dirty marks' (meaning marks made by mud), Robert said 'Oh, you mean sex marks.' He said that Jon would lie and say that he, Robert, touched the toddler's private parts.

Jon also showed increased anxiety when being asked about a possible sexual assault. He suddenly launched himself at his father and started punching him, screaming 'You think I know, Dad, but I don't.'

## A baying mob

When news of the children's arrest reached the locals, many of them gathered outside the various houses where they believed the culprits or their families were and threatened to hang them. Completely innocent children were implicated by rumour and had to flee their homes.

When the case went to court, men and women launched themselves at the van shouting 'Hang the bastards.' A man would later call a phone in radio programme with the suggestion that the judiciary should have hanged these disturbed ten-year-olds.

Commenting on the situation years later on a television programme, a spokesperson for Consequences (which helps victims' families) said 'this lynch mob mentality didn't really care who they took their anger out on' and added 'Britain was disgraced in that time.' It's certainly ironic that a crowd, ostensibly horrified by a violent murder, were willing to carry out two violent murders. And other members of the public with the same mindset attacked women in the street after mistaking them for the mothers of the boys.

## Secure units

Aware of the level of hatred, the two children became increasingly anxious. They were sent to secure units, where they had nightmares and Jon soiled himself twice. They were afraid to play outside - and Robert apparently comfort ate - so they each gained over two stone, a third of their original weight. They were terrified of never having any friends, of going to prison. Robert continued to say that Jon was guilty of all the violence - and Jon was too upset to talk about it.

Their childishness showed through their attempts to be grown up. Jon said that he'd like to be a Sylvester Stallone type figure such as Rocky - then added that he'd also like to be Sonic The Hedgehog. Robert, who had sometimes spent all day in the local video shop watching cartoons, admitted that he liked to collect trolls.

## The trial

Nine months after the murder, Jon and Robert (now aged eleven) were tried at Preston in an adult court. Jon's lawyer later admitted to being petrified when entering the packed courtroom and said it must have been terrifying for the two boys.

Jon cried frequently and often looked back at his parents, but they kept their heads bowed. Robert looked defiant - but he would later tell his mother that he felt like crying but didn't want everyone to think that he was a baby. The press misinterpreted this and described him as diabolical, a fiend. Ann was occasionally in court, heavily tranquillised.

Numerous witnesses testified to seeing the two boys with the increasingly tired and occasionally sobbing toddler. Another witness had seen James laughing. It doesn't seem that the original plan was to kill him as they had taken him into the local pet shop and had spoken to the assistant there. They had also spoken to two other boys they knew, saying that James was Jon's little brother and that they were taking him home.

Forensic evidence was introduced that proved James's blood was on Jon's shoes and that Robert's shoeprint appeared on the toddler's face, suggesting a glancing blow rather than a deep, bruising one. The toddler's lower lip was badly damaged, probably by the batteries. Death had been due to heavy blows to the skull.

There was little doubt that Robert and Jon were the killers so the trial centred around whether they knew it was wrong to take a child from its his mother, injure him and leave him on the railway line. Psychiatrists testified that the boys were of average intelligence and were fit to plead.

The children's interviews were played over the speakers, their voices high and unbroken. Robert looked upset when he heard Jon say that he, Robert, was girlish. (Robert, who spent much of his time in the secure unit knitting gloves for his baby brother, was happiest spending time in the playground with the girls.)

Attending the trial, author Blake Morrison noted that the court was only interested in the children's intelligence, not in the mental disturbance both obviously had.

Robert had put a flower on James's tribute site - and one court observer later said that this 'wasn't the normal action of a ten-year-old.' But Robert wasn't a normal ten-year-old. He'd been neglected, kicked, punched, tied up, tortured and possibly sexually molested. How much normality could the rational world expect?

After six hours of deliberations the jury came back with unanimous Guilty verdicts for both boys. Jon cried and Robert looked confused. Moments later, out of sight of the many spectators, he would hyperventilate. The judge told them that in his judgement their conduct was 'both cunning and very wicked' and that they would be 'securely detained for very, very many years.'

After the eleven-year-olds had been taken from the court, the judge said that violent videos might have played a part. This came as a surprise to those who'd noted the background of violent parenting, violent siblings and violent school bullies. He wished everyone a peaceful Christmas and thanked Mr and Mrs Venables and Mrs Thompson for trying to get Jon and Robert to tell the truth.

## Allocating blame

In search of a scapegoat, the tabloids picked up on the judge's comment about violent videos and had a field day with stories of evil horror films and 'born bad' boys.

But other authors - each of whom wrote a book about the case - brought more understanding to the discussion. Mark Thomas quoted a report on reducing delinquency which said 'poor parental supervision, harsh, neglectful or erratic discipline, parental discord and having a parent with a criminal record' were the childhood factors 'consistently and significantly linked to later teenage offending.'

David Jackson wrote that the 'suggestion that the killing was a freak happening... erodes our personal responsibility for understanding and challenging the individual and social forces that have produced such a numbing event.'

David James Smith was equally aware that children of ten don't think in the same way as adults do, offering a Rousseau quote which tells that 'childhood is the sleep of reason.' He also spoke honestly in a later Despatches television programme about how unhelpful it was to demonise these damaged boys. And Blake Morrison wrote that 'between the ages of eight and fourteen, most of us do something terrible, performed in a childish, first-time daze.'

Other journalists came forward with their own stories of destructive acts they'd carried out in childhood. One could remember prodding a distressed toddler repeatedly into a lake, egged on by his equally bored friends.

Both boys came from the family backgrounds that make a child most likely to become extremely violent. That is, they had abusive childhoods, had fathers who were absent in Robert's case and passive in Jon's case. Both had dominant mothers - and Jon's mother was also over-protective. Both had seen violence in the home.

Both experienced a fear of abandonment - Jon in particular was shown to be terrified of his mother's rejection. Both lived in environments that were emotionally chaotic. The final factor is that the mother may come to fear her children - and Ann Thompson had been hit by one of her older sons.

## Explanations

It's likely that many factors came together on the day that the boys lured little James away from his mother. It seems that the original idea was Jon's - he'd been so excited at school the day before that his teachers couldn't get any work out of him. The theft of the batteries and the blue paint (the latter appearing in the Chucky film *Child's Play*) suggest he may have had some vague plan - based on childish logic - to have access to his very own Chucky-sized living doll.

Robert was initially less interested in keeping the toddler, and was ready to hand him over to a concerned passerby. But Jon told him to take the child's hand, and he did. There was clearly a strong *folie a deux* element to the crime, for Jon admitted later that he did things with Robert that he was too scared to do on his own.

Having taken the toddler to an isolated location, it's likely that Robert - who appears to have been sexually abused - examined him intimately then felt deeply ashamed of this act.

Author David Jackson would later speculate that the boys, forced to grow up too quickly in a violent macho culture, were 'splitting off their fearful, baby parts and projecting them onto baby James.' It's likely that both boys were jealous of their siblings; Jon's brother and sister were given extra attention because of their developmental problems. And Robert saw Ann, now sober, caring for her new baby in a way that he couldn't remember being cared for, given that she'd been a battered wife then a single mother with a drink problem during his formative years.

## Public hatred

The public continued to hate the boys, rather than simply hating their murderous actions. Perhaps reacting to this, the judiciary kept increasing their sentence. The trial judge had originally given both boys an eight year sentence but the then Lord Chief Justice increased this to ten years. Later still, the Home Secretary, Michael Howard, increased this to fifteen years but this last increase was quashed by the English judiciary.

## A second chance

For the next eight years, Jon and Robert remained in separate secure units for juvenile offenders. After a year in such a facility, Robert was given a few hours of freedom by being taken on a long supervised walk. As he moved into his teens the staff would sometimes take him into town to buy clothes when he'd outgrown his old ones. These outings are formally known as 'mobility' and are a way of preparing the child to re-enter the outside world.

Jon was also taken on supervised outings, sometimes accompanied by his dad. There's more information available about Robert's post-trial years because the Despatches team, who produced an investigative report on the boys for Channel Four, were able to talk to a boy who had spent time in the same unit as Robert but they apparently couldn't find a youth who'd spent time in the unit that housed Jon.

## Psychiatric help

The boys both had regular sessions with psychiatrists to help them come to terms with what they'd done. Though Jon had admitted to the police that he'd killed James, it was another two years before he was able to admit his guilt again. Robert apparently remained in denial for much longer; it was five years before he took responsibility for his earlier actions and showed remorse. Even then, he was only able to talk about the crime when his psychiatrist promised not to write most of it down.

The Lord Chief Justice said that the boys had made remarkable progress - and a visitor to the secure unit said that Robert was now an exceptional young man, very thoughtful and caring. He was also an academic success, having gained five GCSE's and gone on to take A Levels. Jon had also made exceptional progress. His earlier writing had been semi-literate, but he'd now made great strides in English and Maths. A psychiatrist specialising in children said that 'for the majority who are amenable to treatment, the outcome is good.'

## Emerging adults

In December 1999, when the boys were seventeen, the European Court of Human Rights decreed that they'd been denied a fair trial, that - as eleven-year-olds - they shouldn't have been tried in an adult court with a jury. This wasn't altogether new thinking: at the time of the trial, many European newspapers had expressed shock that young boys were being tried in such a public way.

The European Court now said that, due to their exceptional youth and distress, the children hadn't been in a position to instruct their lawyers and mount a fair defence.

There was also an awareness within the juvenile justice system that if the boys weren't released at age eighteen they would have to be transferred to adult prisons. There they'd return to a life of intimidation and violence, the life they'd known before.

Two disturbed little boys had apparently been rehabilitated to become caring teenagers. If they were imprisoned with hardened adults, they'd very likely become hardened again - and would be a danger to the public when eventually released.

Lord Woolf, the Lord Chief Justice, said that 'because of their behaviour they are entitled to a reduction in the tariff' and that, subject to a parole board decision, they would be freed early in 2001. They were subsequently released.

## Update

Sadly, large sectors of the British public remain antagonistic to these boys. The tabloid press has sometimes fuelled this, printing 'new facts' about the death that suggested the brutal crime was even more brutal. The Despatches team investigated these allegations and found them to be lies. An interviewee on the television programme *The James Bulger Story* explained that 'in tabloid press terms there is no such thing as rehabilitation,' and that one bad act made you bad forever in tabloid land.

But occasionally there is a glimmer of understanding, an awareness that you can feel horror and disgust at little James's death without having to for-ever hate the ten-year-olds that murdered him. A neighbour, speaking on the Despatches programme, remembered a Robert who was far from the monster the media portrayed him as. She said that she'd like to see him again and added simply 'I'd talk to Robert, I wouldn't tell him to go away, cause there's a reason for everything, isn't there?'

And David Smith wrote in his introduction to *The Sleep Of Reason* that 'Many people... think kids pretend they've been beaten to get off the hook. A good slap never did *them* any harm. Anyone who has seen or experienced the effects of this kind of abuse, or spent time observing and listening to young offenders, will not be so dismissive.'

Gitta Sereny wrote honestly of the case saying that 'Unhappiness in children is never innate, it is created by the adults they 'belong to': there are adults in all classes of society who are immature, confused, inadequate or sick, and, under given and unfortunate circumstances, their children will reflect, reproduce and often pay for the miseries of the adults they need and love.'

# 8

## CAN'T GET IT OUT OF MY HEAD
### Roderick Justin Ferrell

Rod was born on 28th March 1980 to seventeen-year-old Sondra and twenty-year-old Rick Ferrell in Kentucky. Within months the marriage had crumbled and they got divorced. Sondra found it difficult to fit into normal society as her Pentecostal fundamentalist parents hadn't allowed her to go on dates, visit the cinema or attend dances when she was growing up. She admitted that her childhood had been an emotionally and mentally abusive hell so she wanted little Rod to see her as a friend rather than a cold controlling mum.

But despite his mother's good intentions, Rod's first few years were very uncertain ones. Sondra had felt alienated from the other children at school and had left as soon as possible. Still just a teenager herself, she was ill-equipped to support her infant son. Sometimes she'd find work in a burger joint for a few weeks, leaving Rod with her parents. On other occasions she worked as a dancer or lived off benefits.

The teenage mother began to smoke cannabis and drink alcohol in order to relax. She started dating. She continued to have difficulties with her parents and her father told her that she wasn't fit to be a mum.

Rick, Rod's dad, initially visited his son but Sondra kept interrupting their games and made the visits unpleasant. As a result, he saw less and less of the little boy. On the upside, Rod and his mum went to the cinema together and shared pizzas and had some fun times. But her boyfriends and various jobs limited the amount of time she spent with her son.

### Puritanical versus hedonistic philosophies

Meanwhile, Rod was being given very conflicting messages about life. His grandparents said that smoking and drinking were forbidden and that women shouldn't wear makeup or trousers (because Deuteronomy 22 says that a woman wearing male garments or vice versa is an abomination,) whereas Rod's mother was making up for her desperately repressed childhood by partying like mad.

Children need consistency in their lives. If a child runs around singing a song and his mother smiles then he assumes that singing is good, that it brings adult approval. If, the next time he sings he's shouted at, he doesn't know which way to turn. Rod's grandparents would give him one set of instructions - but when Sondra had an argument with them then she'd tell Rod not to do what they said.

When Rod was five years old he allegedly came back from a day trip looking very distressed. Sondra questioned him about what had happened and formed the impression that he had been sexually abused in a ceremony run by a religious cult that involved one of her relatives. Rod would continue to mention this alleged incident every so often - and it would be raised again eleven years later at his trial.

Rod's grandfather was a travelling salesman so the family moved around a lot. The little boy often had to get used to new neighbours, new schools and new acquaintances. Sometimes his mother was away staying with a boyfriend but at other times she and Rod played Dungeons & Dragons together. Rod also played this role-playing game with his father, Rick. The boy had a talent for it as he was highly imaginative and creative. But Rod's grandfather declared it was 'the Devil's game.'

These inconsistencies continued over the years. Rod's grandparents kept telling him to pray and to read the Bible whilst his mother taught him how to cast spells and read the Tarot cards. His school noticed that he'd become increasingly troubled, increasingly strange.

## The lost boy

By the time he entered his teens, Rod was hurting himself physically as a way of coping with all the hurt he had inside. A friend saw him batter himself against a fence. He also had shallow cuts on his arms which he made with a knife or a razor. He was clearly deeply depressed and often talked about suicide.

When he was fifteen, Sondra married again. She moved away to Michigan with her new husband, meaning for Rod to join them later when he left school. But someone gave Rod the impression that his mother didn't want him back. When Sondra heard this she was horrified and travelled to Murray to fetch him. So Rod changed house and school again.

By now he was sleeping all day and truanting from school so he was expelled for bad attendance and poor attitude. Now he had even less structure to his life.

Rod started to experiment with drugs. He also smoked cigarettes and lived off junk food. He often looked anaemic and ill.

## A new identity

Physically, Rod matured quickly, growing to almost six foot tall. He remained reed-thin but grew his hair down to his shoulders and dyed it jet black. With his probing dark eyes, porcelain complexion and narrow nose he appealed to girls who were looking for someone different, someone who seemed superficially strong. Deep down, of course, Rod had little self-esteem or hope for the future. All he could do was invent a persona that would draw other lost young people to him, that would give him a transitory power.

## The so-called cult

The group of people who Rod now spent his time with would later be described as a terrifying vampiric cult - but they were hardly that. They were a loose knit group of around thirty, of which only five would go on the run.

Rod's main man was Scott Anderson whom he'd known since second grade. Scott had been taken away from his unhappy home and had settled down with foster parents but was now back with his biological parents again. He was thin, wore thick glasses, lacked confidence and was desperate to lose his virginity. He saw Rod, who'd had several lovers, as a heroic figure and tended to follow him around.

Charity Kessee, Rod's sixteen-year-old girlfriend - who he called Che or Shea - was the second member of the group. She loved Rod's dark romantic side but feared his violence. (He'd break furniture when he got really angry.) They'd been together for almost a year. She lived with her father in Murray but kept in touch with her mother who lived in South Dakota. She often felt lonely when her father was at work.

Charity told Rod again and again that she loved him but he clearly doubted that he was lovable and kept setting her little tests. She noticed that he'd provoke fights in order to get a reaction, something that was hard for the teenager to understand. But it's common for dysfunctional people to provoke fights as a means of avoiding true intimacy. Such damaged people desperately want to be loved but at the same time they can't allow others to get close. The drama of passionate arguments offers a kind of love - or the closest thing to love that most of them have ever known.

The third teenager who Rod hung around with was fifteen-year-old Heather Wendorf, a platonic friend. Heather's older sister had started dating so Heather was somewhat lonely. An artistic girl, she felt different to the more conventional students at school.

Heather's father was a self-made man who'd been able to give his two daughters and his common-law wife Ruth a good standard of living. They lived in a beautiful house that had many amenities.

Limited information has been released about Heather's home life so it's hard to know exactly where her unhappiness stemmed from - but she'd started to cut her arms to release her emotional pain, something that both her older sister and her mother knew about. She also suffered from insomnia and migraines and thought about death frequently.

People who knew her at school said that she was intelligent but troubled. She had always been a quiet girl but became even quieter after she got to know Rod. She started to dye her hair purple and sometimes wore a dog collar around her neck - but Heather wasn't living a wild child life. Her parents liked her to stay home with them at night and watch TV. Luckily she was close to her seventeen-year-old sister, but her sister was currently the source of family rows as she was staying out late with her new beau.

Heather wrote to Scott that she had 'vengeance, hate, destruction' in her as well as the side of herself that she showed at school, a largely passive side. Heather told Rod all about her unhappiness and Rod strongly empathised.

The fourth member of the cult was nineteen-year-old Dana Cooper, a friend of Charity's who Rod had met a fortnight before. Dana had her own flat and Rod and his mates started to hang out there. Dana was overweight and lacking in confidence so was grateful for these instant new friends.

The teenagers dressed like vampires and often met up at the cemetery. They hung out in a small crumbling outhouse in the woods that they called the Vampyre Hotel. They'd take turns at lightly cutting their arms and licking their own or their friends warm blood.

The press would later refer to this as drinking blood, as if the supposed vampires were opening their veins widely, but the wounds the teens inflicted were just thin razor cuts. One of Heather's boyfriends was so disgusted by this blood-licking act that he finished with her, though he was aware that she was being influenced by Rod.

Rod said that he'd been reincarnated many times and had lived for hundreds of years, inhabiting the best districts of Paris. It wasn't clear why he'd chosen to relocate to rural Kentucky for his current life.


## Soliciting rape and sodomy

Rod's homelife continued to have its difficulties. His mother - by now an attractive thirty-five-year-old - often flirted with his friends. They liked his house as they could just hang out and be themselves with Sondra. But Rod was clearly embarrassed by his mother's behaviour and was always looking for different places to stay. On another occasion a friend saw Rod and his mother arguing and Sondra trashed her son's room and dragged him out of it by his hair.

The tension exacerbated when Sondra developed a crush on one of Rod's fourteen-year-old friends. She wrote the child a letter saying that she dreamed about being 'French kissed and fucked' by him. She wrote a second letter that was equally graphic and suggested the boy move in. Sondra knew that the boy's brother was active in another vampire cult and hoped that this fourteen-year-old would initiate her so that she could become a vampire who supposedly had eternal life.

Rod was incensed by all of this - after all, early adulthood is partly about forging your own identify and separating from your parents. How could he revel in his vampiric differences if his mother was a vampire too? Rod told friends that he wanted to kill his mother and his grandfather, who he described as a sick bastard. But his rage was becoming increasingly free-floating, for he also offered to kill the parents of two of his friends.

At this stage the mother of the fourteen-year-old boy who Sondra desired saw the sexually explicit letters. She went to the police and on 12th November 1996 Sondra was charged with 'soliciting rape and sodomy' from a minor. She would subsequently spend six months in jail.

Rod also had his run-ins with the police as they suspected that - acting with another teenager - he'd mutilated two puppies from the local animal shelter. And one of his friends said that Rod had fatally swung a kitten against a tree.

By now the sixteen-year-old was experimenting with so many drugs that his girlfriend Charity felt frightened. Rod looked stoned and threatened to kill numerous people - yet he thought he was being singled out by the locals simply because his long hair and black clothes made him look different.

All five of the teens felt alienated from their peers and were looking for a new start. They talked more and more about running away. On 25th November 1996 they each packed some clothes and set off on their great adventure in Scott's old Buick. Rod was pleased when Charity told him that she was expecting their child. (She'd been deliberately trying to get pregnant in the hope that he'd settle down with her and not look at any other women.) But he knew that Charity's dad wouldn't be so pleased.

They could hear that the engine was soon going to pack up so they looked around for another vehicle. Rod knew that Heather's parents were wealthy and that they had a sports utility jeep. He'd previously heard Heather say that she'd only be allowed to leave home when her parents were dead - and she'd been overheard telling someone else that she wished they'd both disappear. It suited Rod's purpose to remember these words now as he had so much hate in his heart.

## The murders

The boys let Heather Wendorf think that they were going to collect another friend who was supposed to run away with them. In truth, they went looking for the Wendorfs' house. Rod had lived some distance away from Heather throughout much of their friendship so had never been to her home before but another friend had told him how to identify the place. At first he approached a neighbouring dwelling but looked inside and saw little children playing so knew that couldn't be Heather's home.

The teens soon located the Wendorfs' garage and Rod grabbed a crowbar to use as a weapon. The door was unlocked so he and Scott entered the house, had a drink in the kitchen and looked around. The youths saw Heather's father sleeping on the settee, something the hardworking man often did at the end of another long day.

Rod had allegedly heard Heather complain about her parents many times.

She'd cried on the phone and he'd assumed that she was being abused, just as he'd been. He'd decided, without telling her, that her parents were going to die.

Rod started to batter the man - a man he'd never met - over the head with the crowbar. The first few blows rendered him unconscious but Rod continued to batter him, causing blood and brain tissue to fly everywhere. He delivered more than a dozen blows to the man's skull until he eventually stopped breathing, his face unrecognisable, the bar briefly forced deep into his chest. Faced with the reality of watching a brutal death, Scott froze. He believed, in principle, in blood sacrifices - but seeing all this real blood and brains was completely different.

Moments after killing Rick Wendorf, Rod lifted the dead man's shirt and burnt a V for vampire into his stomach with a lit cigarette then took his credit card. Scott went into one of the other rooms to see if there was any cash available and Rod, holding the bloodstained crowbar, walked out into the hall.

At that moment Ruth Wendorf stepped into the hallway carrying a coffee. Startled at suddenly finding this long-haired stranger in her house, she asked him what he wanted. He lashed out at her, and she threw the hot liquid over him. They fought and she scratched him - the police would later find his DNA under her nails. Enraged, the teenager battered the crowbar into her head again and again.

Then Rod and Scott left, knowing that Heather's older sister would shortly walk into the scene of horror. They'd already cut the phone lines so that she couldn't immediately summon help.

**The great escape**

Scott took the wheel of the Wendorfs' Explorer (an act of theft that, in the eyes of the law, would make him almost as guilty as Rod) and soon caught up with the other car that Charity was now driving. They eventually all transferred to the Explorer and ditched the Buick.

Heather was shocked when she saw that they'd stolen her parents' vehicle and said that they'd be livid - but, after dropping several hints, Rod admitted that they were dead. Heather appeared shocked, then angry for a time, and later said she'd thought about running away from the group but decided to stay in case Rod killed her too.

Independent life is hard - and the five teenagers had little money and only a vague notion of where they were heading. They got lost several times and burgled a house to find cash to buy food. Rod had thought he might live on his wits in the wilderness - but the girls were cold and scared and Charity was two months pregnant with his child. Like most teenagers, he had only a sketchy idea of how he'd survive in the real world, telling the others that they might be able to stay with his former friends in New Orleans.

Meanwhile - as they'd suspected - Heather's sister had come home and discovered the bodies so an APB was out for the Explorer. Charity decided to phone her mum and ask for help. Her mother told them to go to a motel and she'd arrange to pay for it. The police raced to the motel and the teens surrendered immediately.


**Rod's statement**

Rod was questioned in Baton Rouge, Louisiana on 28th November 1996. He said, in answer to their question, that he'd been seeing a psychiatrist at the behest of either his school or his mother. He couldn't remember which. He admitted that he no longer cared about anything, adding 'It's because I don't have any concern for life anymore.'

He went on to answer questions about the proposed trip then said that he and Scott had gone to Heather's garage for 'weapons, food and cash.' Moments later he added 'I went to her dad and smacked the fuck out of him until he finally quit breathing so yes, I'm admitting to murder.' He also said that he'd rained numerous blows on Ruth Wendorf's head 'until I saw her brains falling on the floor.'

His statement showed that Scott hadn't taken part in the bloodshed, because 'he totally froze,' adding later that 'the most he did was move the bodies a little bit.'

Rod added that they hadn't gotten caught until he let his girlfriend phone home as she was the only thing he cared about. By then they were lost and hungry and walking through a bad neighbourhood which scared Charity.

Rod was very amicable with the Baton Rouge police saying that they didn't beat him like the Murray and Florida cops had. He said that such violence had made him wary of everyone. Asked if he'd seen a murder before he replied

'I've fucking seen murders all my life, ever since I was five...' He implicated a male relative in one such murder and added that the cult the relative was part of had raped five-year-old Rod as part of an initiation rite.

Moments later he asked if he'd get the death penalty. When told that he probably would, he said 'I was kind of hoping... please go ahead, ha!'

He added that he didn't currently know where his mother was, but that she was staying with a new boyfriend who had just gotten out of prison for forgery. Earlier in his statement he'd talked about one of her ex-boyfriends who, he alleged, did drugs.

Towards the end of his statement he said that he hoped the police who were coming to collect him were as nice as the ones currently interrogating him. He said that if they weren't he would clam up, adding 'I didn't speak for two years at one time so I can do it again.'

## Scott's statement

Scott said that he'd planned to kill Ruth Wendorf whilst Rod killed Rick Wendorf. But when he'd seen Rod strike Rick for the first time he knew that he couldn't go through with it. He said that they'd told Charity and Dana minutes before the deaths that they were going to kill the couple and steal their car. Scott said that Heather hadn't had prior knowledge of the murders. He was unable to explain to the police why he'd agreed to kill the couple or why he'd let Rod go ahead with such vicious acts. The girls had remained in the Buick whilst the murders were taking place in the house so there was little they could add.

## The trial

It was a foregone conclusion that Rod would be found guilty of killing Rick and Ruth Wendorf, a couple who had done him no harm and whom he'd met for the first time moments before he bludgeoned them to death. His skin had been found under Ruth's fingernails as she'd scratched his arms whilst they wrestled. His footprints were also found at the scene. He had told Dana and Charity that he and Scott planned to kill the couple and the police had his full confession on tape.

It's not a court's place to explain why an act occurred, only that it did. But obviously the defence wanted to show any mitigating circumstances. They spoke of Rod's miserable childhood, being moved around from one place to another. They spoke of Sondra's prison sentence for soliciting sex from a fourteen-year-old child. An expert who'd interviewed Sondra said that she had the maturity of a twelve-year-old and was sometimes delusional.

Rod had also told them that he'd been sexually abused by his grandfather - and by other men - at age five or six as part of a Black Mass. As he was also claiming to be a vampire who had lived for hundreds of years, no one paid much attention to these allegations. But Sondra said that Rod's grandfather had taken him out for the day fishing when he was five and that he'd come back looking hugely traumatised and vomiting. He'd later drawn pictures of demons and pictures that suggested oral and anal abuse.

Sondra's sister Lyzetta spoke up in court saying that her father - Rod's grandfather - had kissed her and fondled her, and that he'd rubbed her childish body against his. As a result of this she had left home at age fourteen.

Rod's grandfather has never been charged with any sexual offence so must be assumed innocent. But he told reporters that a Christian wouldn't do such things, and in this he was wrong for professionals who have studied sexual addiction have found that men and women who act in sexually inappropriate ways have often spent years adopting the moral high ground. As a result, they are well known for their strong moral values both by their families and in the wider community. When the man - or woman – is then arrested for, say, flashing or making obscene phone calls, everyone refuses to believe it at first because it contrasts so strongly with the values he or she has always professed.

Such men and women are often desperate for outside approval so they try harder than normal to appear extra good. But deep down they believe that they are bad people who are not lovable and whose needs will not be met. They see sex as their most important need and will risk their careers, marriages and children's happiness to have these needs met.

Patrick Carnes, author of *Out Of The Shadows: Understanding Sexual Addiction* has noted that such sexual obsessives are often drawn to helping professions such as the ministry, social work and nursing. These are all professions in which people can either nurture or dominate. Both roles are attractive to the sexual addict who believes that he or she cannot be loved for themselves, only for what they can give to others - or can force from them.

Rod Ferrell admitted to psychiatrists that being sexualised at the age of six had left him a nymphomaniac and that he'd had numerous lovers. The vampire embrace - though he didn't say so - is also a very sexual act. During it the teens embrace closely and one grazes his teeth against the neck of the other. When performed by two same sex members of the clan it had a homo-erotic element.

## Spreading blame

Rod's statement in court seemed to differ from what he'd originally told police. In his statement at Baton Rouge he'd said that Scott just froze when he, Rod, started to bludgeon Rick. But in court he said that Scott smiled whilst watching this first murder and that Scott had seemed high afterwards.

He hadn't said much about Heather initially, but now said that she didn't like her mum and suggested that Heather had masterminded the two murders - but this contrasted with what he'd told Scott and the other girls earlier. Rod now seemed to be trying to spread the blame in order to get a reduced sentence for himself.

Sondra had planned to say in court that she'd overheard Heather and Rod planning the deaths together. But she failed a lie detector test on the subject so her testimony couldn't go ahead.

## Death penalty

Rod now changed his plea to guilty. Later that month (February 1998) he was sentenced to die in Florida's electric chair. He remained implacable, only looking momentarily close to tears when his mother began to sob.

Charity was given ten years for robbery with a firearm or deadly weapon. She was also guilty of driving Heather away from the Wendorfs' home that night. Dana was given seventeen years for similar offences as she was an adult offender rather than a juvenile. Scott, who had watched the killings and stolen the Explorer, was given two life sentences for first degree murder.

A programme aired in Britain about the vampire murders said that the judiciary was looking closely at Heather as they believed she might have played a part in planning her parent's deaths. But subsequent to the programme being aired, a Grand Jury said that they'd found no evidence against her and she was cleared.

## Update

Scott will remain incarcerated for life without the possibility of parole. Charity's original release date was set at 2007 but she will probably be released in 2004. Within weeks of her arrest, she lost the baby she was carrying. It's believed that Dana's sentence will also be reduced. Heather, who was cleared of all charges, moved away from the area and returned to school.

Rod was put on Florida's Death Row. Interviewed in Lake County Jail in Tavares after being sentenced, he said that he didn't realise the impact of his actions. This seems unlikely: he was long-term disturbed but he wasn't delusional when committing the homicides. After all, he'd made sure that the couple didn't have company, had cut the phone lines, gotten rid of his blood-stained shirt and changed the registration of the Explorer to that of the Buick in order to confuse the law.

As is often the case with high profile youthful killers, teenager 'fans' soon set up websites dedicated to the vampire clan and tried to find Rod's prison address so that they could write to him. One boy on a vampire message board said he'd been told by another web-user that he could have the address for seventy-five dollars. The boy seemed fascinated with Rod Ferrell because he sounded articulate, looked impressively Gothic with his flowing black hair and had committed the murders when he was so young.

But appearances can be deceptive. Most of Rod's statements, when carefully analysed, made little sense. And with his dyed black hair shorn off in jail, he looked weak and hopeless. One of the policemen associated with the case summed it up best, saying that he talked a good talk but was really just a scared little kid.

In April 1998 Rod's lawyers tried to have his death sentence commuted to life imprisonment, arguing that the jury hadn't given enough weight to the psychological reports about his multiply-abused childhood. The judge disagreed so he is still likely to die in the electric chair.

# 9

# DON'T CRY OUT LOUD
## Mary Flora Bell

Mary was born on 26th May 1957 to Betty, a seventeen-year-old single mother. She was a beautiful baby with a sweet smile and large violet-blue eyes. But Betty shrieked 'Take the thing away from me' when a nurse tried to put the baby girl into her arms. Betty had been hidden away in a convent for the duration of her pregnancy as she came from a Catholic family and in those days illegitimacy was frowned upon.

No one knew who Mary's father was and Betty - who was deeply religious - just said that he was the Devil. Whatever Mary's true paternity, Betty reluctantly took her home to the house she shared with her widowed mother and younger sister in Gateshead, England. Thankfully her relatives loved Mary from the start.

Betty returned to her factory job leaving her mother to care for the child. Seven months later she met a handsome young man named Billy Bell. They married within weeks of meeting (by which time she was pregnant again) and Billy moved in with Betty and her mum. Billy was very proud of his new bride who had won many local beauty competitions and who loved to dance.

## Mary's mother tries to kill her

Betty continued to look upon her firstborn with unconcealed loathing. She gave the one-year-old some of her own mother's tranquillisers and Mary almost died. Luckily Betty's relatives found the baby and rushed her to hospital where she had her stomach pumped out. Everyone knew that a one-year-old could not have reached the secure hiding place where Betty's mother kept her tranquillisers but no one wanted to believe that Betty was to blame...

That autumn Betty gave birth to a son, Mary's first half-brother. At this stage the rest of the family moved back to their original home town of Glasgow in Scotland, leaving Betty and Billy in Newcastle, England, with their little brood.

Billy soon found that he alone had to take care of the two children. Betty would do the cleaning but she didn't cook and wouldn't get up to feed the babies during the night. When her little boy was six months old she left him and Mary with her husband for a few weeks and no one knew where she'd gone. On other occasions she took Mary with her to stay with an assortment of friends and relatives. Robbed of the routine that young children so desperately need, Mary often looked pale and tense.

She had received so little attention from her mother that she'd had to deny her own need for hugs and now wouldn't let her relatives hug her. (Gwendolyn Graham, profiled in this author's book *Women Who Kill*, had a similarly neglectful mother and also couldn't respond to physical affection when it was finally offered.)


## Mary's mother tries to kill her again

Mary's mother now gave her away to a female acquaintance and the woman cut Mary's hair because it was full of lice. The frightened toddler had no idea what was happening. Unfortunately the woman soon returned the child and Betty explained this rejection by telling Mary that she was a bad child. The following year, it's apparent that Betty gave both Mary and her little brother pills that could have resulted in their deaths. Luckily a relative saw the children eating the tablets - though she didn't see Betty handing them over - and she made both children sick.

A few months later Betty took Mary to visit her grandmother in Glasgow. Betty was holding Mary near the window when she suddenly 'fell' out. Her uncle managed to grab the three-year-old by an ankle, seriously straining the ligaments in his back. The following week Betty left Mary with a stranger that she'd met at an adoption agency but her relatives reclaimed her within hours. The woman, who clearly meant well, had already bought the confused little girl some new clothes.

One of Billy's relatives suggested that she and her husband adopt Mary as they were so worried about her being ill-treated and given away to strangers, but for some reason Betty refused to consider this. Instead, she took the sad-faced little girl back to Newcastle.

Shortly afterwards Mary had yet another 'accident' in which she swallowed some of her mother's iron tablets and spent three days in hospital, iron tablets being poisonous to a small child. By now she was almost four and was able to tell the doctors that her mother had given her 'the sweets.' A neighbourhood child who had been playing with Mary when the pills were handed over verified this.

Mary's relatives made it clear that no child could have this many near-death accidents in four years - but Betty's response was to sever contact with them. Sadly, they didn't go to the authorities and Mary's life now took an even more dangerous path.

For some time Betty had been seeing other men and she now began to turn this into her profession. She became a prostitute and often went to Glasgow to pursue this work but at other times, when Billy was away, she had clients come to the house. Billy - who loved Mary and her brother and was always good to them - was away more and more often, sometimes serving time in jail for petty theft.

Betty's own life careered increasingly downhill. She was often admitted to hospital suffering from her nerves. She complained of stomach problems and sometimes imagined that she had cancer. Her digestion had been poor since childhood, again doubtless as a result of stress. A desperately unhappy woman, she attempted suicide several times, sometimes by overdosing and once by preparing to jump off a bridge. Four-year-old Mary watched and listened to her mother's constant stream of complaints and blamed herself as children do. Her mother contributed to this, telling her that she was no good.

## Strapped for cash

Betty now began to specialise in sado-masochistic prostitution and brought a variety of whips into the home. Usually this speciality is as much about verbal and physical ritual as it is about pain so it tends to be at the higher end of the sex-for-money market. Most dominatrixes don't engage in intercourse and many clients are forbidden to ejaculate. Instead, the specialist simply binds and whips the submissive client and indulges in clever word-play or enacts a script that the client has previously written.

Sophisticated specialists can earn large sums and can afford a flat to ply their trade in, keeping their activities well away from their children. But Betty clearly wasn't in this upscale category. Her home was poorly furnished and she was earning so little that she told the authorities that Billy had permanently left her. This meant she got more social security money as a single mum.

## Paedophiliac abuse

Meanwhile, Betty brought some of her clients to the house where she whipped them for money. But for reasons that can only be guessed at, she now introduced four-year-old Mary to the sex for sale. She would hold her daughter's head back whilst the client ejaculated into the little girl's mouth. Mary would vomit and her mother would then tell her that she'd been a good girl and give her sweets.

It may be significant that Betty's own mother had gone out to work when she was four - the age that Betty introduced her daughter to oral sex. Four-year-old Betty was left with her invalid father who may not have been able to protect her from paedophile activity. By five Betty was refusing to eat with the family and such sudden appetite loss can be one of the symptoms of child sexual abuse. Another sign is trying to be very good - and Betty was constantly drawing religious icons. A third sign is overreacting to criticism and Betty began to believe that she was her mother's least favourite child.

So perhaps Betty felt compelled to abuse her daughter just as she'd been abused. Or maybe the alcoholism that would later cut short her life was already beginning to claim her and she wanted the additional money that paedophiles would pay in order to buy the whisky that she craved. Whatever Betty's conscious or subconscious motivation, the pre-school Mary paid the price.

Mary would later show another sign of child sexual abuse, acting inappropriately by unzipping the trousers of a horrified family friend. And she'd exhibit many of the other symptoms, namely an inability to concentrate, depression, nightmares and several attempts at running away from home.

## Pleading for attention

In the autumn of 1961, Mary went to school. Already she was a world removed from the other children. She'd lie on her back under the desk and refuse to come out. At other times she'd sit on the floor and pull hairs out of her teacher's legs in a desperate effort to be noticed. Misunderstanding, the teacher refused to respond to her bad behaviour. But Mary strived to be noticed by a parent substitute, as being ignored by a parent is devastating for a child. When Betty was at home she'd hit Mary and shout at her and talk about what a sinful girl she was. At other times she'd half choke the child whilst her clients forced their penises into her mouth.

Mary began to copy this behaviour, as children often feel compelled to do. She put her hand around another child's neck and asked her teacher if doing so would make him die. Again, the teacher didn't realise the significance of this strange comment. Mary also kicked and nipped the other children until they all avoided her, then she cried because she was so alone.

Mary's ordeal continued at home. Betty would hold Mary down on her stomach for her clients to abuse. At other times she would take her to the homes of old men and they'd masturbate over her. Afterwards her mother would be nice to her and would buy her chips.

By the start of 1963 the family had moved again to an even uglier neighbourhood. There Betty had a third child, a girl. The birth was soon followed by a nervous breakdown and when Betty got out of the hospital she was so depressed that she stopped cleaning the house. But two years later she had another baby girl; the people who can least nurture children often give birth to the most.

## Cruel punishments

Mary's mother now spent even less time with her than before - and when she did notice the child it was often to shout at her or to beat her. Mary was beaten for such crimes as having a bath and using all the hot water. She was also punished for wetting the bed, something Betty was convinced that Mary did on purpose. In truth, Mary tried to stay awake every night so that she wouldn't lose control of her bladder again.

She remained odd and unpopular at school. Though her clothes were clean, she often had headlice. And her dog - though loving towards her - was the fiercest in the district and barked at everyone who went by.

Mary was so lonely that she used to give her brother coins if he would play with her. She sometimes acquired this money by getting into cars with men then saying that she'd tell her father that they'd touched her. Her mother's actions had shown her that men paid for sex - and that adults of both sexes would pay a child for her silence.

By now her family life had become even more bizarre as Billy and Betty rarely spent a night in the house together. Instead, he stayed with friends but when Betty went away on prostitution trips to Glasgow, he'd move back in to look after Mary, her half-brother and the other two little girls. But sometimes Betty went away while Billy was in prison so the children had to be looked after by one of his relatives.

As soon as Betty moved back, Billy would leave again. Increasingly worn down by his wife's instability he gave up work permanently and lived off the money from small burglaries and handouts from the state. Mary still thought that he was her biological dad but called him her uncle when there were strangers around so that Betty could keep claiming extra social security as a single mum. Mary managed to keep this lie going so successfully that her teachers thought she didn't have a father figure in the house.

The confusing and frightening days merged into sleepless nights, but when she was nine years old her life improved because a new family moved in next door to her. They also had the surname Bell though they weren't related. Mary soon befriended one of the children, a girl two years older than herself called Norma Bell.

Norma had five brothers and five sisters and a father who couldn't work because of ill health. One of her brothers was handicapped and others had suffered serious illness. As a result, Norma didn't get much attention and had run away several times. She admitted to Mary that sometimes she wanted to kill her younger siblings as they took up so much of her kind but overworked mother's time.

That same year, Betty beat Mary and her brother so hard with a dog chain that the police were called. But, as usual, other adults saw the family as sacrosanct and no one did anything.

## Rehearsals for death

On 11th May 1968 Mary and Norma said that they'd found a three-year-old boy bleeding from his head. The dazed child had been pushed by an unseen attacker. The next day Mary squeezed the necks of two six-year-old girls and asked one 'If you choke someone, do they die?' In both instances the police interviewed Mary and Norma but none of the victims were seriously harmed and no charges were brought.

## Martin's murder

Less than a fortnight later, Mary killed for the first time. It was 25th May, the day before her eleventh birthday and she found four-year-old Martin Brown playing in the street. She took him into a boarded up house and strangled him. The act involved so little pressure that it didn't leave any marks on the child's neck. Shortly afterwards he was found by workmen who Mary saw trying to revive him. She hurried to Martin's relatives and told them that there had been an accident but when they reached the house they found the child dead.

There were tablets scattered beside his body, so the pathologist suspected poisoning but the post mortem revealed that the child had a small haemorrhage in the brain. The medics believed he might have had a convulsion, so questioned the family as to whether Martin ever had fits. He hadn't. In the end, his death was ruled as accidental and the CID weren't involved.

The next day - a Sunday - Mary tried to strangle one of Norma's sisters but the girl's father intervened and hit Mary.

That same day, Norma and Mary broke into the local nursery and co-authored some notes, one of which said 'we did murder Martain brown.' (sic)

On the Monday, Mary made a drawing of Martin surrounded by pills with a workman walking towards the body. The wording underneath included the words 'a boy who just lay down and died.' Later that week she asked Martin's distraught mother if she could see him in his coffin. She was clearly desperate to draw attention to herself. A week after that she started screaming 'I am a murderer' but none of the other children took her seriously.

Norma who had run away before suggested that Mary go on the run with her this time. During the first week of June 1968 they did so but were soon brought back in a police car. Poor Mary was beaten for this by her mother. No one asked why girls of eleven and thirteen would want to run away. By mid-June they had absconded again and were picked up by the police and, again, Mary was punished. By now the sexual abuse had stopped but Betty was clearly terrified that Mary would tell someone about it. The physical and emotional abuse that she had suffered all her life continued. She still wet the bed most nights and her mother would rub her nose in her own urine and make her put her mattress by the window for the neighbours to see.

After the running away escapades, the days returned to their usual hell. Eleven-year-old Mary played outside for hours with Norma and with her Alsatian but she had to go home for meals and never knew when she'd find her mother in a violent mood. She frequently read her Bible, just as her mother wanted her to do. Betty went away again to prostitute herself in Glasgow and Billy moved back in to look after Mary and her brother and sisters in the poorly furnished house.

## Brian's murder

But on Wednesday 31st July, this usual routine was to change. That day both Norma and Mary took a four-year-old boy called Brian Howe to an area of wasteground. There, Mary squeezed his neck until her hands tired and Norma began to laugh hysterically (Norma would later claim that she ran away at this point, having told Mary to stop strangling the struggling child.) Brian was still alive so after a brief respite Mary squeezed his neck again until he stopped moving. Then she covered his face and body with grasses and tiny purple flowers.

Mary went home but later both she and Norma returned to the corpse and Mary cut off a lock of Brian's hair. She also lifted his jersey and used a razor blade and broken scissors to make tiny cuts on his stomach. It's possible that she'd seen her mother do this to her clients as scarification (the cutting of the flesh for erotic purposes) is a known sado-masochistic act.

Norma may also have used the razor briefly for handwriting experts would testify that a capital N scored on the little corpse had been changed by one stroke of a different hand to make it into a capital M.

Possibly remembering the penises that had abused her until three years before, Mary made a tiny cut on the dead boy's scrotum. Hearing someone approach, she hid the scissors near the body and both girls ran away.

A search party found his body shortly before midnight. His neck was scratched, his nose was marked and there were small wounds on his legs and scrotum. Death was due to strangulation but so little force had been used that the pathologist was sure the killer was a child.

Police questioned dozens of local children and soon found inconsistencies in both Mary Bell and Norma Bell's statements. Mary tried to blame another boy, mentioning that she'd seen him with broken scissors. It was the break-through - only the killer knew about the broken scissors left by the body as they hadn't been alluded to in the press.

Eventually Norma told the police that she'd tell the truth if her father left the room. She then said that she'd tripped over Brian's body and saw that he was dead. She added that Mary told her she'd squeezed the child's neck and had enjoyed it. She added that Mary had showed her the tiny cuts on his stomach caused by a razor. Norma then took the police to the murder site and showed them the razor which was hidden under a concrete slab.

## My mother hates me

The police now got Mary out of bed and took her to the police station. She continued to deny everything and said that she was being brainwashed, and that she wanted a solicitor. The eleven-year-old child was behaving like an adult - but then she'd had an adult's share of life experience.

The police let her go home that night but saw her laughing strangely at Brian's funeral procession on 7th August. Afraid that she might kill again, they arrested her. At the police station her uncle Peter slapped her across the face and told her to keep her mouth shut. It's unclear exactly what the child was supposed to keep quiet about.

Mary would later say that she was terrified that her mother would beat her to death for bringing the police into their lives. Her parents had always hated the police and Billy was a known lawbreaker. She knew that her family was poor and was terrified that her mother would have to pay a fine.

During her initial interrogation she had seemed clever and self-assured and old beyond her years. But now, in the cells at the police station, her minders saw a very different side to her. She was so frightened of wetting the bed that she went to the toilet constantly and hardly slept at all.

Mary told a policewoman that her mother hated her. The woman replied conventionally that her mother must love her at which Mary asked 'why did she leave me, then?' The policewoman had no idea that Betty regularly took off for weeks at a time leaving Mary with whoever was available. Yet again, no one looked into this neglected and abused little girl's life.


**The trial**

Mary and Norma's trial opened on the 5th December 1968 at the Assizes in Newcastle upon Tyne. Mary looked intelligent and alert whereas Norma appeared frightened and kept glancing at her parents for reassurance. It was to set the pattern for the entire nine day trial. As a result, the public - and doubtless the jury - quickly formed the opinion that Mary was the coldhearted ringleader who had led the educationally-challenged Norma astray. In truth, Mary was suffering from her usual insomnia and was having night terrors when she did get to sleep.

But no one was very interested in the background of either child, though Gitta Sereny - in her book *The Case Of Mary Bell* - became increasingly aware that 'Mary's mother was... the principle source of all her troubles.' Betty Bell attended the trial with her own mother who sat between her and her estranged husband Billy. Billy looked distressed but remained silent whereas Betty frequently broke into histrionic sobs and seemed determined to have centre stage.

Norma said that she'd watched Mary squeeze Brian's throat until he went purple. Then she, Norma, had run away and made pom poms with other girls. Later the two girls returned to the corpse and Mary cut a little chunk off Brian's hair. Mary disputed this, saying that Norma had done the hair cutting and had also cut Brian's knee with the razor blade.

Most of the trial consisted of such childish testimony. There were also psychiatric statements in which Norma was described as 'a simple backward girl of subnormal intelligence.' She was kept in a hospital during the trial whereas Mary was put into a remand home, probably indicative of the way both children were already being pigeonholed by the system and by the press. One court-appointed doctor said that Mary had psychopathic tendencies and that such tendencies were usually partly environmental. Unfortunately the importance of Mary's environment wasn't even touched upon. Her relatives could have testified to the times that her mother had tried to kill her and others could have told the courts of how Betty had worked as a prostitute in the presence of Mary and her brother. By now, Betty was also beating Mary's younger half-brother with increasing severity so perhaps he could have told about the pain he and Mary had suffered at their mother's hands.

Instead, the trial ended with the impression that Mary was simply a bad seed who had led a weaker girl astray. As such, the sentences weren't a surprise for Norma was found not guilty and Mary found guilty of manslaughter on the grounds of diminished responsibility. This applied to both the murders of Martin Brown and Brian Howe. In his summary the judge said that 'quite young children can be wicked and sometimes even vicious.' It was a view soon echoed by laypeople for this author can remember her own mother, a housewife who knew nothing about criminology, stating that 'Mary Bell was a little bitch.'

During the trial, Betty and Billy Bell went to the tabloids and tried to sell the story of Mary's life, but the newspapers refused.


## Conspiracy of silence

Over the years various psychologists and group therapists tried to get Mary to talk about her childhood but she always answered 'My mum said for me not to say anything to you.' Betty had originally phoned Mary's lawyer during the trial saying that Mary must never talk to a psychiatrist. After all, Betty knew that on some level Mary would remember being sexually abused from age four to eight whilst Betty held her down.

Now that Mary was in a reform school, Betty visited every few weeks to reinforce this warning and after her visits Mary was always unsettled. But visits from Billy always cheered her up.

Betty continued to have a strange attitude towards her oldest daughter. One day she got the young teenager to pose in her underwear for a series of photos, with Betty's mother watching. Betty then sold the photos to the press.

## Update

For the next twelve years Mary lived in various remand homes and adult prisons. At first she remained disturbed and allegedly strangled two hamsters in the first remand home she was sent to (She'd also tried to strangle a kitten one night during her trial,). But as the staff of the remand home continued to love and care for her, her behaviour markedly improved. She was considered manipulative as a teenager - but, in fairness, she was still being manipulated by her increasingly alcohol-driven mum.

Becoming aware that the hatred Betty felt for her wasn't normal, Mary asked her mother again who her natural father was. 'Was it your dad?' she asked as she'd found love poems that Betty had written to him and feared she was the result of an incestuous union. But (according to Mary's biographer, the respected Gitta Sereny) Betty's father had died when she was fourteen and she didn't get pregnant until she was sixteen so the dates don't add up. Mary also asked a friend of the family but he simply said 'It's best that you don't know.'

Mary was released from prison in 1980 at the age of twenty-three. She soon found herself a husband and in 1984 she gave birth to a daughter. But after she became ill her spouse became violent and she left the marriage, taking the child with her. For the first few years of her daughter's life, the authorities watched very carefully, ready to intercede if Mary harmed the baby. But it became clear that she was a good and loving mother and that her daughter felt secure. And Mary herself soon formed another relationship, one which has lasted to the present day.

Unfortunately, Betty Bell did much to undermine Mary's newfound security, continuing to sell stories to the tabloids. Betty remarried but eventually her second husband left her, saying that he'd suffered years of misery and couldn't take any more. Mary asked him who her biological father was but he said it was best not to know. Betty still saw herself as a martyr, saying 'Jesus was just nailed to the cross but I'm being hammered.' She continued to emotionally hammer Mary on the few occasions that they spent time together and these emotional cruelties only ceased with Betty's death in early January 1995.

Though Mary has never harmed anyone as an adult, she carries a deep sadness within her, a sadness that was apparent to psychologist Gitta Sereny. She suffers from frequent migraines and finds it difficult to concentrate on work or on any kind of project or educational course. And the love she feels for her own daughter has made her fully aware of the pain she caused to the families of her little victims, Martin Brown and Brian Howe.

She is continually hounded by the tabloids who refuse to believe that a battered child who killed can become a caring adult. As a result she has had to move house several times to protect her family. Yet, as crime writer Brian Masters has stated, her voice is 'one of maturity and remorse.'

# 10

## UNDER PRESSURE
### Kipland Philip Kinkel

Kip was born on 30th August 1982 to Bill and Faith Kinkel, both successful schoolteachers. The couple already had a daughter, Kristin, who was almost six, a high achiever like themselves. Bill and Faith were in their early forties by the time they had Kip, but they were physically fit and sure that they could cope.

The family lived in Springfield, Oregon, in an expensive house at the foot of the Cascade Mountains. The couple taught Spanish and Faith also taught French. They encouraged the children to explore the outdoors on regular camping trips and to participate in various sports.

In what should have been Kip's first year at a local school, the family went to Spain. Kip was put into a class of Spanish children with a teacher who only spoke Spanish. He'd just mastered English and now everyone was speaking in a foreign tongue so he felt understandably frustrated and out of his depth. At the school he was also bullied by a bigger boy and generally had a difficult time.

At the end of the school year, the Kinkels returned to Oregon. By now Kristin was proving herself a natural gymnast who repeatedly earned her parent's approval - but Kip was comparatively unco-ordinated. Bill himself was a tennis ace with a highly competitive nature who forced his little son to keep playing the game. Kip was small and light, and much preferred picking wild berries or swimming to batting a ball about for hours on the court.

But Bill continued to coerce his son to play competitive games, determined that the boy would become a sporting hero. As a family friend would later say 'Bill had his son's future mapped out.' Photos taken during this time show the other family members smiling widely during football games whilst Kip stares at the camera looking lost and sad.

There were similar problems at school. Kip struggled to keep up with the curriculum. He'd work hard in class all day - then come home and be tutored by his parents for hours every night. As the family home was somewhat isolated, he didn't have schoolfriends over with whom to have fun. (Though he did have a neighbourhood friend called Kasey who noticed that he was very young for his age.) For recreation he cycled through the surrounding woods and did chores for the neighbours, playing with their grandchildren and mowing their lawns.

## Starting over

Kip tried and tried but he was never going to be a sporting hero or an A-grade student. Thinking that he might be able to compete better with younger students, the Kinkels asked Kip's school to let him repeat a year. As a result, he lost his few friends and had to make new ones, a momentous task for such an awkward boy.

Kip continued to have problems in second grade, remaining unco-ordinated and having exceptional difficulty with spelling. His teacher noted that he was a hard worker but an extremely anxious child.

## Under pressure

Unable to understand what his parents were trying to teach him, Kip's ability to concentrate on the nightly tutoring sessions decreased. Dog trainers can see the same behaviour in a young dog - if you ask it to do something it doesn't understand, the dog will 'go silly' on you. So Kip started to act out, for example sliding down the laundry chute. Faith and Bill then decided he must be hyperactive and took him to a doctor who duly prescribed the powerful anti-hyperactive drug Ritalin.

Bill's father had been a minister and Bill had a strong moral code that he expected his children to live by. He frequently grounded Kip - or forbade him to watch his favourite television programmes - as a punishment for high spirited pranks. The cute little boy with the freckled face and neat haircut began to feel that he could do nothing right.

A family video taken during Kip's junior school years shows his sister effortlessly performing cartwheels and handstands out of doors for recreation. Kip tries to emulate her and promptly falls over. Behind the camera, his father says 'Kip needs more work' and urges him to try again.

By the time he was in third grade, his school was giving him extra help with reading and trying to allay his frustration at not being able to master

English. It was only with language and motor skills that he had a problem. He had a high IQ and showed promise in science and maths.

That same year, Bill retired from school-teaching so he now had little to do with other teenagers though he continued to teach Spanish to adults at night. He was an excellent tutor and his Spanish students liked him. But Kip still couldn't understand what his parents were trying to teach him, something that was explained the following year when he was diagnosed as having a learning disability, a form of dyslexia.

Kip began to view himself as stupid so made friends with the less academically able boys on the school bus, boys who were disruptive and violent. He started acting like they did, karate kicking other pupils and calling the girls names.

## Kristin leaves

Kristin now transferred from the local university to Hawaii Pacific on a cheerleading scholarship. She'd taken Kip's side in the past, pointing out to her parents that he was high spirited rather than bad. She often had to remind her older parents that Kip was just doing the sort of things their own younger students had done. She'd later admit that 'each little thing that he would do would be awful' to them. They were academically and sports-inclined adults in their fifties who didn't understand their adolescent son at all.

## Bomb-making

Thirteen-year-old Kip really missed Kristin though they often spoke on the phone. Soon he and his friends were using the school computer to order books about making bombs but the books were intercepted as they were mistakenly sent to the bank on which the cheque was drawn.

Later Kip researched the subject on the internet and even gave an illustrated talk at school on how to assemble an explosive device. He took his homemade bombs into the woods and allegedly used them to kill cats and squirrels and birds. He also told friends that he'd blown up a cow.

He believed that his mother considered him a good kid who did some bad things but that this father saw him as a bad kid who did bad things. The father-son relationship was increasingly poor.

Kip was storing up all his anger, unable to articulate his feelings. He started to go to the local quarry to detonate explosives to get rid of his rage.

## First gun

Kip had always been interested in guns, but the Kinkels understandably didn't believe in violent toys so he'd never even had a toy gun. But now he asked for a real gun as a Christmas or birthday gift. Bill Kinkel had inherited a rifle from his own father, and after much soul-searching he gave it to Kip.

The couple thought that guns had become exciting to the boy because they were forbidden fruit - and that maybe he'd get them out of his system now that he had his own rifle. Trying to find some common ground with the teenager, Bill showed Kip how to shoot cans off a wall. He had no idea that his son also sneaked the gun into the woods to kill wildlife.

Kip couldn't create the clever essays and sporting wins that his father desired - but he could become an expert at destruction. He told friends that he was going to join the army when he grew up.

## Police intervention

When Kip was fourteen, he asked if he could go away with a friend on a snowboarding trip and his parents agreed, presumably glad that he'd found a non-violent interest. But after dark, the two boys sneaked out of their accommodation and threw stones from a road bridge. One stone hit a passing car, frightening and enraging the driver. Kip was arrested and immediately started crying, saying that his friend had thrown that particular rock. The Kinkels had to collect him from the police station and drive him home.

By now Faith wanted to get her son into therapy but Bill was against this as he wasn't convinced psychologists truly helped. He may also have wanted to avoid the stigma, as he was a proud man who wasn't used to being publicly shamed.

Kip retreated further into a world where he was competent - a world of guns. He learned everything about them through magazines and through surfing the internet. He told friends that he'd like to kill someone to see what it was like and started carrying a knife to school.

## Treatment

Kip became increasingly distressed, spending hours in his room writing in his diary. He felt that there was nothing good about each day, that he had nothing to look forward to. At last even Bill had to admit that his son needed help.

The boy wept when he spoke to his psychiatrist, explaining that he couldn't please his father no matter what he did. The therapist found the boy easy to talk to and asked Bill Kinkel to lighten up on his son.

The psychiatrist could see the fourteen-year-old was clinically depressed, though talking clearly helped. Halfway through the series of sessions he prescribed Prozac. Kip's spirits and behaviour further improved.

He told the therapist that his main passion was explosives and guns - and the therapist said that he had a Glock which he was pleased with. Kip immediately wanted one. – and several months later his father would indeed buy a Glock for him.

After nine sessions the Kinkels and the doctor agreed that Kip was doing so well that he could discontinue therapy. They also took him off Prozac after only three months.

Kip prepared to start high school. At this stage his father had a word with a teaching friend and they decided that Kip might fit in better if he joined the school's American Football team. The teenager only weighed eight and a half stone and had no aptitude for or interest in the game but, once again, he did what he could to please his dad.

## Guns and roses

Kip's need to be good at something grew. He began to stockpile guns, buying or being given rifles, shotguns, a pistol, a handgun and ammunition. He talked incessantly about them as he moved further into his high school years. The other students began to call him a psycho and twice voted him the boy most likely to start World War Three.

Then, for a few months, the guns were replaced by roses in Kip Kinkel's life. For the first time he fell in love and felt wanted. The girl was an extrovert who liked the fact that he was different to the other youths. Kip's life now had a purpose and he was ecstatic. Photos he had taken with her show him looking animated and proud. At last someone had accepted him for what he was, not what they'd like him to be.

But young love is a very fragile beast and soon the girl tired of him. Kip wrote in his diary 'It feels like my heart is breaking' and added 'I need help.' Shortly after the break up, he studied *Romeo & Juliet* at school and clearly empathised when the young lovers committed suicide.

Death was increasingly on his mind. He wrote in his diary 'I don't know who I am... I try so hard every day.' He wrote that he wanted to kill a partic-ular boy at school but he hadn't yet because he hoped that tomorrow would be better. He added ominously 'as soon as my hope is gone, people die.'

In May he stayed over at a friend's house, and a group of them wound hundreds of rolls of toilet paper around a neighbourhood house as a prank. The next day they had to clear it up. Kip was the only boy whose parents grounded him for it.

Relatively rich children like Kip are seen as lucky by many - but the reality is that when their family scapegoats them no one intervenes. Eventually the child snaps under the pressure and goes mad and at this stage the medical system and the parents conspire to say that the madness was already in the child. If he or she instead - or later - goes bad then the law steps in to find the child's supposed inherent badness. No one looks for the root cause. Told daily that he was too wild, too moody, too loud, too quiet, too intense or too irresponsible, Kip turned his entire focus on his growing collection of guns.

**Receiving stolen goods**

He now purchased a gun at school - but the gun had been stolen the night before from the parent of another student. The police questioned everyone and Kip nervously admitted that the weapon was hidden in his locker. He was promptly arrested and charged with receiving stolen property and hav-ing a firearm in a public place.

Thurston High School had a sensible zero tolerance approach to weapons in school so immediately suspended him. A teacher who saw him at the point of the arrest said he looked totally miserable, unable to make eye contact and hanging his head. The teacher told Kip that he could expect to be suspended for an entire year - a year that Kip realised he would have to spend alone with his parents and without his friends.

Bill went to the police station to collect his fifteen-year-old son and the pair of them went to a burger bar for a meal. Afterwards Bill Kinkel spent the day phoning friends who had counselling experience asking if they could recommend a school for troubled teenagers. He was interested in sending Kip to an army-style boot camp which involved lots of physical activity - but Kip had always hated sports. The deeply depressed boy may have overheard one of these conversations and realised that his father was always going to force this particular square peg into a round hole. His father had also made it clear that his mother would again be disappointed in Kip when she came home.

**Patricide and matricide**

Later that afternoon - 20th May 1998 - the fifteen-year-old fetched his .22 rifle and shot his father through the back of the head. Then he phoned a friend, pacing back and forward whilst speaking. He sounded edgy and depressed but the friend assumed this was because of his school suspension. He had no idea that Kip's father lay dead. Kip said he had stomach pains and that he was waiting for his mother to come home. He wondered aloud why she was so late.

At 6pm Faith returned. As she walked up the steps Kip shot her. She was still alive so he shot her again, totalling five times in the head and once in the heart.

**A further deathtrap**

Determined to kill as many people as possible, Kip placed one of his home-made bombs under his mother's corpse. He dragged his father's corpse to the bathroom. Then - the sign of a killer who has some compassion for his victims - he covered each of them with a sheet. He wrote a note saying 'I wish I had been aborted' then added 'God damn these voices inside my head.'

Kip kept the television on all night for company. At some stage he scattered dozens of bullets over the living room floor. In the morning he put his *Romeo & Juliet* CD on continuous play and cranked up the volume. Then he gathered together his arsenal of guns and drove his mother's car to his school, Thurston High.

## Class killing

Walking into the school cafeteria at 7.30am, Kip started to shoot at the four-hundred students having breakfast there. Within minutes he'd fired forty-eight rounds, hitting twenty-four students. The innocent teenagers were variously hit in the arms, legs, abdomen, back and chest. Two students were shot in the spine and one boy lost part of a finger. Students screamed and moaned, whilst others mercifully lost consciousness as blood spurted from arterial wounds.

Seventeen-year-old Mikael Nickolauson was killed instantly and sixteen-year-old Ben Walker died within hours. Other students would spend weeks in intensive care.

Kip ran out of ammunition and was reaching for another weapon when he was overpowered by one of the larger boys. Like most spree killers, he had planned to shoot himself at the end of the massacre - and had taped a gun to his chest to use as his suicide weapon. Now he screamed 'Just kill me. Kill me now.'

Taken into police custody, he lunged for the knife that he'd strapped to his leg, clearly hoping that the officers would shoot him. Again, he begged them to kill them and was clearly shocked.

The police asked how his father was and Kip admitted he was dead. Police cars raced to the Kinkels' house. They entered to find the *Romeo & Juliet* music still blaring through every room. As they'd feared, they found Kip's parents' corpses and the trail of blood showing where they had initially been shot. They also found over twenty explosive devices, some of which were active, and had to call for specialists to detonate them.

## The rationale

Spree killings such as this, where innocent victims are shot dead, are incomprehensible to the general public. But they do make sense to the killer who believes he has been failed by everyone.

Kip's parents had frequently communicated their disappointment in him. His sister would later say that he tried desperately to please them, 'studying over and over.' He also tried to overcome his lack of interest in sport when his father wanted him to play in the school team and play so-called recreational games.

Bill was an exceptionally strong character. A friend described him as 'tenacious, like a bulldog' and said that he always had to score the last point with other adults when playing sport. He wasn't a bad man - his Spanish students liked him and he had many friends in the community, plus he and Faith had a loving marriage. But his relentless academic and sporting expectations were too much for a dyslexic, unco-ordinated, slightly-built child.

If most of us had to spend even one week on a subject we hated, then we'd be understandably miserable. But Kip Kinkel had to take part in football, tennis and other sporting events almost every day of his life. And when he walked off the pitch at the end of a game, bruised and demoralised, his father would tell him that he hadn't given of his best, that he had to try again tomorrow and the day after that. He also faced similar academic pressures. As a result, he felt an increasingly dangerous mixture of rage and despair.

Anthropologist Elliot Leyton's book, *Sole Survivor*, explores the lives of children who murdered their own families. He found that 'familicide is more likely to occur in ambitious, even prosperous families.' The parents who were murdered by their offspring tended to be very ambitious and over controlling, to the extent that the child felt that he or she could do nothing right. These parents chose their child's hobbies, school curriculum and sometimes even their friends. Eventually, the child felt that he or she was little more than a robot to be programmed and would often retreat into depression and consider suicide. Elliot Leyton wrote the book long before Kip Kinkel killed his family – but his background is incredibly similar to those of the family killers who Leyton describes.

Such parents, he found, subconsciously set out to deny or even obliterate the autonomy of the developing child. This is certainly true of Kip's parents for the Kinkel's mantra was 'we are a sporting and academic family.' Kip was taken to watch games he hated, participate in sports he hated and study well past the point of exhaustion. He was given very few opportunities to be himself. And in the end he decided to destroy himself, but to first destroy the people he believed had psychologically crushed him for sixteen years.

Having studied similar familicides, Elliot Leyton found that laypeople often didn't understand the distorted family dynamics which had taken place. They'd then try to blame the killings on bad blood, peer pressure or mental illness and would label the distressed young killer as 'an evil seed.' Admittedly these children didn't help their own cause, for they were in no fit state to do a realistic postmortem on their family's dysfunctionality. As a result, they'd blandly state that they murdered their parents 'because they were yelling at me.'

But in Kip Kinkel's case, many people were aware that the family dynamics had gone awry. His sister constantly begged her parents to be fair to him. The Kinkels' friends suggested that Bill should ease off on his son during their interminable tennis games. Faith's colleagues saw that she looked increasingly exhausted and knew she shouldn't be making Kip study for hour after hour. The psychologist who evaluated Kip told Bill Kinkel to stop being so hard on his son. Bill complied for a few weeks – and during these few weeks the father-son relationship improved. But Bill soon slipped back into his usual endlessly-demanding parenting style. An old friend with psychological experience even warned Bill Kinkel that his son was a big suicide risk. The friend, who lived some distance away, urged Bill to phone him if he needed advice, but Bill never did.

Psychologist Dorothy Rowe (writing in the late eighties before Kip killed) said that 'If we understand how aggression is a response to frustration, and if we understand how a certain young man has created a structure of meaning in which he sees himself as lacking all recognition except in his knowledge about guns, if he feels that he is frustrated in everything that he wishes to do, then we can see the series of connections which culminated one day in this young man shooting his mother and his neighbours. We do not approve of his act, but neither do we see it as a sudden, inexplicable action.' Ironically, many crime writers made Kip's parents out to be saints and said that the multicide had come completely out of the blue.

Prescription drugs may also have played a part in Kip's increasing sense of malaise. He was prescribed Ritalin when he was eight years old - and the drug's many opponents say that it causes a stunting of growth, loss of muscular control and self-esteem. Over time it also shrinks the brain.

Ritalin is a schedule 2 drug, ranked alongside cocaine and opium. If overused it can lead to violence. The manufacturers themselves admit that, if the drug is abused, psychotic episodes can occur. Even coming off the drug can be dangerous as one of the side effects of Ritalin withdrawal is the risk of suicide.

The seratonin-enhancing drug Prozac also has its problems. Shortly before killing his parents and his schoolmates, Kip had been prescribed this drug. Like many users, he noted a swift improvement in his mood - but this improvement tends to be shortlived. Children who take the drug can find it increasingly hard to differentiate between dreams and reality and can have appalling nightmares. Between 1988 and 1992, over ninety children were violent towards themselves or others whilst taking the drug and researchers noted in 1999 that it could cause manic episodes.

Sometimes it's during the withdrawal phrase from the drug that the user becomes exceptionally violent. A 1995 Danish study concluded that withdrawal from such drugs could cause - amongst other symptoms such as fear, restlessness, irritability, aggression - an urge to destroy.

## The verdict

At first, fifteen-year-old Kip offered an insanity defence, but later withdrew this. He was kept under constant suicide watch and charged as an adult. He also received so many death threats that he appeared in court wearing a bullet proof vest.

In September 1999 Kipland Kinkel pleaded guilty to four counts of murder - and twenty-six charges of attempted murder - and was sentenced to 111 years in prison. He was immediately sent to the MacLaren Youth Correctional Facility, a prison for violent young men. He will stay there until his early twenties, when he'll be transferred to an adult prison.

## Update

After the trial, various friends of the family spoke publicly in his favour, explaining that he'd been pushed towards academia and sport all his life by a father who just couldn't let him be himself.

## 11
# THE GRASS WON'T PAY NO MIND
## Wendy (Gweneviere) Gardner & James Evans

Gweneviere was born in October 1981 to Jann and Clarence Gardner. (The latter was always known by his nickname, Buzz.) Jann had taken heroin and cocaine during the pregnancy and continued to do so after Gweneviere's birth. Buzz also enjoyed experimenting with soft drugs and alcohol, and the couple - who lived in New York - had a very volatile relationship.

Gweneviere was a sunny natured and loving little girl. She was delighted when, at two years old, her parents gave her a sister, Kathy. But the new baby put pressure on an already rocky marriage so it was an increasingly unhappy home.

When Gweneviere was three her parents had a fight about cigarettes during which her mother lunged at her father with a knife. Some reports say she stabbed him. Buzz fled, permanently ending their relationship.

Jann's drug addiction was getting worse so Buzz's mother, Betty, applied to the courts for custody. Betty and her late husband had failed Buzz (who said that his father was a violent ogre and his mother a strict disciplinarian) but presumably she thought she'd succeed in parenting this time around.

Betty was given custody of both girls and they moved to her Saugerties home in upstate New York. Meanwhile Jann had turned to prostitution to support her drug habit and moved to another part of the city, living in a squat.

At first Gweneviere seemed to thrive in Betty's care. After all, she now had three meals a day and was no longer neglected. Betty's home was modest but well tended. She decorated the girls' bedroom and made sure that they were neat and clean.

Unfortunately, Betty followed the rules of a bygone age. She told friends that she lived her entire life by the teachings of the Bible. This seemed to include the maxim of 'spare the rod and spoil the child' for she beat Gweneviere and Kathy with a fly swat and a paddle. Neighbours sometimes heard shouts and screams emanating from the house.

Gweneviere was glad to escape to school, where the other children shortened her name to Wendy. She will be known as Wendy in this profile from now on.

Wendy learned to play the flute at school. She did well in her exams and on the sports field. Neighbours thought her a very well behaved child who clearly adored her younger sister. She also tried to please the devout Betty by frequently attending church. But whenever she did anything that Betty considered to be wrong, Betty would tell her that she'd end up like her 'no-good mother' who Betty despised.

Wendy became an increasingly beautiful girl with long dark hair and sad dark eyes. Like any other human being, she yearned for love and acceptance rather than constant complaints. A neighbour even saw Betty dragging Wendy into the house simply because she'd lost a sewing needle in the grass. Betty made ongoing financial sacrifices in order to feed and clothe the girls, but what Wendy needed most was approval. At an alarmingly early age, she tried to charm this from the opposite sex.

By ten or eleven she'd found herself two 'boyfriends' and wrote in her diary that she'd come close to going all the way with them. (Admittedly, her idea of going all the way might not have been anatomically accurate.) Friends noted that she was desperate for the boys' acceptance, but one boy finished with her and the other told his friends that she was a slag.

Betty had no idea that these early sexual relationships were taking place. She still treated Wendy as a baby, telling her that she couldn't use the telephone to talk to boys or go to the shopping mall. But Wendy was becoming her own person and refused to take confirmation (a kind of adult baptism) in Betty's church.

In turn, Betty made it obvious that she loved Kathy more than Wendy, giving the former new clothes and the latter hand-me-downs.

## Love at last

In the late summer of 1994, twelve-year-old Wendy was out playing tag with a group of other children when she bumped into fifteen-year-old James Evans, who'd just returned to the area to live with his mother. There was an immediate attraction between them and by November of that year, with Wendy now thirteen, they were having sex. Betty, who'd always hated the so-called sins of the flesh, said that James was evil and tried to stop the teenagers seeing each other. But Wendy loved the tall, thin youth and started playing truant to be with him.

## James Evans

James had been born in 1979 to Dinah Evans. She and her husband already had a son and a daughter who were both at secondary school. The family lived in Kingston, New York.

Dinah, whose own childhood had been violent, got into trouble with the law so she wasn't around for part of James's early years. When she was there she was sometimes beaten by her husband and James witnessed this violence. (Children have been known to copy their parents' violence when they are as young as eighteen months.)

When James was two, his parent's marriage ended. He spent some time with his grandmother who he really cared for. He also spent some time with Dinah and some with other relatives. He was described as cheerful with a high IQ. By the time he was six his mother was a more permanent part of his life though she still had her problems. But James loved her and he also loved his older sister so he was a child with hope in his heart.

When he was eight his father applied for custody on the grounds of Dinah's instability. He won his case, the judge noting Dinah's many brushes with the law and her various personal problems. But for some reason James's father didn't take up custody for another three years. By then James had become so close to his family that he had to be physically dragged from their home.

He kept running away from his father's house, which was a hundred miles away from his mother. Onlookers would describe his father as a hard worker but a disciplinarian.

The arguments between the parents continued and in the end - at age fourteen - he was placed in a community home. Psychologists found him depressed, angry and tearful, though he tried to hide the latter emotion behind a wall of indifference. Like some of the other unhappy children in this book (Robert Thompson and Kip Kinkel) he found it hard to eat.

The lonely, dispossessed teenager was overjoyed at finding love with tiny, slender Wendy who he described as 'perfect.' It would take a few weeks for him to discover just how troubled she was.

## Banned love

Wendy was happy for the first time in years but Betty Gardner - and most of Wendy's other relatives - didn't approve of the match. Betty thought that fifteen-year-old James was too streetwise for her thirteen-year-old grandchild. He had a reputation for bullying, but his mother would later say he was hassling older kids for picking on the younger ones.

Betty tried to break up the young lovers - but for once her grand-daughter stood up to her. The elderly woman continued to insult the boy.

## Self-harm

Wendy became increasingly distressed. She thought she was pregnant and, terrified, asked James to punch her in the stomach. On another occasion after an argument she grabbed a knife and cut herself. James's sister, a paramedic, also saw a deep slash on one of Wendy's wrists as if she'd tried to commit suicide.

In October she ran away and phoned home to say that she was living in a different part of America - but when the police were called in they found her hiding at James's home.

In December she again cut herself several times, deeply hurt by her grandmother's ongoing assertion that she'd inherited her mother's sin.

Towards the end of December the situation at home was so tense that Wendy all but moved in with James and his mother. They knew that the clock was ticking, that her grandmother would eventually phone the police.

But this time Betty started to make arrangements to have Wendy put into a home. She also told Wendy (according to a phone call which James overheard) that she could hit her at any time. A neighbour had seen welts on Wendy's face which she claimed were inflicted by her grandmother and Wendy told James that when she was younger Betty had pushed her down the stairs.

Wendy was hurt by the abuse and terrified of losing James. She'd effectively lost her parents - by now she hadn't seen her mother, Jann, for years and the woman was dying of HIV-related complications. And when her father Buzz visited, he and Betty usually had huge verbal fights.

On 29th December 1994 James suggested that Wendy phone her grandmother and ask if she could stay the night with James and his mother. Betty said no and Wendy told her to 'fuck off' and slammed down the phone.

## Death wish

Turning to James, she said she wished the old lady was dead. James seemed to have acted as peacemaker at first, suggesting she try again, but Wendy's subsequent phone calls to Betty failed to resolve anything. She repeated that she wanted to kill her - and James tried to change the subject suggesting that they get married as soon as they were old enough and live far away.

Wendy continued to talk about murdering Betty Gardner. This was probably the equivalent of fantasising out loud - many who've suffered for years at the hands of a violent parent or guardian have lain in bed night after night and imagined killing them. Finally, James said he'd kill Betty if that was what Wendy wanted. Wendy agreed it was, but said she didn't think he had the guts.

Further fantasising took place, with the teenagers planning grisly ways to dispose of Betty Gardner. In the end, James decided that snapping the old woman's neck would be easiest.

## Killing time

The young lovers walked the few streets to Betty's house and went downstairs to the TV room to confront her. They'd rehearsed that Wendy would say 'You abused me. Now it's your turn.' But Wendy - like most children faced with their abuser - lost her nerve.

Betty told James to get out. Ignoring her, James kept asking Wendy what she wanted to do - and in the end Wendy shouted 'Just do it.' As he lunged at Betty, eleven-year-old Kathy began to scream. Wendy grabbed her younger sister, dragged her to their bedroom and rammed her head into the wall. She held onto Kathy to prevent her racing downstairs to her grandmother's aid.

James yanked at Betty's neck, but it didn't obligingly snap the way it had in his fantasies. He managed to get her onto the carpet and pulled a kite string from his pocket, looping it around her neck. He also put his foot on her back to keep her in place as he desperately tightened the string.

Betty continued to shout and scream - and Wendy started singing songs upstairs to help drown out the noises. After a few minutes the sixty-seven-year-old's face changed colour and blood seeped from her throat where the string was cutting into it. Ugly death gurgles began to emanate from her convulsing body. Only when her bladder let loose its contents was James sure that she was dead.

When he confirmed that he'd killed Betty, Wendy started to sob. She hadn't actually believed that he'd go through with it. Neither wanted to look at or dispose of the body. Like most children who kill, they hadn't planned what they'd do after their nemesis was dead.

Wendy cried several times that night and the next day. James was also shaken and tearful. Wendy deliberately cut herself with the scissors and James had bad dreams. Kathy would later say that she overheard Wendy moaning so she thinks the teenagers had sex (as usual, that particular detail was the one emphasised by the prurient press).

Unable to sleep with the corpse in the adjoining room, James and Wendy carried Betty Gardner's body to her car. They hid it in the trunk then returned to the house and swore Kathy to silence. For the first time in years they could do what they wanted. They even had money, for they'd taken the seven-hundred dollars that Betty had in the house.

**Life after death**

The next day Wendy and James took Kathy out for a pizza. Later they took her bowling. At other times, when the eleven-year-old was tired, they locked her in the house and went shopping at the mall.

They drove the car to various fast food joints with the corpse still locked inside the trunk. At one stage they drove to the Catskill mountains where they could easily have dumped the body, but for some unknown reason they brought it back home again. They also showed the body to at least one of James's friends.

On the third day Kathy left the house whilst the young lovers were asleep and ran to a neighbours'. She told them of the murder and the neighbour phoned the police. The body was found and the teenagers were immediately arrested. Buzz was located and raced to Wendy's side.

He was shocked that his daughter had encouraged James to kill Betty - but he could understand her motivation. He told a journalist that the Child Protection Services had failed to investigate reports that Betty was abusing Wendy. He said that he'd tried very recently to get custody but had been turned down.

James's mother and older sister gave him emotional support but both children were refused bail and remained in youth detention centres until their trials.

## James's trial

James went on trial in July 1995. He had no money so was reliant on the public defender's office. Wendy would fare better, with Buzz getting her a lawyer who he'd used in the past.

A psychiatrist testified that James had murdered Betty in order to protect Wendy. He had been unable to protect his mother from his father's violence but was determined to be protective this time round. He also spoke about how terrible James's early years had been.

It wasn't until little James was six that his mother had been a consistent presence in his life - and by eight he knew that he might lose her at any time as his father had been granted custody. As an eleven-year-old he'd had to be physically carried to his father's house and had run away numerous times.

James had been clinically depressed before he met Wendy. He often couldn't eat, couldn't sleep and was frequently tearful. Their relationship gave him love and acceptance, a reason to get up in the morning. He was also planning a future with her and couldn't bear for Betty to separate them.

James's lawyers said that Wendy had been the mastermind behind the murder, that James was a troubled boy rather than a cold-blooded murderer. The prosecution argued that he was a sociopath who would kill again.

Yet whatever James's faults, he doesn't appear to have been a sociopath. He was capable of loving Wendy and adored his disabled grandmother. He didn't lack empathy - instead he empathised with Wendy's unhappiness to such an extent that he was willing to do anything to alleviate it. He was traumatised after the murder and still found it hard to eat and sleep.

The jury deliberated for a few hours then found him guilty of second degree murder rather than the lesser charge of manslaughter. A month later he was sentenced to the harshest penalty available, nine years to life.


## Wendy's trial

It was February 1997 before Wendy had her day in court. She'd been thirteen when she heard the homicide being committed - but she was now tried, at age fifteen, as an adult.

The prosecution made the trembling teenager out to be a scheming Jezebel who had charmed her lover into carrying out the murder. But her defence pointed out that her grandmother's treatment had amounted to physical and psychological abuse. The defence lawyer admitted that 'This is the hardest case I ever tried in my life because she is such a little kid.'

The defence also gave the impression that the murder was all James's fault. This was hardly fair as Wendy had asked him to do it and had restrained Kathy whilst he choked the old woman to death.

James agreed to testify for Wendy's sake. As he'd already been found guilty of murder, his presence in court was likely to make her look the less culpable teenager. He had told his psychologist that he was still in love with her.

Wendy insisted on testifying in her own defence, believing that if the jury heard what she'd been through at her grandmother's hands they'd be more understanding. Unfortunately, like many abuse survivors, she sounded flat and cold.

She also said that James had been violent towards her and that she'd stayed with him out of fear after the murder. Unsurprisingly, the jury weren't convinced by this.

Her defence was further undermined by her sister Kathy who said that the beatings with the paddle and the fly swat hadn't been so bad. She admitted under questioning that Betty had gotten physical in other ways, including slapping Wendy's face.

Buzz testified in Wendy's defence. This essentially meant that he had to sever all ties with Kathy, as she was living with other relatives. And Betty's relatives were hotly contesting the abuse.

Buzz said that Betty's hitting Wendy had been a bone of contention between them for a long time - and that it had also distressed some of their relatives. He agreed that he'd failed her by leaving her with his disciplinarian mother. Looking over at Wendy in the dock he added 'I should be sitting where she is.'

It seems that Wendy was badly advised in several ways, as she was seen carrying a teddy bear after her arrest and she turned up at court in a little-girl dress. These made her look false and manipulative. Yet she was very young in some ways as Betty hadn't liked her going out with other teenagers, instead taking her out socially to see relatives. Indeed, a psychologist testified that she had an emotional age of eight. Her mother Jann had finally died a few months previously, adding to her distress.

That April, Wendy wept as she was found guilty of second degree murder. Her sentence was seven years to life.

## Stereotypes

As they so often do, many laypeople bought into the traditional stereotypes of James as a remorseless teenage psychopath and Wendy as the perfect child who was led astray by him. But Wendy's problems began long before she met James. She was so desperate for love that she came close to having sex with two previous boyfriends - and when they broke up she wrote about killing them violently. She also wrote that if anyone read her diary, she hoped they'd 'burn in Hell.' She was clearly a mixture of fear and despair and rage, living with a woman who constantly told her that she was turning out just like her dying mother. Eventually, something had to give.

The feminist interpretation took a different tack, suggesting this was statutory rape with Wendy as the clear victim. But, though both teenagers were under-age, the sex was consensual. James wasn't using Wendy as a sex object. His mother said that they were clearly devoted to each other and tried not to spend a single moment apart. He bought her gifts and talked about their future and kept every one of the troubled letters she sent.

Meanwhile those who subscribe to a wholly genetic basis for crime said that Wendy was violent like her mother was. But studies have shown that if animals are removed from an aggressive mother and placed with a non-aggressive foster mum, the young animals own aggression significantly diminishes. (One example of such a study is *The Effect Of Maternal Environment On Aggressive Behaviour In Inbred Mice*, a research paper by C.H. Southwick, published in a biology journal in 1968.) Similarly, studies have shown that animals are more likely to fight if they see the animals in the next cage fighting. Wendy was being hit by her grandmother and saw her grandmother and father have regular shouting matches, factors surely more pertinent than biology.

Betty Gardner had her good points, giving her grandchildren physical care and helping to run a support group for widows. But her repressive parenting made both her son Buzz and grand-daughter Wendy deeply unhappy and desperate for fun.

## Update

James passed several exams in a young persons institution. As his sentence was nine years to life, his time in prison remains indeterminate. His 1999 appeal was turned down.

Wendy is currently incarcerated in a detention facility near Albany where Buzz visits her weekly. Assuming that she isn't released early on appeal, she will be eligible for parole when she is twenty-one.

## 12

## NOBODY'S CHILD
### Sean Richard Sellers

Sean was born on 18th May 1969 to Vonda and Rick Sellers. Vonda had been only fifteen when she became pregnant with Sean and was sixteen when he was born. The family lived in Concoran, California but by the time Sean was three the marriage had broken up. This did nothing to improve Vonda's volatile temper and she often hit the little blonde boy, frequently slapping him across the face.

By the time he was five his mother had met Paul Bellofatto, a former Green Beret. Paul told Sean that he had killed the enemy whilst on duty in Vietnam. He was now a cross country trucker and Vonda decided to join him on the road.

She gave Sean to her father and his second wife. At other times he was cared for by his great-grandparents. His mother and stepfather came home every few weeks for a short visit then left again. Each time Sean would wave them goodbye then lock himself in the bathroom and cry.

At school he had to explain that his surname was Sellers after his natural father although his parents had the surname of Bellofatto. Plus his grandfather who he lived with had yet another surname. He knew that he was different.

Sean was a bright little boy who liked animals and said that he wanted to be a vet when he grew up. He loved his pets but was sometimes separated from them when his mother took him away to her latest living quarters. He'd stay with Vonda and Paul for a few days or weeks then be shipped back to his grandfather or to other relatives. He had virtually no stability in his life. To the outside world he seemed unusually self-reliant - but deep down he was filled with fear, low self-esteem and an increasing rage.

### Sexual abuse

When Sean was eight his parents again took him to live with them, this time in Los Angeles. The couple were living with relatives in an apartment block that was supposed to be childfree so he was constantly being told to keep quiet. Various relatives shouted at him and one of them made the child give him oral sex. Like most abused children, Sean thought that this was his fault. Within weeks it was clear that they were never going to play happy families so his parents shipped him back to his grandfather's house in Oklahoma and he returned to school there.

The next seven years passed in this way. Every so often Vonda and Paul would take Sean to live with them in their latest house. They never stayed in the one town for more than a year so he often had to cope with new schools and new friends. By now Vonda's violence had increased and she hit her son with a belt, a hairbrush and wooden spoons. Sean tried very hard to please her then opted for trying to avoid her by staying in his room. Meanwhile Paul spent little time with his stepson and Sean came to the conclusion that the man - who he thought of as Dad - didn't like or admire him at all.

Vonda and Paul smoked dope and by age twelve Sean had joined them in this. He also started playing Dungeons & Dragons games.

By the time Sean reached his teens he was filled with rage. He turned to the martial arts to improve his self-esteem and read up on how to kill people. During this period he was sent to live with an aunt and uncle who laughed at him for his interest in Ninjutsu. But Paul took him to see the film *Rambo* and said that soldiers should be able to kill people and not worry about it.

When Sean was fifteen they moved him again, this time to Colorado. For the first time in ages he was happy. He joined the Civil Air Patrol and became a cadet commander. This pleased Paul and their relationship improved. But the couple decided to move back to Oklahoma which would mean Sean losing everything he'd built up. Sean begged them not to go - or to let him stay on his own - but they made him return, showing his wishes didn't matter. Like many children, he was being given no respect.

His needs ignored once too often, the boy gave up trying to be part of everyday life. He no longer tried to make friends and began to read up on Satanism in the hope that it would give him some control over his days.

He and his friend Richard would talk about what it would be like to rape and kill people. They also planned robberies but didn't carry them out.

## In pursuit of power

The teenage Sean increasingly turned to the occult in the hope of acquiring power. He wrote in his own blood that he served Satan and added 'to my enemies, death.' He told his schoolmates that he saw flying demons. This isn't unusual in poorly parented individuals. Under intense stress, people often hallucinate and see or hear things - usually of a frightening nature - that aren't actually there.

He got into a fight at school about satanism and when a teacher intervened she discovered he had the occult book *The Satanic Bible*. She called his parents who discovered he'd set up a satanic altar in his room. Sadly, this started yet another shouting match during which his stepfather yelled 'You don't exist.'

Sean was now even more desperate to prove that he did exist, to exert some form of power. He decided he'd enhance his satanic status if he broke the Ten Commandments. His seventeen-year-old friend Richard was also interested in murder and the two youths decided to kill a shop clerk called Robert who Richard knew.

## The first murder

On 8th September 1985 the boys entered the convenience store where thirty-six-year-old Robert Bower was working the night shift. Richard was angry at Robert who had previously refused to sell him beer because he was underage.

The boys went to the store and spoke to him for the next hour. They joked that he was at risk because the store didn't have a security camera but Robert explained that there was only fifty dollars in the cash register at any one time. He had no reason to fear Richard and had no idea that Sean - who he didn't know - was toting Richard's grandfather's gun.

Moments later, Sean aimed the gun at the clerk's head, fired and missed. The shocked clerk ran and Sean fired again. This shot also missed as Robert had slipped and fallen to the floor. He screamed and grabbed hold of a jacket, trying to hide behind it. Sean could see his terrified eyes. Nevertheless, he fired a third time, hitting the man and sending blood spurting everywhere. Laughing, the youths raced from the store.

## Aftermath

No one connected the brutal killing with the withdrawn teenage boy. Sean didn't think about the death for days - but when he did he felt superior. He wondered if his stepfather would be pleased with him for taking a life and not feeling upset about it. Paul had given him the impression that soldiers who suffered from post traumatic stress were weak.

Sean got a job as a bouncer for a youth club. There he met a teenager called Angel and for the first time, he fell in love. Unfortunately, Sean's mother couldn't stand the girl who smoked and was a high school drop out. Sean thought that Angel reminded his mother of herself as a girl, acting tough but feeling lost. Vonda called Angel a tramp and a bitch and tried to split the couple up.

The next six months were increasingly unpleasant at home. Sean brooded in his room and practiced the so-called black arts. He took driving lessons to have more control over his destiny. Meanwhile his mother threw him out of the house so Sean decided to sleep in his van but Paul promptly went to Sean's work and fetched him back. His mother then threatened to send him to his natural father in California, presumably to separate him from his girlfriend.

During one of their many arguments, Vonda attacked Sean - but this time he pushed her back, meeting violence with violence. He alternated between just wishing he could leave and wishing that she was dead. He even put rat poison in her coffee but it had no effect.

Sean had been counting the days until he turned eighteen and could leave home, but now he just couldn't wait. He was only sixteen - but during those sixteen years he'd had good reason to build up a lot of hate.

## The second and third murders

On 5th March 1986 he waited until Vonda and Paul went to bed, stripped to his underwear and went through one of his satanic rituals before creeping into their bedroom with Paul's .44 revolver at his side. He would later say that he felt like he was shooting his way to freedom, knocking down the door of a prison cage.

He put the gun close to his forty-three-year-old stepfather's head and fired, killing him instantly. He turned the gun on his thirty-two-year-old mother and shot her too. As she rose, wounded, from the bed he shot her again, watching the blood run down the side of her head. He laughed, just as he had done after killing the shop clerk. Then he showered and staged the scene to make it look like a burglary.

Afterwards he drove to Richard's house and they talked about what they'd say to the authorities. Sean contacted them after pretending to discover the bodies the next day.

## Arrest

The police went to his school and were told about his problems with his parents and his interest in satanism. He was soon arrested. The police also spoke to Richard who agreed to testify against Sean to save himself.

## Neglect not board games

The media immediately blamed the young killer's crimes on Dungeons & Dragons. (Many journalists would have run out of things to say years ago if the game had never been invented.) Meanwhile the Christian community decided it was his interest in the occult that was to blame.

As usual, few people bothered to notice that, by the time he was nine years old, Sean had only spent a total of six months with his parents. Instead, he was passed around like an unwanted parcel - and in the years leading up to his becoming a murderer he'd lived in six different towns. Largely friendless and completely powerless he'd turned to an ostensible source of solace and power, the occult. But it wasn't any so-called demon that committed these crimes - just a badly neglected teenager with a gun.

## The trial

Sean's defence team failed to have him tried as a juvenile so they entered an insanity defence, saying that his interest in satanism constituted madness.

The prosecution alleged these were thrill killings. The jury were back with a guilty verdict within three hours.

At the time of the trial, in October 1986, Oklahoma didn't allow life sentences without the possibility of parole. Some of the jurors were allegedly worried that if they gave the youth life he'd be paroled in as little as seven years. Whatever their various motivations, they voted for the death penalty and Sean was sent to Oklahoma's McAlester Prison.


## Update

For the next thirteen years Sean Sellers remained on Death Row, saying alternately that a demon or drugs had made him kill his parents. He got religion and started to write religious poetry, becoming a pin-up for many born-again Christians. Unsurprisingly, the family of the innocent clerk he'd shot were wishing that he hadn't been born the first time around.

Christian visitors flocked to the triple murderer and his new friends included those who performed exorcisms for money. He gave interviews to ministers about the supposed dangers of satanism. He also published a book that blamed the world's ills on black magic, heavy metal music and drugs.

Yet he'd made the connection between the violence he'd endured and his own violent murders, writing that 'Mum... slapped me in the face... mashed my mouth into my teeth... hit me in the head with butcher knife handles, hairbrushes, whatever she had in her hand... I tried to live in my room as much as possible. I hated her as much as I loved her.'

Sean now decided there was a deity out there who loved him. He appeared on talk TV renouncing the occult and saying that he'd seen the light.

This usually goes down well with parole boards and those who oppose the death penalty - but it shouldn't as many children who kill come from religious backgrounds. The same is true of adults who murder. Some of the world's most sadistic serial killers - including Ted Bundy, Rose West, Dean Corll, Richard Ramirez and Robert Berdella - had deeply religious upbringings. The same is true of necrophile killers like Ed Gein. And the very devout John List murdered his mother, wife and three children when his prayers went unanswered and his family started to move away from the church.

During his years on Death Row, Sean produced many devout words. He also married a born-again Christian in 1995 who said that when watching him on TV she'd 'seen Jesus in his eyes.' (Another woman had said the exact same thing about serial killer Aileen Wuornos, adopting her and proclaiming she was innocent. But the eye-reading proved unreliable as Aileen later confessed.)

By 1997 Sean's marriage had been annulled. By early 1999 he'd run out of appeals and on 4th February 1999 he entered the McAlester Prison execution chamber singing hymns. He was twenty-nine years old.

Sean was strapped down and both of his arms were injected with a drug designed to render him unconscious, stop his breathing then stop his heart. Watched by fourteen witnesses, he was pronounced dead at 12.17am.

Sadly, there are still groups and individuals trying to blame his crimes on the medieval concept of demons rather than looking at the violence and neglect he endured for sixteen years.

# 13

## NINETEENTH NERVOUS BREAKDOWN
### Johnny Frank Garrett

Johnny was born in 1964 to a young woman called Charlotte Garrett who lived in Amarillo, Texas. It was a difficult birth during which he suffered oxygen deprivation. This alone was enough to leave him slightly-brain damaged, but it wouldn't be the last trauma dealt out to the unfortunate child's brain. He came into the world to find that he had an older brother, and that brother (and other young relatives) would also be abused.

The first father he remembered - who may or may not have been his real dad - battered his mother and beat his brother with a baseball bat. Meanwhile Johnny's mother, a Jehovah's Witness, had one nervous break-down after another and couldn't cope.

When Johnny was a toddler his mother was incarcerated in a mental hospital yet again and he was sent to stay with his maternal grandparents in their freezing cold, cockroach-ridden home. They frequently half-starved him and hit him, just as they'd previously done to his mum. They did the same to Johnny's cousin, Kathalene, who also lived with them.

When he was three and a half his mother was discharged from hospital and decided she wanted him back. She divorced her husband but soon married again and introduced the child to the man he'd think of as father number two. He beat Johnny repeatedly on his backside and either he or Johnny's grand-mother deliberately held the child against a hot stove when he wouldn't stop crying. His cousin Kathalene would never forget the terrible screams he made - and the scarred gouge in his flesh would remain for the rest of his life.

Johnny's mother continued to bear children and to have breakdowns that prevented her from looking after them. And so, for the next few years, Johnny made his way between his grandparent's isolated old house and his mother's extremely cramped trailer. His grandmother kept telling him that he was a bastard and was always hitting him about the head. She also dressed him up as a little girl and gave him to his grandfather for the old man to sexu-ally abuse. His cousin Kathalene heard Johnny crying during these sessions, which happened twice a week.

At one stage his mother got the whole family back so that Johnny, his older brother, his two little sisters and his little brother were all staying in the trailer at the same time.

## Sexual abuse

Johnny's mother married again. This third 'father figure' made Johnny fellate him and another adult male. He made him strip and provide such oral sex on numerous occasions. Soon the abuse extended to forced sodomy. The man was keen to increase the child's humiliation, making him bend over and spread his legs.

Johnny's mother was at work when the abuse was going on and sometimes his younger siblings were sleeping in the other room. Johnny looked increasingly shell-shocked but no one was looking out for him. The man would also fetch the boy from school and abuse him, threatening him with further beatings if he refused to comply.

## Child pornography

Johnny's mother divorced this violent man too but he remained in Johnny's life, and began to take him to a friend who made porn films. There the boy was coerced to have sex with other adults and a dog. Johnny wasn't the only minor taking part in such exploitative videos - he saw children as young as seven being forced to participate.

By the time Johnny was in his early teens, his stepfather was setting him up with various older men for cash. Johnny was so slim that he looked much younger than his years and the punters liked this. He'd later claim that a judge and prominent businessmen were amongst the men who had sought out his sexual services.

The relentless beatings and sex abuse took its toll. Johnny attacked another child at school, throwing a glass tumbler at him. He was sent to a reform school where he became increasingly paranoid, fearing that strangers were about to attack. He also began to insert thin bottles into his rectum whilst masturbating - abuse victims sometimes do this as a way of taking control of previously involuntary invasive acts. Meanwhile his mother had descended into alcoholism and had married and divorced for the fourth time.

For years this multiply-abused boy had disassociative episodes where he tuned out of his body and tried to believe that the intense pain was happening to someone other than himself but it wasn't enough to save his sanity. As more and more bad memories filled his every waking moment he became increasingly bizarre, attacking strangers before - in his deranged mind - they could attack him.

## School's out forever

Viewing Johnny as a neighbourhood bully, the authorities sent him to a school for delinquents. In the summer of 1981 they released him and he again began shuttling between his mother's and grandparents' house. He skulked around the neighbourhood, at one stage stopping to watch the nuns entering and leaving the local convent. Many were the same age as his violent grandmother, someone he had good reason to hate...

On the last day of October the seventeen-year-old went to see his grandparents but they humiliated him so he hurriedly left and started drinking. He went on to his mother's and could remember leaving her trailer feeling even more upset. He didn't know what had happened when they were together - his ongoing brain damage plus the constant abuse had left him frequently confused and delusional - but could remember that she was clad only in a slip. A relative who saw his mother standing in the doorway of the trailer would confirm this.

## Rape and murder

In the early hours of that morning - 31st October 1981 - he crept across the fields to the St Francis Convent. Under cover of darkness, he cut a window screen and broke a pane of glass. Then he dropped the knife he'd used, knowing that he had another sharper one in his possession. (Other accounts say that he stole this second knife from the convent's kitchen but it's impossible to know which statement is accurate as Johnny's testimony was frequently confused.)

Entering the convent, he walked until he found an open bedroom door. Sister Tadea Benz, also known as Sister Catherine, was lying in the darkness.

He could hear that the seventy-six-year-old Catholic nun was deeply asleep.

Johnny put his hand over her mouth so that she couldn't scream. He either undressed the old woman or made her undress - her body would be found naked. He raped her, choked her and stabbed her. One newspaper report suggests that during the rape she recited The Lord's Prayer. But no one came to deliver her from Johnny Garrett so her nude body was found on the floor a few hours later. Blood had seeped from her nose and further blood was found on the walls.

## Arrest and trial

Witnesses had seen Johnny hanging around the convent so the police quickly arrested the seventeen-year-old who alternately admitted and denied the crime. The evidence against him was overwhelming. His fingerprints were in the nun's bedroom and on the knives and his pubic hair was found on her thighs.

He was sentenced to death and put on Death Row at Huntsville, in his home state of Texas. There, the guards frequently overheard him speaking to imaginary people, loud conversations that sometimes went on all night. Prison wardens are used to very disturbed prisoners but they had to admit that Johnny Garrett was the most insane inmate they'd ever known. Dr Dorothy Lewis, who evaluated him, ultimately became convinced that he had multiple personality disorder. In other words, he'd created additional personalities to take the pain inflicted on him by the numerous abusive adults in his life.

The prison psychiatrist decided the boy was schizophrenic and administered various strong drugs, none of which could quell the voices in Johnny's head.

## Death penalty

In January 1992 Pope John Paul II asked for clemency in the Johnny Garrett case. The nuns at the convent also asked that his life be spared. Several medical experts argued that a twenty-eight-year-old mentally-ill man should not be put to death for a crime he committed when he was a multiply-abused child of seventeen.

Defence lawyers said that he had been abused by his mother and by his alcoholic stepfathers. They also referred to his recent diagnosis of multiple personality disorder. But after due consideration the authorities decided not to grant clemency.

On 11th February that year Johnny entered the execution chamber in Huntsville. His mother and his sisters, Jeane and Janet, watched and sung hymns. His mother said several times that she loved him and added 'It's okay to go to sleep, baby.' Outside, thirty members of Amnesty International chanted anti-death-penalty slogans whilst approximately seventy students from San Houston State University shouted 'Kill the freak.'

When he was strapped to the gurney, Johnny said 'Thank my friends who tried to pull me through all this... my guru who helped me go through this. I'd like to thank my family for loving me, and the rest of the world can kiss my ass.'

He stared at the ceiling as the lethal injection took effect and died within minutes, his death much more humane than his life.

# 14

# SENSES WORKING OVERTIME
## Recognised Typologies Of Children Who Kill

Criminologists have defined at least ten different types of children who kill. They are the family killer, school killer, mentally ill killer, gang-based killer, incidental killer, hate killer, self-killer, infant killer, cult killer and sex killer. But if you look at them carefully you'll find that they mostly stem from the same source - that is, the child hasn't been loved and nurtured by his primary carers and this has spawned sufficient rage and hurt to make them want to kill. Examples of each of the typologies are:

## The family killer

These killers, who are mainly male, are overwhelmed by parental cruelty or parental demands. Some crime writers believe that children kill their families for financial gain - but a look at many such cases shows that these wealthy parents have also been abusive. The financial motive, if it exists, is very much secondary.

For example, numerous writers have suggested that Wendy Gardner had her grandmother killed in order to enjoy spending her money and partying in her home. But a quick glance at Wendy's life shows that her grandmother beat her and constantly told her that she was turning into her mother, a drug-addicted prostitute.

Similarly, much has been made of the fact that William Allnutt stole several sovereigns from his grandfather - but William only killed after his grandfather knocked him down for the umpteenth time and threatened to murder him next time. These children didn't kill to enjoy a few days prosperity - they killed out of terror, desperate to escape further physical pain.

Criminologists and psychotherapists such as Kathleen M Heide have found an overwhelming connection between patricide and child abuse. The children who killed their fathers had been physically and emotionally ill treated and neglected. Some had also been sexually abused. For case studies of children who have killed abusive guardians, please see the chapter Children Who Kill Their Families.

## The school killer

Such killers - who often take out more than one victim - have often been bullied mercilessly for weeks or even years before they finally snap and take a gun to school with them. Most of these killers are male and often the hatred for the institution is so intense that they kill everyone in sight - but some have warned the one or two pupils who were kind to them to stay away from school that day. Kip Kinkel, profiled earlier, was bullied at school and wrote of how much he wanted to kill one particular pupil. Numerous other stressors occurred at home as he couldn't be the academic and sporting success his parents craved. Luke Woodham, also profiled, was endlessly abused at school and mocked at home to the extent that he spoke about 'being beat his whole life.' Luke expected to be killed by police at the end of his rampage and Kip planned to kill himself after the shootings, their respective plans being to take as many lives as possible before meeting their own deaths.

These school killers meet most of the requirements for spree killers as laid down by author Pan Pantziarka in his book on the subject *Lone Wolf*. That is, the male plans the violence in advance, kills semi-randomly, is controlled during the killing, tries to take out as many people as possible and makes little attempt to escape.

Pantziarka also notes that adult spree killers tend to have a dominant father who crushes the son's emergent identity. Kip Kinkel perfectly fits this profile. Luke Woodward doesn't as his father was absent - but Pantziarka notes that another strong-willed male often takes the father's place. This holds true for Luke who idolised his satanic-games-playing mentor, Grant Boyette. And Grant himself said that he was like a father to Luke.

## The mentally ill (pathological) killer

A tiny percentage of children will, through some chemical imbalance or brain tumour, become mentally ill - and this illness can cause them to kill themselves or others. These are the No Known Fault diseases.

But many children become mentally ill (or at least have their mental health brought into question) because of their abusive backgrounds. Their parents have such strange childrearing methods and such mercurial temperaments that the child can do nothing right. Johnny Garrett and Peter Dinsdale aka Bruce Lee, both profiled, fit into this unfortunate category.

Most of us would find it hard to survive life with *one* violent parent but poor Johnny Garrett had four such brutal stepfathers - and psychologist Dorothy Lewis noted that it was after abuse from his third father-figure that Johnny's mind snapped irreparably.

One particularly senseless murder by mentally subnormal boys occurred in Britain in February 1947. Ten boys (all aged fifteen and sixteen) from an approved school decided to kill the headmaster, steal his car and drive away. To this end, they stole three rifles. They were busily loading them when they were apprehended by one of their teachers and promptly shot him in the groin. As he lay on the ground, badly injured, one of the boys reloaded and shot him in the chest. He died within half an hour.

All ten of the boys were quickly traced and stood trial at Stafford Assizes where their headmaster admitted that eight out of the ten had a mental handicap. They were sent to various borstals and prisons. Meanwhile there was an enquiry into the running of the approved school which resulted in it being closed down.

## The gang-based killer

Again, children who join violent gangs tend to be children from violent homes. Sometimes the gang acts as an alternative parent, giving them a skewed respect and stature. For the first time, they have a sense of belonging - and, in order to keep their status in the group, they will maim, rape and kill. Such gangs invariably have a leader. They also tend to have at least one member who is reluctant to carry out the murder, and who is likely to confess to the police.

The most widely reported teen gang rape-murders have been American ones, but in December 2001 a gang of thirteen and fourteen-year-old boys carried out a gang rape in the leafy town of Guildford, England. The five youths separated a fifteen-year-old from her friend and dragged her to a car park where they repeatedly raped her, thankfully stopping short - or being stopped short - of murder. They were apprehended and released on police bail.

Such rapes give the group a purpose - after all, they are often comprised of very inarticulate youths who have no employment or hobbies to talk about. J W Messerschmidt's book *Masculinities And Crime* suggests that such acts 'help maintain and reinforce an alliance among the boys by humiliating and devaluing women, thereby strengthening the myth of masculine power.'

Whether the victim lives or dies is often incidental in such group rapes. One London gang repeatedly raped a tourist then asked her if she could swim. She lied and said no, at which point they threw her into the freezing dark water. She was able to swim to safety and survived.

But a thirteen-year-old boy from Swansea wasn't so lucky. He was found unconscious in a car park in January 2002 and later died of his injuries. Six children (four boys and two girls) aged between twelve and sixteen were charged with grievous bodily harm. The six children were bailed to appear later at Swansea Juvenile Court. Meanwhile a seventh child - an eleven-year-old girl - was also investigated for the murder but released without charge.

## The incidental killer

These are children who perhaps plan to rob or play a prank on a victim but end up killing him or her. Robert Thompson and Jon Venables may fall into this category. That is, they said they planned to take a child and 'get him lost' - though it's more likely that they first planned to examine him sexually. They didn't initially intend to kill him, believing childishly that if they threw one piece of brick he'd be quiet and they could leave - but 'he wouldn't stay down' and they hit him again and again. They had both been on the receiving end of repeated cruelty and this made it comparatively easy for them to carry out violence.

Recently there has been an alarming increase in children mugging other children for their mobile phones. A home office study released in 2002 showed that most of the muggers were male and aged fourteen to seventeen whilst most of the victims were aged eleven to fifteen. The muggers picked on a child who was younger than themselves, sometimes just snatching the phone but at other times punching and kicking the owner. In the worst reported case - that of attempted murder - a young man shot a nineteen-year-old woman in the head in broad daylight simply to steal her phone. It's a safe bet that these young muggers have been hit throughout their childhoods as children who haven't been hit by their parents usually don't behave in such an unprovoked violent way.

**The hate killer**

The victim of such a murder may be from a different religious group, colour or sexual orientation to the child who murders him. Again, though, we invariably find that the killer has suffered during his or her childhood and is passing that hatred on.

Sometimes the actual target (eg homosexual men) is the same target of the violent parents. In other instances, the parents hit and humiliate the child who then goes looking for a safe target to harm, perhaps setting fire to a sleeping tramp or kicking a homeless woman to death. These children are often so young that their names and details are withheld from the press.

But in one Russian case the children were named. Ten-year-old Volodya, thirteen-year-old Vitya and fourteen-year-old Andrie (all with the surname Yakovlev) were Moscow-based brothers living with their mentally ill mother. They survived in total squalor. In 1994 they admitted to battering several down-and-outs to death, though only the fourteen-year-old was brought to trial. Such children are often so traumatised by their unhappy upbringing that violence is their primary voice.

This author taught adult basic education on a voluntary basis and can remember speaking to the tutor of a youth discussion group. (Attendance at the group was obligatory as it replaced a school academic module that these young men didn't have the IQ for.) The tutor said that the youths mainly sat in sullen silence but on the few occasions she could persuade them to speak they started every bigoted sentence with 'My dad says...' She was baffled that they didn't have their own voice.

But violent and immature parents simply don't give their children conversational or action-based options. Instead, every independently-voiced thought or act of their children is battered down. Eventually these children end up virtual automatons, extolling the racist or sexual bigotry that they've heard all their lives.

## The self-killer

Psychologists say that everyone who attempts suicide has at one stage wanted to kill someone else - and suicidal children are no exception. Adverse circumstances (parental abuse, school bullying or intense academic pressure) lead to low self-esteem. If the hatred turns completely inward the child will only destroy his or herself rather than the annihilating external source of their misery. Sometimes the pathologist will put this down to accidental death in order to spare the parents additional pain. If the hate is both inward and outward directed then these children are more likely to become spree killers, murdering their parents or the school bullies before turning the gun on themselves.

One particularly unusual suicide took place in January 2002 when a fifteen-year-old schoolboy deliberately flew a light aircraft into a Florida skyscraper. The boy was half Arabic and had sympathies with Osama Bin Laden who masterminded the destruction of the World Trade Centre.

Once again, though, the unhappy childhood comes first and the rationale for violence comes second for the teenager was from a broken home. He had rejected his father's Arabic name and used his mother's surname but remained deeply troubled. He was described as a loner who was very shy.


## The infant killer

Children who give birth are often terrified of what their parents will say. These youngsters usually suffocate their newborn baby as it utters its first cry. Often they are so in denial about the impending birth that they are in a public place (such as a school toilet or the restroom in a department store) when they go into labour and commit the infanticide.

One Canadian sixteen-year-old hid her pregnancy until the birth then stabbed the newborn baby to death. Clearly too confused to dispose of the evidence properly, she merely concealed the little corpse in the garage of her family home. When the body was eventually discovered she told police that she was terrified of her parent's reaction. Sadly, these girls find censure from their parents more frightening than committing murder. Spending nine months in denial at such a young age must put them under a phenomenal strain.

Some of these girls fear intense disapproval rather than physical assault, but in other instances their mothers have warned them that 'if you ever get pregnant your father will kill you.' If there has been previous violence shown to her, the girl takes this threat literally.

## The cult killer

Children who kill as part of a cult have usually suffered highly abusive backgrounds. Being part of an alternative group - be it based on vampirism, satanism or some other religious belief system - gives them a sense of identity. It's also a very visible way of rejecting an outwardly more conventional society which has failed them utterly. The so-called vampire killer Rod Ferrell, profiled earlier, fits into this category.

Seventeen-year-old Dylan Klebold, who killed thirteen people and wounded numerous others at Columbine High School before turning the gun on himself, even sent an email explaining his motivation. It read in part 'do not try to blame it on the clothes I wear, the music I listen to... Parents and teachers, you fucked up... I did not choose this life but I have indeed chosen to exit it.' Ironically, before the note was made public, the media had blamed heavy metal music and violent films.

## The sex killer

These are often anger-retaliation rape-murders where the lust is fuelled by rage. This is sex as a weapon. Again, the killers - like Kenny Houseknecht who stabbed a near-naked girl over ninety times then ejaculated on a pair of her panties - have invariably been abused themselves. For fuller details of the Kenny Houseknecht case and this typology, please see the Youthful Sex Killers chapter later in this book.

# 15
# CRY ME A RIVER
## Further Classifications


As well as the ten typologies described in the last chapter, it's possible to group children who kill by age or by the particular function (such as babysitting) that they were carrying out when the murder occurred. This author also found that some children are encouraged to kill by a family member, usually a violent parent who wants to involve others in his deviancy.


## Exceptionally young killers

Most of the killers profiled in this book were between ten and seventeen, but occasionally even younger children commit murder. Owing to their own small stature, their victims are invariably even younger - or very old and weak.

In 1968 in Islington a four-year-old boy and a three-year-old boy together battered a seven-month-old baby to death, while in 1978 two Wolverhampton boys aged four and six beat a pensioner who subsequently died. And in 1986 a five-year-old girl took a three week infant from its pram and swung it against the wall, killing it.

That same year, in Miami, a five-year-old boy who had been abused by his parents pushed a three-year-old boy from a balcony. The three-year-old died.

Another three-and-a-half-year-old from a violent American home was cited in a 1962 article in *Social Research* by Dr Douglas Sargent. The child, Ernest, had been abused by his father. The little boy went on to batter his older brother over the head with a bottle, hit another child with a baseball bat and break a puppy's leg. Yet when removed from his violent home he was trouble-free.

When Robert Thompson and Jon Venables killed two-year-old James Bulger in 1992, the world press gave the impression that this was an unprecedented event brought on by violent videos and declining moral standards. But as this book has shown, there are a score or more such killings - usually by abused children - in Britain every year.

173

Over a hundred years ago two little boys committed a murder that has many parallels with the Thompson/Venables case. In 1861, eight-year-old friends James Bradley and Peter Henry Barratt took a two-year-old boy, George, from the wasteground where he was playing. A woman saw him crying and being led by the hand by the bigger of the eight-year-olds. She later saw that they'd stripped him naked - and one of her sons saw the boy break a twig from a tree and aim it at the naked child. The three then disappeared from sight.

Later, the toddler's body was found in a stream. He'd been hit with a stick on the buttocks, legs and head and subsequently drowned. The children were too upset to explain their motivation, but as so much violence is learned behaviour it's likely that one or both of them had been beaten in a similar way. They were found guilty of manslaughter and given five years in a reformatory.

The younger the child is, the less likely that they have full understanding of the murderous event. This was the case with two four-year-old boys who were living in a homeless shelter. They bit and battered a baby belonging to one of the other residents and the infant died.

When background details are known in such cases it's usually said that the child who killed had a 'very sad life' or 'was in care.' One four-year-old American boy who killed a baby had earlier had his arm broken by his abusive father. Paul Mones, who specialises in defending abused children who kill their parents, has noted that many of these children are abused from birth, being thrown into their cribs from the time they are a few days old. Later x-rays will show the numerous fractures that the child has endured over the years.

## Babies who babysit

Sometimes unnurtured children are left in charge of much younger children and they simply can't cope. One such case unfolded in 1992 when an eleven-year-old British girl couldn't get the eighteen-month-old baby she was babysitting to stop crying, a situation that even balanced adults can find exhausting. She hit him against the bars of his cot but this presumably just increased his screams so she placed a hand over his mouth, whereupon he suffocated. She was found guilty of manslaughter.

More is known about an American case, that of eleven-year-old Arva Betts. Arva had been abused all of her life and was suicidal. She was frequently left in sole charge of her half-brother and half-sister, aged two years and fifteen months respectively. Unable to cope, she strangled her half-brother to death and attempted to strangle her half-sister, causing brain damage. In October 1989 she was sentenced to twelve years probation, the judge commenting that she was the third victim in this tragic case.

Occasionally the child who babysits is mentally ill. This was apparently the case with sixteen-year-old Robert Ward, who babysat for his neighbours on Valentine's Day 1986. He shot both pre-school children dead then fired a shot at his father when the man went to investigate. He was found to be mentally ill and was sent to an Oklahoma mental hospital under the proviso that if his sanity returns he'll be transferred to an adult prison.

That said, there is sometimes method in a killer's madness. Gavin de Becker - in his illuminating book about surviving violence *The Gift Of Fear* - tells of one boy, Michael Perry, who was shoved against a radiator by his mother and was badly burnt in the process. He was also cruelly controlled by his father who got a neighbour to tell him exactly what young Michael did. The father explained his all-knowningness by telling the child 'when I go to work I leave my eyes at home.' By adulthood Michael had become insane and stalked various innocent celebrities. But there was an ironic twist to his eventual killing spree - for he shot out the radiator that had burnt him and also shot out his mother and father's all-seeing eyes.

**Children who kill strangers**

As the profiles and case studies in this book have shown, children who kill have usually suffered from neglect and/or repeated emotional or physical violence. Sometimes that violence will have been meted out months or even years before the child kills.

In the hours after being physically and verbally humiliated, the traumatised child comforts himself by having a violent revenge fantasy. He or she may also act out the violence by torturing a small animal, the creature of choice most often being a neighbourhood cat. However any live creature can be used to pass the suffering on - Jesse Pomeroy strangled his mother's canaries, Bruce Lee wrung the necks of numerous pigeons, Rod Ferrell was accused of butchering puppies and Kip Kinkel allegedly bombed farm animals including a cow.

But occasionally we can see a linear approach where the child is beaten and goes on immediately to beat another who may be a stranger. This happened in 1971 when a fourteen-year-old girl was savagely hit by her mother, one of many instances. Within hours the bruised teenager had lured a five-year-old girl to a quiet spot where she beat her to death with a stick and a stone. She was indicted for manslaughter.

Similarly, in a 1996 case in Kansas City, a victim was simply in the wrong place at the wrong time. The killer was sixteen-year-old Candy McDonald who was desperately unhappy at home and had run away numerous times. When she was fifteen she met a man who was six years older and within months had moved in with him. She started planning their wedding but her parents wouldn't give their permission and soon the man had started dating someone else.

Candy confronted his new girlfriend and her friend Nikki Majeed in a restaurant car park. There was a fight during which Candy stabbed Nikki once in the neck, severing her jugular. The fourteen-year-old, who had nothing to do with the ménage a trois, bled to death.

Candy fled the scene with her boyfriend then went back looking for the knife. Only then did she realise how seriously she'd cut the other girl. Charged with second degree murder, she was given a ten year sentence and may be paroled in 2004.


**Child as a weapon**

Sometimes a woman in an unhappy marriage will tell her child repeatedly that she wishes his father was dead. (Mark Chapman, who, as an adult went on to murder John Lennon, came from this kind of background.) These children are forced to grow up incredibly quickly and take the role of protector. Chapman's mother made the child pray with her and his hatred for John Lennon partly stemmed from the musician's lyric 'Imagine there's no Heaven.' He remained a religious zealot after shooting dead the talented singer.

In one such 1988 case, a three-year-old Detroit boy shot his father whilst the man was beating his mother. Witnesses and gunpowder residue linked him to the event. In similar circumstances, eleven-year-old Mary Bailey murdered her abusive stepfather because she knew that when he woke up he'd beat her mother again.

These women, due to their own passive-aggressive natures, make their children pay an appalling price. Even if the child is legally absolved from the crime, they often have recurring nightmares. And those who have been brought up to believe that there is an afterlife also fear being visited by the dead parent's ghost.


## Parentally-encouraged killers

Our society likes to believe that parents are good and children are bad - so many inadequate parents of children who kill are absolved by the media and often by the court system. But in some cases there is no doubt about where the blame should lie, cases where the parent encourages the child to take a life.

One such American case occurred in the seventies, when sadistic father Joe Kallinger began to take one of his children, thirteen-year-old Michael, out with him on robbery and raping sprees. These escalated into murder when Joe, who had been raised by religious adoptive parents, heard God telling him to kill everyone on earth. In July 1974, he persuaded Michael to help him kidnap, gag, rectally torture and cut off the penis of a ten-year-old boy. The emasculated victim died from suffocating on the gag.

Later that same month, Michael and his father lured one of Michael's older brothers, Joseph junior, to a demolition site where they drowned him for the insurance money. Michael had been so brutalised by his father that he showed no emotion after these deaths. On another occasion Joe demanded that thirteen-year-old Michael rape a woman but it seems that Michael, though willing, was physically unable to complete the act. But the teenager clearly enjoyed taunting such victims, doing to them what his cruel father had done to him.

Six months later, Joe and Michael forced their way into a party and tied up all of the adults, Michael guarding some whilst Joe stripped and terrorised others. Then Joe stabbed a young nurse to death while the teenage Michael watched. The boy also warned his father when he sighted danger, ensuring that they could flee the scene. A few days later both were caught.

The judge noted how much Michael and his siblings had suffered at their brutal father's hands and said that the boy was salvageable. Michael agreed to plead guilty to the robbery charges and the murder charges were dropped. He was fostered prior to the trial and then sent to prison until the age of twenty-one. He is now free and his violent father is dead, having choked on his own vomit in prison in 1996 at age fifty-nine.

Another American case in which a father persuaded his son to kill occurred in 1990 in Houston, Texas. Sixteen-year-old Delton Dowthitt had visited a bowling alley and bumped into a girl he knew, Gracie Purnhagen and her nine-year-old sister Tiffany. The girls were presumably pleased when he offered them a lift home in his father's borrowed pickup truck. They had no idea that Delton had only recently been reunited with his father - and that the older man had a history of assaulting girls.

The teenagers Gracie and Delton got into the back of the truck to chat and nine-year-old Tiffany rode up front with Dennis Dowthitt. Before long the forty-eight-year-old man had stopped the vehicle and assaulted the child. The little girl ran from the truck and Dennis turned his attention to Gracie and tried to rape her. But he'd been impotent for years and settled for stripping her and assaulting her anally with a beer bottle instead. He also cut her throat and knifed her in the chest but she wasn't yet dead.

Dennis now ordered his sixteen-year-old son to kill Tiffany. Delton did so, grabbing a rope, throwing it around the nine-year-old's neck and pulling it tight. The injured Gracie screamed as she saw her sibling being strangled, at which point the older man returned to her and cut her throat again - this time fatally - then the two killers fled.

We may never know the exact motivation that sixteen-year-old Delton had for killing the nine-year-old. With his hard expression and his tattoos he looked streetwise but he told various people that he committed the murder because he was frightened of his dad. The powerfully built Dennis had been overheard threatening his son - and the older man had a history of sodomising young female relatives with bottles and with broomsticks, so it's a safe bet that Delton hadn't had a loving childhood.

When first brought into custody, young Delton seemed willing to take his share of the blame - then he heard that his father was trying to link him to both murders. At this stage Delton told the full story and testified against his father and evidence backed up much of his story. But the teenager presumably tried to reinvent history when telling the court that he'd kissed Tiffany on the head and told her that he was sorry before he strangled her, making himself into a cross between Charles Manson and The Waltons. He was sentenced to forty-five years in prison and his father got the death penalty.


## Children who are wrongly convicted

A final category that appears to have been ignored in books about young murderers is children who are innocent. Sometimes they are manipulated by a parent who persuades them to take the blame for the violent death of the other parent. Or they are framed by an antagonistic community or bullied into a false confession by the police.


## The West Memphis Three

There may well have been such a miscarriage of justice in West Memphis, America, where three eight-year-old boys were tortured, mutilated and murdered in May 1993. The bodies had been left in the creek so that forensic evidence was washed away by the water and yielded few clues. And some of the injuries could have been caused by so-called legitimate punishment as one of the eight-year-olds had been beaten with a belt by his stepfather an hour or so before he disappeared.

Rumours of these being satanic killings went around the religious small town and caused the police to bring in three teenagers who had an interest in wicca. Eighteen-year-old Damien Echols suffered from depression, seventeen-year-old Jessie Missakelley junior had a low IQ and was susceptible to suggestion and Jason Baldwin, sixteen, spent time with them and seems to have been charged because of - as his defence team put it - guilt by association. A few fibres found on the bodies that were 'similar to' clothing that the teenagers wore was the only forensic evidence. Despite this, the three teenagers were found guilty and, in Damien's case, sentenced to death.

Since then, there has been an ongoing campaign including internet appeals and televised documentaries to 'Free The West Memphis Three.' A full account of the case can be found in *The Blood Of Innocents*, a book written by the investigative team which covered the story from the start.

As previously mentioned, one of the West Memphis Three had a low IQ.

The same is true in the following case, that of Stephen Downing, and of many other instances where youths are wrongly convicted by over zealous or corrupt police.


## Stephen Leslie Downing

Stephen was a gentle boy who lived with his parents and his sister in Bakewell, Derbyshire. He enjoyed hand-rearing orphaned baby hedgehogs in his garden shed. He was classified as educationally subnormal and could barely read and write.

By September 1973 seventeen-year-old Stephen was employed by the council to work as a groundsman in Bakewell Cemetery. After lunch one day he returned to work and found a half naked and badly battered woman lying face down on the cemetery footpath. He also noticed the weapon, a pick axe handle, lying nearby. Stephen did what any caring passerby would have done - he turned her over and felt for a pulse.

At this stage the victim sat up so the teenager ran to get help. Meanwhile the bloodied woman got to her feet and fell heavily against a gravestone. The police and ambulance arrived forty minutes later and she was rushed to hospital.

The local police asked Stephen to help with their enquiries. The seventeen-year-old - who had the reading age of eleven - was happy to do so. He had no idea that they might suspect him.

But for the next nine hours they questioned him relentlessly. They shook him awake each time he started to doze off and they refused to let him see his parents who turned up at the station several times. He was only given one small sandwich to eat so was very hungry and cold. He also had a spinal problem at the time of the interview so was in pain from sitting on a hard wooden chair for nine hours. The police didn't offer him a solicitor but suggested that if he signed a confession he might get to go home. Eventually the hungry and bewildered boy signed a confession that was not in his own words and, indeed, contained many words that he didn't comprehend. He thought at this stage that the woman would regain consciousness and tell the police that he wasn't to blame. Unfortunately for him, Wendy Sewell died of her massive head injuries without regaining consciousness.

But the youth should have had nothing to fear. After all, his fingerprints weren't on the murder weapon. The blood on his clothes wasn't consistent with the blood spatter there would have been if he'd attacked her. And a bloody palm print belonging to another person, plus hair and fibres that didn't come from Stephen, had been found. The police had got the boy to say in his statement that he'd sexually assaulted her - but despite her partial undress it was later confirmed that she hadn't been sexually assaulted. They'd also got Stephen to say that he'd hit her twice whereas the later autopsy showed that she'd been bludgeoned seven or eight times.

Wendy had allegedly told a friend that she was going to meet one of her lovers in the cemetery that day. An attractive woman, she'd had several boyfriends who lived locally and it was rumoured that at least one of them held high office and had links with the police.

Meanwhile, Stephen went on trial for her murder. Incredibly, the jury weren't told about his mental handicap or learning difficulties. After a three day trial they took just one hour to find him guilty and he was sentenced to be detained at Her Majesty's Pleasure, with the judge recommending a minimum sentence of seventeen years. Poor Stephen almost collapsed at the verdict and his family was also in shock.

Prison isn't easy for most prisoners - but it was an especial hell for this gentle boy from a loving family. In prison he was assaulted by other prisoners, had boiling water thrown on him and was beaten up numerous times. He was also ill-served by the prison authorities on the basis that he was what they call IDOM - in denial of murder. As such, he was wasn't sent on training courses or given the better prison jobs. Instead he was penalised again and again for asserting his innocence.

His parents and sister also continued to assert his innocence, going to MPs and newspapers and constantly reiterating that the evidence simply didn't point to Stephen but they often met with hostility or indifference. They watched the years slip by without Stephen being granted parole as he 'refused to show remorse.' But how could he show remorse for a terrible murder that he didn't commit? He even told his parents that he'd rather die in prison than pretend that he'd killed Wendy in order to go free. Because of his continued claim to innocence, his seventeen year tariff passed and the authorities didn't let him out.

When their son had been in prison for twenty years the Downings were joined in their campaign by Don Hale, a journalist who had become editor of the local paper, the *Matlock Mercury*. He became convinced that this was a miscarriage of justice and obtained a court order which forced the police to release relevant documents.

## Hale, the conquering hero

For a while after this, Don Hale's life became almost as frightening as Stephen's. He had his phone tapped and was followed by the security services. He received death threats and survived three attempts on his life with vehicles been driven straight at him as he walked home at night. It was very clear that someone didn't want the case reopened and was willing to use violence to keep the caring editor quiet. He also faced hostility from the police who threatened legal action claiming obstruction and defamation - but they backed down when challenged via the courts.

As the authorities became increasingly aware of Don's campaign, Stephen was transferred to the freezing 'troublemakers' wing in Dartmoor Prison - his only troublemaking being to continually protest his innocence.

For the next seven years Don fought to clear Stephen's name. During these years, various witnesses contacted him and explained why they'd been too afraid to come forward. Others had been given the impression that Stephen was a pervert so thought that it didn't matter if he was doing time for a murder he didn't commit. But it turned out that these were rumours put about by people with a vested interest, determined to blacken the innocent teenager's name.

Stephen Downing had by now become the longest serving prisoner to be detained at Her Majesty's Pleasure - and he was being detained on no evidence. But after seven years Don's crusading paid off and in November 2000 the case was referred back to the court of appeal and by January 2002 his conviction had been quashed.

Don Hale - and Stephen's parents - had mainly battled alone to end this travesty but the press were out in force when Stephen, now forty-four, was freed. By then he'd spent twenty-seven years in prison. 'I could have done with the cavalry a few years ago, but nobody wanted to know' Don Hale said ruefully.

But it should have been obvious from the start that Stephen didn't fit the profile of a violent killer. He was from a loving home and he cared for animals. He had no history of violence - and we know that children who kill have usually displayed previous episodes of more minor violence towards animals, other children or towards themselves.

This author interviewed Don Hale in April 2002 immediately after publication of his inspiring book on the Stephen Downing case, *Town Without Pity*. Asked why he'd fought so determinedly for a teenager he didn't originally know, he said that 'there were so many anomalies in the original evidence that it soon became obvious that Stephen was innocent.'

The facts do indeed prove that the gentle teenager was innocent - so why were so many people happy to believe in his guilt? 'He was working class, from the wrong side of the tracks,' Don says sadly, 'If something went wrong in the town, the locals would say they were sure it was someone from the council estate. Stephen and his parents lived on that council estate.'

Don also got the impression that Stephen's comparative solitude was enough to make him appear different - and some people are very threatened by anyone who isn't like they are. 'He was a bit of a loner in that he wasn't involved in lots of clubs and societies. He liked to do mechanical work rather than go to discos with the local lads.'

Did the boy's age at the time of his imprisonment make Don more sympathetic to his situation? 'To a certain extent - but it was more about his low IQ. He was considered backward yet the police treated him very badly. He was a very naive boy, the ideal patsy really.' Don's own son was seventeen at the time he began researching the case so this made him additionally aware of how terrible it must be for an innocent teenager to lose everything he'd ever known.

So could this happen to another child or has the introduction of PACE in 1986 (a criminal law which ensures that prisoners have access to legal advice) put paid to such high pressure interrogations? 'Well, it wouldn't happen in the same way now,' Don admits, 'Interviews are taped, monitored, and the prisoner is accompanied but I'm sure there are still cases where the wrong suspects are rounded up and put in the frame for someone else. It's especially difficult for teenagers who are loners to provide an alibi.'

In *Town Without Pity* Don describes how he was alternately mocked and ignored by prison wardens on his first visit to Stephen. 'The wardens don't like journalists getting involved in a case. Maybe they think that it will raise the prisoner's hopes of an early release unfairly. But Stephen had already done ten years over his originally suggested time.'

Thankfully Don's message - that innocent children sometimes go to jail -

will reach an even wider audience in due course for he's been co-writing a screenplay about this gross miscarriage of justice. He's aware that the situation could have been even more dire for Stephen than it actually was. 'If the boy had been convicted a few years earlier when we still had the death penalty he could have been hung.' He would like to see a different judicial set-up that doesn't send vulnerable seventeen-year-old boys to adult prisons.

After twenty-seven years in such prisons, Stephen is at last free. When he first left jail he found work as a trainee chef, but at the time this author talked to Don Hale he had just changed employment to become a security guard. Meanwhile, Derbyshire Police have announced that they intend to reopen the investigation into Wendy Sewell's murder, so perhaps at last her killer will be tracked down.

# 16

## HEARD IT THROUGH THE GRAPEVINE
### Children Who Kill Their Friends

There have been instances of children killing their friends in America because of the ready availability of guns. The argument that would once have been ended by juvenile shouts or blows turns into a fatal episode when one child shoots the other dead.

That said, many psychologists have pointed out that children who have never been hit by their parents don't have this level of anger. Speaking at the *Children Are Unbeatable* seminar in January 2002, bestselling author Dorothy Rowe said that people who have never been hurt and humiliated by their parents have the capacity to talk things through without violence, to reach a compromise.

Sometimes the juvenile's rage has been simmering under the surface for months, as in the following case of teen killers Karen Severson and Laura Doyle who murdered Missy Avila, their seventeen-year-old friend.

### Karen Francis Severson and Laura Ann Doyle

Karen was born on 17th October 1967 to a single mother who immediately gave her up for adoption. Three days later her new parents, Loyal and Paula Severson, took her to their Californian home. She was a lonely child who made up stories about having lots of brothers and sisters. She overate and was clearly lacking in confidence.

When Karen was eight she befriended one of her schoolmates, Michelle Avila, who was always known as Missy. Karen started to spend most of her time at Missy's house and started to call Missy's mother 'mom.' For the next few years - up until weeks before she killed her - the girls appeared to remain best friends.

But the differences between them became more obvious as they matured into teenagers. Missy was less than five foot tall with pretty features, a little waist and long silken hair. The boys at school loved her. In contrast, Karen was plain and still overweight. And Missy was a first class scholar whilst Karen struggled to pass her exams. Missy also had an incredibly close relationship with her mother Irene and could tell her anything.

Karen watched for day after day as her best friend was admired and asked out by various boys. When someone at last asked her, Karen, out she was ecstatic. She soon slept with him and became pregnant at age fourteen.

She gave birth to a baby at age fifteen but couldn't cope. She often fled to Missy's house, leaving the baby with her adoptive parents. But being at Missy's house just made her more envious - Missy could have fun with boys and had a freedom that Karen now lacked.

Karen had gained over three stone during her pregnancy so was mocked even more than before by the local youths. She started to smoke marijuana and drink alcohol. Meanwhile, Missy's parents had separated and Missy was very upset and even more reliant on her best friend. So when Karen enrolled in a less academic school, Missy joined her there.

But Karen became increasingly jealous of her friend. She started to set various schoolmates against each other, telling each of them that it was Missy who had started the ugly rumours. As a result, four of the girls jumped on Missy, causing facial bruising. They implicated Karen but Missy refused to believe that her best friend would set her up.

Soon afterwards Karen could see that sixteen-year-old Missy had fallen in love. She herself started dating a boy who had a crush on Missy. Karen was so terrified of losing him that she warned Missy to stay away.

Suddenly bereft of Karen's friendship, Missy made friends with another pupil called Laura Doyle, a girl who - along with Karen Severson - would plot her death.

Laura had been born on 1st May 1967 to a couple who had problems with alcohol. They argued constantly, oblivious to the effects it was having on their little red-haired child.

Laura matured into a thin, anaemic-looking teenager. All the problems she'd had at home had made her awkward so her mother decided to send her on a modelling course. But being surrounded by natural beauties made the insecure child feel even worse about herself and she became increasingly withdrawn. Luckily she was allowed to leave the course prematurely because her family ran out of cash.

Laura was very glad to have Missy as a friend. She started spending lots of time at her house and also started to call Missy's mother 'mom'. She found a warmth in the Avila household that she'd never known in her own unhappy home.

When Laura was sixteen she started dating a boy who she liked a lot. She was terrified that he'd go off with someone else so clung to him tightly. But he said that she was too possessive and finished with her. He also started spending more time with Missy, who'd dated him in the past.

Laura now felt angry towards Missy for this supposed betrayal. Karen also became enraged when she saw her own boyfriend holding Missy close. Karen was pregnant for the second time and longed to get married. She was unjustifiably afraid that Missy would get in the way.

On 1st October 1985 Laura drove Missy up the local mountain road to a wooded area. Karen Severson and another girl (whose identity is secret so she'll be called Annette throughout this case study) followed close behind in Karen's car. When the cars stopped, Laura and Karen grabbed Missy, hauled her into the woods and shouted at her. They said that she'd 'fucked' their boyfriends and that she'd have to pay. In turn, Missy wept and looked to Annette for help, but Annette looked away.

When they'd run out of insults they proceeded to beat her. The seventeen-year-old tried to deflect the blows and received abrasions to her arms and hands. Other blows caused bruises to her chest and face.

Laura pulled Missy's hair then Karen produced her penknife and cut shards of it off. Next, they dragged her into the stream in a standing position. A frightened Annette now ran back to the car. But Karen and Laura continued the assault, forcing their former friend into the shallow water whilst she pleaded and screamed. One girl grabbed Missy's feet to stop her from kicking whilst the other twisted her arm behind her back. Then they held her face in the stream until she stopped writhing and was presumably dead. Even now the girls weren't happy with their handiwork so they pushed, pulled and rolled a huge log from further upstream until it covered Missy's small body, pinning her down.

Laura then phoned Missy's house and said that Missy had gone off with some boys in a car and was she back yet? She and Karen would stick to that story for many months whilst Annette kept quiet and tried to put the death from her mind.

Karen and her little daughter went back to Missy's house after the funeral and stayed for hours. They came back the next day and the next. Within a fortnight they'd moved in and Karen was helping with the housework and emotionally supporting the bereaved mother. It comforted Irene to have her daughter's best friend there.

She noticed that Laura wasn't coming around any more, then heard that the girl had left school and found a job in a bakery. And Laura sent a condolence card which said that Irene had been like a mother to her and that she still felt Missy's presence all around.

But there were increasing clues that Karen wasn't coping with the pressure of Missy's death. Her weight soared to over fifteen stone. She started to imagine that she heard and saw Missy's ghost - or at least she told Irene she did. She kept naming possible culprits and trying to set traps to catch the boys she said were Missy's killers. She intermittently spoke to the police and probably acted strangely, but they suspected a man or men in this homicidal death.

When Karen was five months pregnant with her second baby she had an argument with her boyfriend and aborted his child. She began to visit Missy's headstone most days and speak to it. This became so alarming that Irene asked her to get professional help.

Laura was equally lost. She'd originally avoided alcohol in favour of soft drugs as she didn't want to emulate the drinking problems she'd witnessed throughout her childhood. But now she increasingly turned to drink. She looked blank when the police asked her questions about the youths that Missy had gone with and it was soon rumoured that she'd turned to cocaine. She lost so much weight that she was in constant ill health and looked skeletal.

It's unlikely that either girl would ever have confessed but the third girl, Annette, remained troubled by Missy's death. Three years later she told the full story to the police and Karen and Laura were arrested. In 1990 the case went to court. Both were found guilty of second degree murder and sentenced to fifteen years each, to be served in a Californian prison.

Laura's mother was honest enough to write a letter to the authorities explaining that she hadn't been strong enough to remove Laura from a very unhappy home situation. She admitted that Laura had suffered greatly as a result.


## Why they killed

This case is atypical in that the children who killed got away with the murder for so long - most children are caught within hours or days of the homicide.

Having immature and usually traumatised minds, they rarely think beyond getting rid of the abuser (or in this case the love rival) who is ruining their lives.

Karen and Laura succeeded in deflecting attention from themselves because both clearly loved Missy's mother - and they seemed, until the year of her death, to love Missy. The fact that they were female also stopped the police from looking too closely at them. Indeed, detectives at first thought that Missy's murder was a sexual assault from an unknown male that had escalated into a homicide.

Yet statistically a female killer or killers was more likely, for the FBI have noted that girls mainly kill acquaintances or friends or their own family. It's boys who are more likely to kill strangers - and these strangers are usually other boys rather than girls.

The police should have been alerted by the fact that both Laura and Karen were incredibly unhappy teenagers who were desperate for love - and who would do anything to keep that desired love object. (Such as getting pregnant at fourteen as Karen did or virtually stalking an ex-boyfriend as Laura did.) Such fear makes people suspicious to the point of paranoia so they saw Missy, in truth a good friend to them, as a rival who they had to kill. Their hate was such that they mocked her and damaged her face and hair before drowning her and covering her body with the log, as if afraid that she'd rise up to tempt away their supposed chance of happiness. A film loosely based on the crime, *A Killer Among Friends*, suggested that Karen was the leader and Laura the follower.

In another case where one friend killed another, there wasn't a prior history of jealousy towards the victim. Instead, the victim was apparently seen as a symbol of authority at a time when the soon-to-be-killer, Jennifer Tombs, was desperate to have fun.

## Jennifer Lee Tombs

Jennifer was born in 1981 to a mother who was unable to keep her. At eight months old she was adopted by Pastor Madlyn Tombs, a single woman who ran a Christian church.

Jennifer was a beautiful baby and Pastor Tombs gave her a beautiful home in Denver, but by Jennifer's early teens there was trouble in this supposed

Paradise. Clearly unhappy, the child had begun to steal. In turn, Pastor Tombs began to wear her jewellery at all times to ensure that it didn't go missing. She also put a lock on her bedroom door.

Pastor Tombs had been raised in a family where she was constantly supervised and she brought her daughter up the exact same way. Perhaps Jennifer felt suffocated and needed more freedom. It's clear that she suffered from low self-esteem as by fourteen she was having sex and by fifteen she'd had many boyfriends, most of whom treated her very casually.

Jennifer told one of these boyfriends, who was five years older than her, that she was pregnant with his baby. He faded out of her life after that but she phoned him several months later to say that she'd had the child. Again, he didn't go to see her - but if he had, he'd have found that she'd invented the baby. She was clearly a very troubled girl. She also tracked down details of her birth mother and had the woman's name tattooed on her arm.

The police often visited the Pastor's home after one of Jennifer's minor brushes with the law, but at fifteen her crimes became more serious when she stole a car. She was put on probation and given an electronic tag, which effectively put her under house arrest. Given that she had a poor relationship with her adopted mother - and had even stayed with a friend for several months in order to have more freedom - this possibly wasn't an appropriate solution.

But in September 1996 Jennifer saw the chance to party when Pastor Tombs said that she was going away on a religious retreat for the weekend. At school, Jennifer invited several friends round promising that she'd cook them a shrimp dinner. Unfortunately Pastor Tombs then added that she was arranging for a live-in babysitter for Jennifer.

The baby-sitter was a twenty-three-year-old woman called Tanya Lavallais who Jennifer thought of as her cousin. In truth, the two families weren't related but they were both heavily involved with the same church.

Tanya arrived at Jennifer's house - and shortly afterwards Jennifer's friends arrived. She sneaked them upstairs into her bedroom, telling them to be quiet until Tanya went out. In reality, Tanya - a responsible young woman - had no intention of going out and was relaxing in the downstairs Recreation Room.

Jennifer now went downstairs taking her ex-boyfriend's gun with her. Tanya was sitting on the couch with her arms stretched back behind her head. Fifteen-year-old Jennifer shot the innocent young woman six times, the bullets entering her upper arms and her head. She collapsed, bleeding heavily, back on the couch and Jennifer pulled her dead body to the ground.

At some stage Jennifer decided to clean the couch and poured detergent over the blood stain. She emptied the boot of her cousin's car, probably intending to put her in there. But Tanya weighed a lot more than Jennifer did and she only succeeded in dragging her body a few yards across the room. Jennifer then phoned an ex-boyfriend several times saying that she'd done something bad, that she'd killed a female intruder. She was doubtless hoping that he'd come over and dispose of the body but he was ill and refused to visit her house.

Jennifer must have gotten blood on her clothes for she went and had a bath, leaving her friends playing records and cards. At some stage she appeared wrapped only in a towel and her friends told her to get dressed again. They had no idea that there was a cooling corpse in a downstairs room.

But Tanya's family were concerned when they paged her and she didn't answer. They phoned Jennifer's house and even went round there but Jennifer refused to let them in, just saying that Tanya had gone out to a club.

Jennifer acted entirely normally for the rest of the night. Eventually most of her friends left but she asked one boy to come back later. He did and they had sex in the early hours of the morning. He, too, left and Jennifer and a female friend then retired for the night.

The next morning Jennifer pretended to discover the corpse. Telling her friend that she'd be blamed if the police saw the gun, she disposed of it in a nearby drain. This naturally made the police suspicious - and when they found out that someone had attempted to clean the couch they knew that this was an inside job.

The trial was unsurprisingly brief. Jennifer, by now sixteen, was tried as an adult and found guilty of first degree murder. She was sentenced to life imprisonment without the possibility of parole. Her adoptive mother said that the judicial system wasn't over and that Jennifer should pray - but the prayers didn't help and she lost her subsequent appeal.


## Adopted child syndrome

Both Karen Severson who helped to murder Missy Avila and Jennifer Tombs who murdered Tanya Lavallais were adopted as very young children. Statisticians have noted that a disproportionate number of serious offenders are adopted or foster children. In some regions 45% of all felonies committed by children are by adoptees. Some adults have made the leap to suggest that these children become violent because the 'vital mother-baby bond' is broken. As a result, they're campaigning to abolish adoption. But the truth is doubtless more complex than that.

For starters, it's a myth that a biological parent is automatically good to a child. Most of the children in this book suffered hugely at the hands of their biological parents. Some of these children flourished when taken away from their birth parents - most notably the younger children such as Robert Thompson, Jon Venables and Mary Bell. And Dr Dorothy Lewis has noted that young prisoners often change markedly if treated well by prison staff.

Second, sociologists would have to make a study of the adoptive parents before concluding what went wrong in the child's life. Were the parents who adopted very strict or in some other way restrictive? Or were the adoptive parents older when they adopted and too set in their ways so that they continually criticised and restrained their energetic adopted offspring? Did these parents have fulfilling lives prior to adopting or were they underachievers who put all of their own unfulfilled hopes onto the child?

Every one of the sex killers in the next chapter was raised by his biological parents and in almost every case there is a clear link between the lust murders and early parentally-caused abuse.

## 17
# HUNGRY LIKE THE WOLF
## Youthful Sex Killers

The teenage sex killer - like his adult contemporaries - has made a lethal connection between sexual pleasure and fatal levels of violence. He's often highly sadistic and may enjoy picquerism (cutting and stabbing), inflicting most of the wounds on the pubis or breasts or, in the case of a homosexual killer, on the penis and the scrotum. Lust and rage have become so interlinked in his damaged psyche that he seeks to destroy the parts of the body which arouse him most.

As most of the following case studies show, the teenage lust murderer usually fits into the category of the *disorganised* killer. That is, the crime is often committed on impulse so he doesn't bring a weapon with him, instead making use of bindings and implements available at the scene.

Such disorganised killers tend to leave the body at the crime scene. In some cases, this is the teenage lust killers bedroom or workplace, making discovery virtually inevitable. In contrast, an organised killer often takes the body to another place and disposes of it carefully.

Disorganised offenders often turn to religion after the crime, something that the organised offender (who has a higher IQ and is able to maintain relationships) avoids.

The following double murder, which took place in 1944, shows that teenage sex killings are not a new phenomena. The case is also interesting because the fourteen-year-old killer was executed within weeks of being found guilty and was the youngest American convict electrocuted by the state in the twentieth century.

**George Stinney**

George Stinney lived in an agricultural region of South Carolina with his family. The fourteen-year-old could neither read nor write and appears to have been of limited intelligence. He was slender and just over five foot tall. George was black but his victims would both be white. (Black males who rape and kill white women are the most likely to be executed by the state.)

On 24th March 1944 he was walking along the railroad track when he saw Betty Binnicker, age eleven, and her eight-year-old friend, Mary Thames, looking for wild flowers. The girls knew George so had no reason to fear him. They were presumably unperturbed when he followed them into the woods.

But George wanted to have sex with eleven-year-old Betty - and determined he'd have to get Mary out of the way. Picking up a heavy metal railroad spike, he battered the younger girl over the head, fracturing her skull in several places. She collapsed on the ground, bleeding profusely. She had only minutes left to live.

George now turned his lust-filled rage on Betty as she turned to flee, battering the railroad spike into her head at least seven times. Two of the blows actually produced holes in her skull, whilst others produced similar fractures to those endured by her younger friend. Betty also collapsed, seriously injured. The baby-faced killer remained unperturbed. It's unknown if at this stage George sexually assaulted either girl. Sexually-sadistic killers often spontaneously ejaculate during the violence - and after this their lust may be temporarily spent.

George now threw the bodies into a ditch that had filled up with water and went on his way. Residents would later say that his demeanour was entirely normal, so he may have been too dim-witted to understand the enormity of his actions or else may have been a remorseless psychopath. Though the crime has been well documented, this author could find little about the youth's childhood except that he lived with his parents and sister and that the latter continued to protest his innocence. In a photograph taken in jail he looks considerably younger than his fourteen years.

Early the next day the girls' submerged bodies were found and autopsied. George had been seen in the area and within an hour had confessed to the crimes. He initially said that the girls had attacked him and that he'd battered them in self-defence but soon changed his story to admit that there was a sexual motive to the assaults.

Less than three months after being found guilty, a weeping George entered the Death Chamber clutching his Bible. There the double killer - now aged fourteen years and five months - died in the electric chair.

Twenty years earlier in Britain, a white teenager called Harold Jones had also killed two white girls - but this case had a very different result.

## Harold Jones

Harold Jones gained notoriety as a teenage sex killer because he escaped justice only to immediately kill again. He lived in Wales with his father, who was an unemployed miner, and with his mother and younger sister. The family were poor so he had to share his bed with an adult male lodger. Harold himself had a job, working in a grocery store.

With his blonde hair, robust complexion and strong body he looked healthy and his visible hobbies of reading and harmonica-playing were laudable. He was also a hard worker - but dark passions were brewing beneath his pleasant facade. Whenever he went egg-collecting with his young friends, he'd pull the wings off the baby birds.

He may have been suffering from ongoing sexual frustration as presumably it was difficult to masturbate at night when sharing a bed with an adult lodger. But none of the crime writers of the day appear to have considered this.

On 5th February 1921 Harold was working in the shop when an eight-year-old girl called Freda came in to buy grain. The fourteen-year-old said that they kept it in the shed so Freda followed him there - but once he'd closed the door, he pounced.

Little Freda screamed and he grabbed her shawl and stuffed it into her mouth. He tied her arms and legs with string, rendering her helpless. Then he pushed her juvenile underclothes aside.

Only now did Harold realise the difference between fantasy and reality - for raping an eight-year-old child is physically very difficult. He attempted to penetrate her again and again but failed. At some stage he may have digitally entered her as grain from the shed floor was found in her vagina and in her clothes.

Possibly overcome by frustration, he hit her on the head - but the blow didn't kill her. Exhaustion and shock was the reason that the coroner would give for her untimely death.

That night Harold dumped the body a few yards from the shop then asked his friends to help him lock up the shed. He clearly wanted them to see that the building didn't contain Freda's body. He knew that the police would soon be asking questions as he was the last person to see her alive.

And indeed the police soon arrested him - but the nation thought that they were just using the teenager as a scapegoat because they couldn't find the real murderer. The defence argued that Harold had left the shed door unlocked and that the killer had brought Freda there. In less than two hours the jury returned with a Not Guilty verdict and Harold was free to go home. It was a fateful ruling that would lead to another child's death.

A fortnight later, Harold started chatting to one of his sister's friends, an eleven-year-old girl called Florrie. He lured her into his house, knowing that his parents and their lodger were going to be out for several hours. Locking the door, he immediately struck her on the head with a metal boiler lid, knocking her out. Then he tore at her knickers and tried, in vain, to penetrate her. During these attempts he ejaculated on his own clothes.

But Harold's blood lust wasn't spent. He fetched a knife and carried the unconscious child to the sink. There he cut her throat and left her there for a quarter of an hour whilst the blood drained from her. When she was dead he wrapped an old shirt around her head to avoid any blood stains smearing the walls or ceiling. Then he tied a rope around her body, went up into the attic and pulled her corpse up after him.

Whilst Harold was washing the blood from his body, Florrie's mother called to ask where she was. Harold chatted to her quite amicably, saying that she'd been at his house but had left.

Several witnesses had seen Harold talking to Florrie so the following morning the police arrived at the Jones's house. The child's corpse was found in the attic and Harold confessed that he'd given in to the urge to kill again.

It's likely that Harold was a teenage psychopath. He lied easily in court when questioned about Freda's death - and he was totally calm when talking to people within moments of both murders. Psychopaths don't learn from experience, which would explain Harold killing an eleven-year-old within a fortnight of being found Not Guilty for the murder of an eight-year-old child.

Harold Jones falls into the disorganised category - his crimes were impulsive and opportunistic and he left the bodies in his workplace and in his home.

He spent more than twenty years in prison then was released to serve in the Second World War. Incredibly, thereafter he returned for a visit to his home town. Again, this is the act of a psychopath, indifferent to the hurt that his presence might cause the victim's relatives. Locals were amazed to see him drinking in the local pub, a man without a care. He remained in the area for the rest of his life and ultimately died in hospital in his seventies.

Ironically, after Harold's first murder he could have enjoyed consensual relations with girls. Several had written to him after his trial declaring that they loved him, just as women do with adult male serial killers today. But Harold became aroused through totally controlling a girl - so an active, willing partner simply didn't have the same appeal.


## Psychopathy

Relatively little was known about psychopaths in Harold Jones day - so his smiling and unperturbed demeanour after eight-year-old Freda's death was originally taken as proof of his innocence.

Nowadays we know that psychopaths simply don't get nervous as they have very low levels of emotional arousal. They don't learn from experience, which explains how Harold could commit a second sex killing within days of being released from jail after the first. And psychopaths don't fear punishment, so Harold was equally blasé when the police found Florrie's blood-drained corpse in his parent's attic.

Harold Jones' two sex murders were highly opportunistic. The girls came to him whilst he was alone - and trusted him enough to follow him - so they died. He had the superficial charm that is the hallmark of the psychopath but also had the homicidal psychopath's obsession with control, need for sensation and lack of shame.


## Socially inept killers

More usually, disturbed teenagers commit lust murders because they don't believe that they can have a consensual relationship with a girl. They'll desire a female from afar but know that they lack the social skills to impress her. As a result, more and more anger gets mixed up in the lust. They feel stupid and clumsy when they think of approaching a pretty young female - but they perversely blame her for making them feel bad.

George Stinney probably fits into this category as do several of the other lust murderers whose case studies appear later in this chapter. In other instances, there are multiple motives, with the anger and lust mixed up with the need for excitement and monetary greed.

## Multiple motives

Adult burglars often go on to commit rape or sex murders and occasionally this is also true of teenage burglars. These are crimes of both wrong-thinking and opportunity. Sometimes the burglar will find women's lingerie and be aroused by it so he'll wait until she gets home and will attack. In other instances, he'll think that the house is empty - then find a woman ill in bed or in the shower. Already sexually excited through the act of entering her home, he moves on to a sexual assault. Kenny Houseknecht fits into this category.

## Kenny Houseknecht

Kenny Houseknecht is a good example of social ineptitude stemming from insufficient nurturing, mixed up with a robbery that went wrong. At age fourteen, Kenny was a six foot tall and heavily built American schoolboy living in New Jersey. He had a history of bedwetting and was very stressed. He turned to a neighbour for parenting but the man instead introduced him to burglary and drugs.

Kenny owed a friend fifty dollars and the friend kept asking for it. Kenny said he'd steal it from a neighbour's house - The Andersons - as they left lots of money lying around.

On 19th April 1988 he sneaked into the house after the adult Andersons had left. He'd just grabbed a piggy bank when twelve-year-old Kim Anderson confronted him in the hallway. She'd probably just left the shower as she had a towel around her breasts.

He'd later say that she grabbed the knife, but that's very unlikely. What's known is that they struggled in the hall then she probably raced into the bedroom to phone for help and was pursued by him. They landed on the bed for there was blood all over the bedspread and on the carpet. He hit her with the telephone, causing heavy bruising but she remained conscious. By now he was on top of her.

As she tried to fight him off, he stabbed her in the hands nineteen times. He received cuts to his own hands during the struggle but continued to stab her, moving his knife to her chest so that the blade punctured her lungs.

By now Kim was unable to fight back, but the fourteen-year-old flipped her over onto her stomach and continued to stab her, reigning blows on her back. He also stabbed her in the head, and the tip of the knife snapped off and remained embedded in her skull.

At some stage during or after the assault, Kenny ejaculated, for a pair of women's panties with his semen on them were found in Kim's garden. It's not unusual for such sex killers to take away a trophy and he may have dropped it in his rush to flee the house.

Kenny then went to school and had the nurse bandage the cuts on his hands. Several people noticed that he was acting jumpy and an acquaintance told the police that Kenny had planned to rob the Andersons' house that day.

Meanwhile, Kenny went home and wrote a naive letter to Kim's family, suggesting the killer was someone else who would try to pin it on Kenny. He also drew a naked woman, a large vagina and a couple having anal sex.

Police searched his home and found the incriminatory letter in his bedroom. They duly arrested him. As he was only fourteen, the police asked one of his relatives to sit in on the interview. At this stage he was still technically innocent - yet the first thing the relative did was slap his face.

Social workers at the trial testified to his unnurtured childhood which included abuse and abandonment but psychiatrists said he was sane at the time of the killing. In July 1991 he was sentenced to life imprisonment.

## Tony Craven

Sometimes it's impossible to know if the teenage sex offender is solely attracted to children (that is, a paedophile) or if he only vents his lust on a child because he believes that an adult woman will spurn him. One British killer whose motivation is indeterminate is Tony Craven. He was a very immature seventeen-year-old who only looked thirteen and was mercilessly teased by his more worldly workmates about his virginity.

That said, Tony fits the pattern of a young paedophile. He spurned other young adults in order to spend all of his time with children. And he immersed himself in their games and in their favourite pastime of riding their bikes. Local parents approved of the well mannered and cleancut youth though it's unclear if he formally babysat for any of their children - 48% of paedophiles find their victims through babysitting work.

By August 1991 Tony Craven was determined to lose his virginity. He lured a seven-year-old girl called Angela Flaherty into the woods near their Huddersfield homes where he persuaded her to take off some of her clothes. When she hesitated he took the rest of her garments off and stared at her immature body. He then raped her and told her not to tell.

But the badly injured little girl couldn't stop crying and he panicked and semi-strangled her then beat her to death with a rock, causing a brain haemorrhage. Thereafter he tried to 'help' the police solve the fatal crime. He was eventually arrested and tried to commit suicide three times before being sentenced to life imprisonment by Leeds Crown Court. He will become eligible for parole in 2009.

## Mother-son incest

Because most teenage sex offenders - and adult sex offenders - who are caught are male, there's an erroneous belief that women don't commit sex crimes. In truth, they do but their victims are less likely to report them. Even if they do report them, they are much less likely to be believed.

Johnny Garrett (profiled in chapter thirteen) wasn't believed when he said that his mother had initiated sex with him - and we can't know for sure that she did, given that Johnny had increasingly lost touch with reality. But we do know that he'd been forced to have sex with his grandfather and that his grandmother - his mother's mother - encouraged this. Clearly the older woman had no incest taboos to overcome.

In the book *Female Sexual Abuse: The Ultimate Taboo* twelve men told of being sexually abused throughout their childhood by women. (The other cases featured are those where girls were sexually abused by women.) The offenders were mothers, stepmothers and aunts - but therapists have also heard of boys being abused by female teachers, babysitters and nuns. The phenomena is more commonplace than lay people imagine - after a television debate about women who abuse, the TV station received over a thousand phone calls in a single day.

Of 127 people who talked to a counsellor about being abused by a woman, 42% had been abused by their mothers. The abuse had often begun before the child was five years old. The mothers were often abuse victims themselves and some were mentally ill.

Johnny Garrett was abused with his grandmother's aid in the sixties and seventies - but this crime still isn't believed by many today. Only three percent of convicted sex offenders are female - but some field workers estimate that the true figure may be closer to ten percent. When children grow up and admit they'd been molested by a female relative they are often told by therapists that they must be confused, that the abuse has been committed by a man.

There is also confusion about what these women do to their victims given that they don't have a penis. In truth, the abuse is varied. Female sex offenders have made their victims perform oral sex on them or have had full intercourse with them. Other offenders abuse more covertly, perhaps rocking themselves against the child's body until reaching orgasm.

In the next case study, that of Kevin Peanut Hughes, the mother has frequent intercourse in front of her children and often demands that they join her in sexual acts.

## Kevin (Peanut) Hughes

Kevin's life was blighted whilst he was still in the womb, for his schizophrenic mother drank heavily throughout the pregnancy. He came into the world in March 1962 to find a home that was desperately poor and a mother who was increasingly turning to drugs. Kevin, who was black, was never to know his father and all five of his siblings were fathered by different men.

The next few years were a living hell for the child and his brothers and sisters. His mother often left them alone without food or warmth. As a result, Kevin and his siblings often missed school. And when their mother was at home she invariably had an equally disturbed man in tow who would beat her and the children. Often the couple had sex with the six children watching and Kevin's mother would try to involve them in these sexual acts.

Kevin's IQ was only in the seventies which is borderline retarded. As a result, he was picked on by his mother's many lovers. After all, there's nothing a loser likes more than finding someone more inadequate than himself. He was frequently beaten by these drunken males and also had to watch them raping his mum. At least one of them also sexually assaulted the helpless boy.

By the time Kevin reached his teens, the link between sex and extreme violence had again and again been made clear to him. One of his mother's lovers even made the point verbally, telling young Kevin that women should always be forced.

In 1976, Kevin, now fourteen, raped an eleven-year-old girl. He threatened her with a knife and was clearly prepared to use it. She identified him and he was put on three years probation. It was too little too late. Perhaps he decided at this stage that he would silence any future victims - or perhaps his own rage was just spiralling. By now his mother had made numerous suicide attempts and Kevin had joined her by taking at least one failed overdose.

He began to believe that he was protected by magical powers. This may have been the earliest signs of schizophrenia as schizophrenics often think that they are protected by a god or that they have an especial affinity with wild beasts such as lions. Obviously this is a fallacy and when they break into the lion enclosure at the zoo they are seriously mauled.

Kevin's odd fantasies - which would definitely have included sexual fantasies - continued. In March 1979, aged almost seventeen, he lured a nine-year-old girl called Rochelle Graham to an abandoned house. He attempted to rape her but failed so turned her over and sodomised her instead. Then he strangled her and stuffed a burning pillow into her vagina, the flames burning her sexual organs before spreading out to char much of her flesh. Adult rape-murderers such as John Duffy have carried out such post-mortem vaginal fires in order to destroy forensic evidence - but it's unlikely that Kevin was bright enough to understand the importance of destroying DNA traces, so perhaps this was just another delusional action. He then burnt his nickname, Peanut, into the ceiling above her corpse.

Kevin continued to suffer at home - and to fantasise about making others suffer. By now he was becoming increasingly mentally ill and had terrible mood swings. Like the previously-profiled Johnny Garrett, who came from a very similar background, Kevin was increasingly out of touch with reality.

In January 1980 he grabbed a twelve-year-old girl from behind as she walked down the street and forced her into a vacant house. There he made her strip and forced her to fellate him. His rage still unassuaged, he proceeded to batter her and stamp on her face. Then he strangled her and left her for dead. But the child revived and was able to identify Kevin from his previous police photograph. He was arrested and soon confessed. Moreover, police found the name Peanut burned into the ceiling above his bed.

The prison noted his severe mental illness before the trial and had him admitted to a psychiatric unit. One psychiatrist said that he wasn't fit to stand trial but two others said that he was, providing he remained on anti-psychotic medication. This was duly provided and at the trial the anti-psychotic drug Thorazine made him so spaced that he sat and wrote nursery rhymes. Incredibly, the jury weren't told how appalling his childhood had been. (It isn't an excuse, but it is an explanation.)

Kevin was found guilty and formally sentenced to death on 27th October 1983. For the next few years he worked his way through the appeals process. In 1989 the judgement was upheld and in October 1995 a warrant for his execution was finally filed. The following month, the Philadelphia County Common Pleas Court granted a stay of execution. After that there was a moratorium on the death penalty in Pennsylvania - but on 11th April 2000 Governor Tom Ridge signed a warrant for Kevin Hughes execution by lethal injection, a move that was condemned by Amnesty International. At the time of writing, he remains on Death Row, a forty-year-old man who killed when he was a teenage boy.

Boys who are as multiply-damaged as Kevin Hughes possibly can't be rehabilitated - the connection they've made between extreme violence and sex is foremost in their sexual identities. The earlier the authorities can intervene and help the abused child who abuses, the greater the likelihood of a return to normal life.

If a child's sexual assaults on other children aren't taken seriously, he is more likely to reoffend, sometimes with tragic results. Speaking on the programme *Manhunt: The Catching Of A Child Killer* which looked at the paedophile murders of Robert Black, sexual offences expert Ray Wyre said that teenage sex crimes are often misclassified by the authorities. (Robert Black is one of the case studies in the chapter Children Who Kill Again As Adults.)


## Matricide and necrophilia

One of the most unusual sex murders committed by a child is told in Greggory Morris's *The Kids Next Door*, a book about children who kill their parents. It profiles a young man called Garry who was frequently beaten by older bullies at school for being artistic and different. The teenager started to steal and stay out late and his mother would shout at him and encourage his father to do the same.

Garry retreated more and more into a fantasy world fuelled by sniffing large quantities of glue. He also started to masturbate outside the home of a girl he fancied. (Men who grow up to be rapists, child molesters or sex killers are often Peeping Toms from a very early age.) He felt unsure of himself around women but he was desperate to have sex.

Six weeks after his father's death, Garry had yet another argument with his mother about his glue addiction. Deciding to kill her, he battered her over the head with a metal bar. The assault fractured her skull but she was still breathing so he raced to another room for a knife and slit her throat then had intercourse with the still-warm corpse. He'd later explain that 'I had Mother's dead body there. There was nothing left to do but make use of it.' So, at eighteen years of age, he entered his mother's corpse and lost his virginity.

A psychiatrist later said it was likely that the boy was a psychopath but that he wasn't insane. He was sentenced to twenty-five years in prison for this sexual killing.

## Early sexual experimentation

It's entirely normal for children to become interested in sex as they mature and most children will play doctor and nurses games as a way of finding out about their own and others' bodies. But children who are sexually abused will be much more extreme in their search for a sexual outlet, and more likely to use force.

Psychologist Patrick Carnes has written that 'masturbation is an essential part of being a sexual person.' He found that many sex addicts come from proscriptive families who often see masturbation as a sin. Ironically, people from such disapproving families are often inappropriately sexually active when they grow up. Carnes tells the story of a Lutheran minister who picked up men in the park for casual sex, despite the fact that he found these encounters humiliating. He was badly beaten up, but continued cruising - and only sought help after having sex with one of his young parishioners who he feared might tell.

Another man, who went on to molest his children's babysitters, had been sent to confession as a child where his penis was fondled by a paedophile priest. The priest said that Gene wasn't supposed to touch himself as masturbation was a sin.

## Sibling sexual abuse

Often such abused children carry similar abuses out on their younger brothers and sisters. Serial killer Rose West was sexually abused by her father and went on, in turn, to masturbate one of her younger brothers. One of Robert Thompson's brothers was investigated for sexual assaults on a younger child. Mary Bell carved letters, post mortem, on one of her little victims - and it's very likely that she was copying her mother who, as a sado-masochistic prostitute, might have been asked to carry out scarification (cutting for erotic purposes) on the flesh of her male clients.

When normal development takes place, sexual exploration is healthy and simply gives rise to pleasure. But with abused children, masturbation also becomes a form of desperately-needed self-comfort. As a result, this masturbation will be frenziedly carried out as a replacement for parental love and nurturing. As such, it becomes something pathological rather than something good. As so much is wrong with the child's life, the urge to masturbate can become all encompassing in a futile attempt to put things right. These children can become addicted to sex by the time they are adults, and are unable to cut down on self-pleasuring even when they've made their genitals bleed.

Unfortunately most reportage of child sex offenders doesn't include details of what they've endured, only of their crimes. For example, in November 2001, an eleven-year-old boy was tried at Cardiff Crown Court for sexually assaulting an eight-year-old girl. He was found guilty and placed on the sex offenders register for two and a half years (but found not guilty of unlawful sexual intercourse) with the judge commenting that the boy knew he'd done wrong. It would have been helpful if his background had also been reported so that readers could understand what made a child offend so seriously at such a young age. Similarly, a programme about the crimes of Robert Black - whilst offering first class information about his crimes and their effect on the victim's parents - said only of his own tragic life that he'd had a troubled history.

## Animal sexual abuse

Sometimes the person who has been frequently abused gives up on people altogether and turns to animals for sexual experimentation. One woman who'd had a terrible childhood wrote a fan letter to serial killer John Wayne Gacy in which she admitted that she liked to 'jerk off' her dog. And a documentary about bestiality included a man who had been so strictly raised by his Christian Fundamentalist parents that he found women terrifying and preferred to have sex with a horse. That said, this man felt romantic love for his horse and would have strongly objected to their 'relationship' being labelled as animal abuse.

In fairness, it should also be noted that brutalised children don't always remain cruel towards animals. Often they are animal lovers who, after removal from their abusive backgrounds, grow to love animals again.

Aware of this, violence expert Gavin de Becker launched and continues to fund a scheme called Patient's Pets which gives criminals of all ages in secure hospitals access to small animals. He's seen for himself how some of these violent men from violent homes have broken their hearts over the death of a guinea pig. He writes that 'many of these men will be locked up for life without a visitor and a mouse or bird might be all they have.'

An article by Peter J Lewis published in the *Insider* magazine backs this up. It told of how staff at a maximum security centre in Ohio allowed the inmates on one ward to keep pets and 'within a year suicide attempts were down to zero, and prescribed medication down by a half.' The pets in prison scheme was so successful during its various American trials that it has now been adopted by South Africa, Australia and Spain.

Sadly, Britain has opted out of the scheme and inmates at Garth Prison in Lancashire have been told that they can no longer breed budgies. As the inmates were giving the surplus baby budgies to senior citizens, everyone has lost out.

The thinking behind this seems to be that we have to be tough on criminals - but some of these adult and young offenders have known nothing but toughness all their lives. Caring for a pet has been shown to reduce prisoner violence. It also reduces the recidivism rate.

Many young offenders have been verbally and physically harangued by their parents then mocked as underachievers by their teachers. The pet they're given in prison may be their first experience of unconditional love.

## 18
## BORN TO RUN
### Children Who Kill Their Families

Children who kill are least likely to kill a member of their own family. This is probably because these families are so violent that to risk their retaliation is terrifying. It's easier to take that childish rage out on a stranger, usually an even smaller child (as Jesse Pomeroy, Robert Thompson, Jon Venables and Mary Bell did) or to choose an elderly weaker victim, the choice of Johnny Garrett, Cindy Collier and Shirley Wolf.

Another reason that children don't kill their abuser is that most children consider their childhoods to be normal, no matter how dysfunctional. The child has lived with the violent or neglectful parent since birth and has no other yardstick with which to judge his or her background. Plus that child is sometimes being told at school that he or she is a bad child, not that they are the result of inadequate or cruel parenting.

Numerous parents emotionally and physically abuse their children and in the UK one child per week dies at its parent's hands. The few children who do turn the tables have usually been abused so relentlessly that they can see no other way out. Even so, the child who kills a violent parent invariably blames himself and is filled with remorse.


### Bernard Smith

Abuse that ends in patricide - or, even more rarely, matricide - is not a modern phenomena. Bernard Smith was born in 1923 to a drunken father. The man was incredibly violent, a violence which increased towards Bernard when his mother died. Indeed the beatings were so bad that by the time the helpful child entered his teens the NSPCC had been called in. Neighbours noticed that no matter how hard Bernard tried to please, he was emotionally and physically demeaned by his hate-filled parent. Everyone pitied the youth and feared for his life. In 1937 the fourteen-year-old shot his drunken father dead, at last putting an end to a life of torment. The jury took pity on him and found him not guilty, an unusual decision for the time - and for now.

## Richard John Jahnke

Sometimes the jury is unsympathetic but there is public sympathy when full details of the child's life emerge. Richard Jahnke junior snapped after years of extreme physical and emotional abuse from his father - and years of knowing that his father was also abusing his sister. Richard had sought help from various authorities but no one intervened. From the age of two he was severely beaten for such so-called sins as coughing at the table. His father was a former army sergeant who ran the family along military lines.

By 1982 Richard had turned sixteen and his sister was seventeen. With her agreement, he lurked in the family garage waiting for his parents to come home. When they did, he shot his father six times. Four of the bullets entered his chest, killing him instantly.

Adults who don't understand the nature of child abuse sometimes have no sympathy for the child because the killing wasn't carried out in the heat of the moment. They suggest that if the killing was really about self-preservation the child would kill whilst being beaten by his mum or dad. But to retaliate against a fist-swinging man or woman is too terrifying for most children. They dread the next beating and kill when the parent isn't expecting it such as when they are asleep. An adult faced with another abusive adult (as with women who kill their abusive husbands) does the exact same thing.

Richard Jahnke was initially given a long sentence but there was a public outcry when the level of abuse he'd endured became known. He was released at age twenty-one.


## Matricide

Richard Jahnke and his sister had considered killing their mother but didn't go through with it. Indeed, matricide is one of the rarest crimes committed. When it does happen, it usually follows especially prolonged abuse. Paul Mones, an expert in abused children who kill has noted that 'sons kill mothers under almost identical circumstances. The father is physically or emotionally absent, the mother physically abuses the boy as a toddler and up to puberty, when she switches, albeit unconsciously, to a pattern of emotional abuse, the centre-piece of which is complete domination.' Steven Cratton, who Paul Mones profiles in his groundbreaking book *When A Child Kills*, perfectly fits this category. (Paul made up the name Steven Cratton to avoid revealing this cruelly abused boy's true identity.)


## Steven Cratton

Steven was born to the mother from hell, a woman who demeaned most adults she came into contact with. Relatives saw her telling Steven to grow up and not be a sissy when he was only one year old. Ruth Cratton also hit Steven for eating too slowly or for falling over. As a result, the toddler would wet the bed and she'd hit him for that too. One relative saw the marks from a wooden spoon imprinted on the child's buttocks when she went to change him. Others frequently saw the little boy crying and being verbally put down by his mum.

His father, Roger, couldn't cope with her domineering ways and left when Steven was four. Now the child was entirely at his mother's mercy. His next few years were so horrendous that he blocked them out and it was neighbours and relatives who later testified to the numerous instances of cruelty they'd seen him endure. People saw him with bruises and with a bleeding nose but Ruth told them that he fell over a lot. Steven himself, like almost every child who is abused, assumed that every child was treated in this way.

Even at school, Steven couldn't escape from his mum. She frequently sought out his teachers to check on his academic prowess. (Luke Woodward's mother did likewise.) She made him study for two hours every night and hired a private tutor for him. Ironically, Steven's IQ was university-level, but the frequent abuse made it impossible for him to concentrate. Like most abused children, he daydreamed all the time as an escape from the horror, frequently going into a fugue state.

By the time Steven turned twelve he was being bullied at school. He wasn't allowed to go out with the other children and Ruth didn't like him having friends home plus he was constantly tuning out of lessons and conversations. He was clearly different - and children often pick on anyone that's different.

His father Roger had kept in touch with him by letter and was still paying maintenance. Eventually he asked the deeply unhappy boy to come and live with him and his second wife. Steven did so and the couple found that the thirteen-year-old was still wetting the bed. They gave him love and he got on brilliantly with his stepbrother and started to do well at school.

The couple also sent him to a psychologist who found that the child was unhappy and nervous and that he had a lot of anger and guilt about his mother. But Steven apparently didn't talk in detail about the numerous cruelties he'd suffered at his mother's hands.

That summer he went back to her for a week long visit. He didn't return to his father, Roger. Instead, Ruth had a legal letter sent to Roger saying that Steven would be staying with her from now on. But even Ruth recognised that Steven was disturbed and she got him a psychologist. Roger wrote to this woman explaining that Steven had been physically abused by his mother for years and that she was still emotionally and mentally putting him down. But no one acted on this information and the teenager's misery increased.

The physical abuse continued until Steven turned fourteen after which his mother continued to disparage him emotionally and flaunt herself before him physically. His friends parents felt so sorry for the teenager that they invited him to stay with them whenever possible and treated him like a second son. But Steven was still desperate to win his mother's love so would try to please her again and again.

Ruth clearly didn't believe that she was worthy of love - and probably set out to destroy it. She'd make the shy American teenager start his chores at 6am and clean the house for hours before starting school. He got home before his mother did but he wasn't supposed to watch TV. When she got back she'd check the set to make sure that it wasn't warm.

Such actions make no sense to rational adults - but they do make sense to very controlling people like Ruth Cratton. It's a safe bet that she had little or no control afforded to her whilst she was growing up so was determined to control every facet of her life now that she was in charge. And as toxic parents blur the boundaries between themselves and their children, that meant controlling Steven - including what he watched on TV.

## Attempts to escape

Like many mistreated teenagers, Steven ran away. On his first two attempts by foot he only got twenty miles or so and was returned by the police exhausted and hungry. The third time he stole a car to aid his escape attempt, was caught and spent ten days in juvenile custody. The police didn't ask the fifteen-year-old why he'd stolen the vehicle, and, like most children damaged by their parents, he didn't volunteer the information. The police and psychologist saw the groomed, concerned side of Ruth Cratton so didn't even ask Steven about his relationship with his mother. But Steven's one friend often heard Ruth calling Steven a bastard and said that she ordered the boy around as if he was a servant and never once said anything positive to him.

## A suicide attempt

Steven now followed the pattern of most of the abused children in this book - he tried to commit suicide, in his case taking painkillers. But he vomited them up and lived to endure another day. He fantasised again and again about jumping from high buildings or shooting himself dead. He probably also fantasised about killing his mother, a woman who had made his life a living hell.

## Matricide

Steven turned seventeen - but he remained much younger in his looks and in his attitude. He'd never been allowed to make his own decisions or explore the world. His only escape from hardship was watching TV and he could only do so if he let the TV set cool down before Ruth came home as he was forbidden to watch programmes when she wasn't there. He always sought out the cartoons, disappearing into their safe, wholly make-believe world.

Ruth, like most controlling parents, kept telling Steven that he'd be nothing without her, that he couldn't survive on his own. Steven's self-esteem was so low that he believed her. He knew she wouldn't let him go away to college when he was eighteen.

One night the seventeen-year-old had two beers with his only friend. He came home and apparently found his mother watching television. No one, except Steven who may have blocked it out, knows what happened next. Paul Mones, who represented Steven, believes that Ruth may have slapped the teenager's face during an argument, something she often did. Maybe further abuses followed. Ruth could be lifethreatening - when Steven was fifteen they'd rowed and she had tried to choke him to death.

Whatever happened, mother and son went to their beds. But Steven got up at 5am, took the family gun and walked up to his sleeping mother. He shot her twice through the head. Years later he'd say that he'd done it to relieve the pressure in his head, to put an end to coming home with fear in his stomach and dread in his heart. (Luke Woodham and Sean Sellers also endured years of misery then rose at dawn and killed their mothers in pre-planned assaults.)

Seen as suicidal, Steven was briefly sent to a mental hospital where he was seen as 'guilty but mentally ill.' He was sentenced to ten years to life yet, despite the hospital's evaluation, he has received no therapeutic help. He told children's attorney Paul Mones that, though prison is regimented and limiting, it's still better than being with his mum.


## Jerry Ball

Another abused boy who snapped and murdered his family was Jerry Ball of West Virginia. The mild-mannered teenager was frequently beaten by both of his religious parents. He had to wear long sleeved shirts even in the height of summer to hide the bruises on his arms. He took beating after beating without complaint and did everything that he could to please his parents, including becoming a youth leader at the local Baptist church. He showed a real talent for baseball, joined the school band and did well in his studies - and still his alcoholic father and psychotic mother mocked and hurt him. His friends were amazed that he could cope with such frequent emotional humiliation and physical pain.

One day in January 1983 the sixteen-year-old snapped when his mother started to curse him. He took the baseball bat that he was holding and started to batter her with it. He also rained blows on his equally violent father and eleven-year-old brother. When his six-year-old brother began to scream he beat him too. The battered family members collapsed but kept moaning so he hit them all again.

Jerry immediately phoned a friend. His mother betrayed signs of life by gurgling during this call so he fetched his father's rifle and shot her through the head. His friend still didn't believe that he'd massacred his entire family so he drove to the friend's house, collected him and drove back to show him the corpses. He felt sorry that he'd killed his little brother as the boy had done him no harm.

Jerry had so little insight into his life of hell that he said he had no motive for what he'd done. He pleaded guilty to all four murders. Only then did witnesses start to come forward, testifying to the life he'd endured. Psychologists who examined him in hospital said he'd been maltreated since birth and found that he had brain damage caused by his parents hitting him about the head but said that it was the years of abuse - rather than the brain lesions - that had led to him killing everyone in the house. Seen as a high suicide risk, he was sent to a Boston hospital with ongoing mental health difficulties.

## No exit

Children who are abused by their parents simply cannot win. Neighbours often hear screams but hesitate to get involved, because it's currently legal in most countries for a parent to inflict pain on his or her children. If the child runs away he is demonised by the police and perhaps by the juvenile court system for doing so, is brought back and is punished by the parents again. Even when social services get involved (as they did with the parents or guardians of Jon Venables, Robert Thompson, Peter Dinsdale, Cindy Collier, Shirley Wolf and Wendy Gardner) they often decide that there is no abuse case for the parent to answer or that there has been abuse but that it 'isn't bad enough' to take the child away from the home. These children are failed by their communities, the police and the social services - yet if they finally snap and kill the violent parent, they are criticised by the public and by the courts for not seeking an alternative remedy.

## Historical injustice

Children's rights campaigners are often appalled at the way our modern legal system treats abused children who go on to commit murder. But there have always been elements of the judiciary who don't understand.

In 1748 William York, aged ten, was living in a workhouse where he had to share a bed with a five-year-old girl. He killed her after she soiled the sheets. William was sentenced to hang as the judge said this would be a deterrent to other boys and girls.

213

But the judge's comments showed a complete misunderstanding of child psychology. Even nurtured children have comparatively poor impulse control - and it's a safe bet that a little boy raised in the workhouse would have suffered a great deal of violence. He did what many abusive adults do to young children. That is, they make the assumption that the child has *chosen* to soil the sheets. Studies have shown that such immature, violent parents see a level of bad intent that a baby or toddler simply isn't capable of. They view the soiled child as bad and lash out. Ironically, such trauma causes the child to wet or soil the bed again that night, leading to further abuse. Abused children like Mary Bell and Steven Cratton, both profiled earlier, are often still wetting the bed in their teens.

Hanging ten-year-old William would have made absolutely no difference to the thought processes of any other wounded child. Indeed, such children often exist in an almost constant daydream to mentally avoid the reality of their daily existence. They can be indifferent to what's going on in the outside world. The reigning monarch, George 2nd, may have recognised this. Leastways he pardoned William York.

## The truth

Society tends to see parents as good and children as potential wild cards - so when Zein-Hassan and Maria Isa called the police and reported that their teenage daughter Palestina (known as Tina) had attacked them with a knife, the authorities believed them. Zein, a Palestinian national living in America, added that he'd grabbed the knife from the sixteen-year-old and killed her in self-defence.

The police went to the Isa's home in Louis, Missouri, and found that Tina had been stabbed six times. Zein Isa painted a picture of his daughter as a wilful child who had become Americanised rather than maintaining her parent's culture. He said that she'd come home from the first day of her after-school job and lunged at him.

But an examination of the high school student's body showed that she'd sustained six deep stab wounds. Clearly a man merely trying to defend himself would not have stabbed so often or so viciously. The police started to make further enquiries and found out that Tina had been terrified of her parents - and that she'd told a friend that if she died then they would be most likely to blame.

The case went to trial with Zein Isa's defence suggesting that he was a good religious man with a disappointing and thoughtless daughter. Tina's friends came forward to refute this, explaining that she was an intelligent honours student who also excelled in athletics. She abhorred racism and was dating a black student. Her parents had hated that. They had also hated the fact that she'd taken a part time job after school as they believed she should spend each night and weekend at home.

The trial might have ended with Tina's name still being besmirched if it hadn't been for the FBI coming forward. They'd suspected that Zein Isa was a terrorist so had bugged his apartment and taped everything that went on there. They'd just listened to the latest batch of tapes - and found one that chilled them. The tapes told the true story of what had happened to the beautiful honours student that night.

Tina comes home from the first shift at her job and her father tells her that this is her last night on earth. She makes a little noise, clearly not comprehending. At this stage Maria Isa screams 'Listen to your father' and other commands in her native Brazilian and pins her to the ground. Obviously seeing the knife, Tina begins to plead for her life, promising them that she won't go to work again - but her father begins to stab her as her mother holds her down.

Tina keeps screaming and begging him to stop but he shouts 'Die quickly daughter, die' and continues to plunge the knife into her. Her mother also shouts at her and keeps her arms down so that she can't defend herself.

The tape was so harrowing that the first Brazilian translator was in floods of tears. The court was similarly moved when they heard it. Both Isa's were given the death penalty but Zein Isa died of diabetes-related complications in prison before his death sentence could be carried out. Maria Isa appealed against her death sentence and for some reason the judiciary commuted it to life imprisonment.

But imagine if the scenario had been slightly different. Imagine if the day before her father stabbed her, he'd lashed out at Tina as he had many times before and she'd picked up a kitchen knife and stabbed him. The police, the courts and the media would then have painted her as a heartless psychopath who, for example, wanted to spend more time with her boyfriend so killed a good religious man.

Sadly, most scenarios aren't on tape. Sadly, society ignores the fact that most violence starts with the parents. Relatives, neighbours, teachers and social workers turn away from the abused child and minimise the hell he or she is going through. And when he kills as a response to his environment, he'll find he has even fewer members of the public on his side.

# 19

## ALONE AGAIN, NATURALLY
### Children Who Kill Again As Adults

Child killers who are removed from a dysfunctional environment and placed in a loving one can mature into sensitive adults. Mary Bell is an excellent example of this healing process. But children who aren't given sufficient care - or older teenagers who are too brutalised to respond to treatment - may kill again in adulthood.

### Edmund Emil Kemper

An example of an abused child who killed and was then returned to his abusive home is Ed Kemper of California, born 18th December 1948. His parents' marriage was an unstable one and little Ed was emotionally starved and neglected. His father deserted the family when Ed was nine but his life was still made hell by his mother who became an alcoholic after the divorce.

At ten he showed some sexual interest in one of his older sisters and his mother banished him to the shadowy basement to sleep from then on. Soon, like many abused children, he had turned his rage onto cats and tortured several of them to death. The animals had no chance as by now he was over six foot tall. (His father was six-foot-eight.)

Ed was so lonely that when he was fourteen he tracked down his father and asked to live with him. But the man had remarried and produced another son and there was no place for Ed in the new family unit. Instead, he was shunted off to his father's parents' remote Californian farm. Unfortunately his grandmother had a very similar personality to his domineering mother so his life remained one of being ridiculed and ordered about.

At age fifteen he snapped and shot his grandmother in the back of the head as she sat at the kitchen table. He also stabbed her three times in the back. When she was dead, he took the gun and hid in the yard, waiting for his grandfather to return from a shopping trip. When he did, Ed also fatally shot him through the head.

The fifteen-year-old spent the next few years in a mental hospital where they found that he had a very high IQ. Taken away from a life of verbal cruelty and rejection, he proved to be a gentle giant. In 1969 he turned twenty-one and was released. Incredibly, the release was into his emotionally-destructive mother's custody. This was despite the objections of two state psychiatrists who knew that she'd ridiculed him constantly.

Soon life returned to the endless mocking that it had consisted of before - and soon Ed returned to murder as a way of assuaging his rage. This time his first six victims were student hitchhikers who he offered lifts to. He shot them, stabbed them, suffocated them, mutilated their corpses and had necrophiliac sex with various body parts. Some of these 1971 and 1972 murders occurred after vicious quarrels with his mother and were substitutes for the real target of his rage.

But in the spring of 1973, he at last turned his violence upon the person he really hated. He crept into his mother's bedroom as she slept and battered her about the head with a hammer. He also cut out her larynx - the voice box that had nagged him so relentlessly - and put it down the waste disposal unit and in a final literal 'fuck you' had intercourse with her corpse. He also cut off her head and threw darts at it and went to sleep with the corpse in the house.

Ed Kemper had also hated his mother's best friend so when she called around the following day he choked her and cut off her head. He then drove around for three days, briefly free of his demons, before phoning the police and turning himself in. But his childhood horrors returned to haunt him and he twice cut his wrists whilst awaiting trial. Somewhat surprisingly, his life sentence allowed for the possibility of parole, though he has so far been turned down for this numerous times.

Since 1987 Ed Kemper has been making tape recordings of books for the blind. He still has a macabre sense of humour, telling a visiting FBI agent that he could break the man's neck before help could be summoned. It was true, but he made no attempt to carry out any attack.

He remains intelligent and well spoken. Clearly, if he'd been taken from his mother much earlier he could have offered much to the world. But that very intelligence and smoothness of manner may still conceal a murderous rage towards women - after all, his mild manner was the second last thing that his student victims saw.

## David Wynne Roberts

In 1969, when David Wynne Roberts was fourteen, he called on one of his mother's seventy-three-year-old friends in Anglesey, Wales. He knew that she was a wealthy widow and he'd decided to steal her cash. But when she caught him in the act and threatened to tell his mother he followed her into the kitchen, grabbed a knife and stabbed her to death.

The teenager, a gifted pianist who was on his way to a music lesson, then stole her purse and drove her car out of the garage. He stalled it in her drive so fled on foot. He seemed to feel no remorse for the murder and spent the money on books.

The fourteen-year-old was found guilty of this killing and spent the next seven years in an institution. When he was released he became a drifter, sometimes picking up men in gay bars and staying with them for as long as he could. He remained volatile and many people were chilled by the rage in his staring eyes.

When he was twenty-six he spent a few weeks in a Lake District hotel, living with a member of the hotel staff, a male waiter. When the waiter asked him to leave he became increasingly violent. He also made it clear that he resented the sixty-seven-year-old hotel owner's lifestyle - though it was a lifestyle she'd worked very hard to build.

Shortly after his gay relationship ended, he returned to the hotel and attacked the owner. He tied her up with various flexes, battered her around the face and kicked her so hard that five of her ribs were broken. He also stabbed her in the neck, strangled her with a scarf and wrapped a plastic bag around her head. He then fled with some of her money and her car. The hardworking entrepreneur's body was found by her distraught son the following day.

He was found guilty of murdering the hotelier in December 1986. Aware that he was an ongoing danger to society, the judge gave him life imprisonment. Only then did the jury hear that this was the second time he'd killed an elderly woman who had done him no harm.

But David Wynne Roberts may eventually be released as the Court of Human Rights in Strasbourg is expected to rule that the British government should no longer be empowered to demand that killers spend their entire life in prison.

This author found few examples of children who killed again as adults - but did find case studies where it's clear that a disturbed child's attempt to kill wasn't taken seriously and these children went on to murder as adults. The motive may be similar as in the case of David Wynne Roberts who chose elderly victims, killed them, then stole their possessions. Or it can be entirely different as in the case of Gordon Wardell whose teenage attempted murder was for sexual pleasure and whose second murder, as an adult, was for material gain.


## Gordon David Wardell

Gordon was an intelligent but troubled youth - and would allege that his unhappiness stemmed from life with a domineering mother. He had fantasies about controlling and about being controlled. By his midteens he had developed an obsession with the actor Paul Newman and wanted to emulate the actor's most macho roles.

In June 1970, when Gordon was seventeen, he heard that his geology teacher was away on a field trip. He realised that the man's young wife would be alone with their pre-school children so he phoned her up and pretended he'd found a rare plant of interest to her husband growing in the countryside. He added that he couldn't convey the plant safely back to his Coventry school as he was on his bicycle. The young woman obligingly agreed to meet him to take a cutting of the plant and drove to the meeting place with her sons, age four and five, in the back of the car.

But when she and Gordon got to a wooded copse, he produced a knife and held it to her throat. He said that his name was Paul Newman and asked her for cash - then immediately upped the ante by telling her to lie down so that he could bind her hands. It was increasingly apparent that this was a potentially violent sexual attack. Wisely she refused to be tied up, at which he shoved his knee hard into her back. He also tried to force her onto her knees but she again resisted. Then he manhandled her into the passenger seat and took control of her car.

Moments later he parked and struck her about the head. Then he tore her briefs off. Her oldest child tried to intervene but Gordon struck him too. He drove on then parked again and slashed one of the car's tire - then leaned in the open door and slashed the woman's throat and stabbed her twice in the back of the neck. The blood arched out and he stepped back for a second. The badly wounded victim saw her last chance and swiftly locked the door. He lunged at the car but she was able to drive off and soon summoned help from another motorist.

This was clearly an attempted murder, for only the woman's desperate escape attempt had prevented her bleeding to death in the vandalised car. As it was, it took nine pints of blood to save her life.

But for some reason the charge was reduced from attempted murder to grievous bodily harm and Gordon only spent four years in Grendon Underwood prison. He was released at twenty-one.

Four years later he met Carol, a former Sunday school teacher who now worked in a building society. After a four year courtship they married in church. She was a kind, quiet woman who was well-liked in the community. The marriage looked contented enough to outsiders but Gordon still wanted more. He began to visit prostitutes and urged them to tie him up and to be rough with his penis. (Men with cold or dominant mothers often ask for such treatment from their sex partners as a way of turning an abusive experience into an ultimately orgasmic one.)

After twelve years of marriage, all still looked well to outsiders but Carol must have been aware that Gordon was under-achieving. He'd drifted from one job to another whilst she'd been promoted to assistant manageress at the building society. And whilst she was cleaning and tidying the house, he was out spending money they could ill afford on bondage prostitutes.

Gordon needed to feel important and he wanted money. He could rid himself of Carol's real or imagined disapproval and get himself a good few thousand pounds if he disposed of her and robbed the building society where she worked.

He proceeded to do just that, chloroforming her after Sunday lunch and probably suffocating her after she lost consciousness. Then he used her keys to enter the building society where he stole fourteen thousand pounds, money which has never been found. He dumped her body in a ditch, went home, struck himself about the face and tied himself up.

When the robbery was discovered and Carol didn't arrive for work, police went to the Wardells' house. They freed Gordon who claimed that a gang had knocked him out and tied him up then abducted Carol. But he showed none of the trauma that someone who'd been tied up for sixteen hours would normally show. Indeed, he hadn't even urinated once in all that time. And the gang, supposedly professional enough to kidnap a vital staff member, had relied on bindings from the Wardells' home...

The police's suspicions were further aroused when Gordon insisted on giving a press conference in a wheelchair despite the fact that he was medically able to walk. As they continued to question him, more and more of his statements simply didn't add up. The authorities put him under surveillance and noted that he strolled around in perfect health but began to limp and look anguished when he went to the building society to talk about his wife's death-in-service pension, money that would now be given to him.

On 23rd October 1994 he was charged with Carol's murder and with stealing from the building society. In December he went to trial and was found guilty. A programme about the case that was televised in 2002 suggested that he is still denying his guilt.

Another case of a damaged youth who attempted to kill and who wasn't taken seriously is Robert Black. Robert would ultimately be charged with three child murders but he may well have committed many more.


## Robert Black

Robert was born in April 1947 to a single mother who lived in Grangemouth, Scotland. She wanted to keep him but her strict parents were horrified by his illegitimacy. They wouldn't let her live at home whilst she was pregnant so she had to stay with various relatives. Within six months of his birth she reluctantly put him into an orphanage.

He was soon fostered by a Scottish couple who had draconian views on childcare. His foster mother used to undress him below the waist and beat him with a belt, causing frequent nightmares. He would wet the bed during these night terrors and was beaten for that too. Neighbours saw the little boy covered in bruises, looking unbathed and unkempt.

It's likely that he was also sexually abused. By the time he was eight he was pushing objects up his own anus - just as the sodomised child Johnny Garrett, profiled earlier, did. This doesn't necessarily imply homosexual desire - Robert's later victims would all be little girls - but is simply a way for an abused child to take control of a formerly hated and forced act.

Robert continued to have a very troubled life. Beaten at home, he would go on to beat other children in the playground. He loved swimming and would use these outings to the pool to stare at little girls. Years later he would take girls' swimsuits from the poolside and use them as a masturbatory aid.

222

By the time he was eleven both foster parents had died and he was returned to care. At twelve he and two friends took a twelve-year-old girl into a field, pulled down her pants and tried to gang rape her. Robert was moved to a care home that didn't include girls - but received no therapeutic help.

At his new residence, one of the staff made the child fellate and masturbate him. Robert was still the underdog, but his fantasies of controlling a child victim intensified.

At fifteen he left the residential home and rented a room, working as a delivery boy. During his deliveries he made clumsy passes at numerous girls. It's unclear how old these females were - but the fact that none of them reported him suggests that they were innocently young.

Within two years the touching wasn't enough, and the seventeen-year-old persuaded a seven-year-old girl to accompany him into a disused air raid shelter. There he grabbed her and strangled her into unconsciousness. When she was completely passive he pulled her pants down and digitally raped her, breaking her hymen and causing her to bleed. Then he masturbated over her, enjoying the fact that she was unable to resist.

He left her for dead - but the little girl revived and the teenager ended up in court. There, a psychiatrist said that the event was an isolated incident. Yet Robert Black had already been moved from one care home to another after attempting to rape at age twelve and had inappropriately approached dozens of girls when he was a fifteen-year-old delivery boy. Despite this dangerous history, he was merely put on probation for a year and moved to a new area where he found building work. In truth, a charge of attempted murder would have been more appropriate.

Again within two years - now age nineteen - his paedophile desires had surfaced and he digitally entered a nine-year-old. He was discovered and hounded out of town - but in his new abode he did the same thing to a seven-year-old. This time he served a year at a borstal where he remained a loner. His life experience had been so loveless that people said they could see the emptiness in his eyes.

After serving his sentence, he left Scotland and moved to London where he began to collect child pornography. This isn't a victimless crime as children are forced to strip and pose for such photographs and are often abused whilst the photos are being shot. Robert also hung around playgrounds and beaches, where he took his own photographs of children to use as masturbatory aids.

Unable to make friends and undoubtedly haunted by his own past, the young man retreated further and further into his fantasy life. He'd been a gifted sportsman but eyesight problems put an end to his hopes for an athletic career. Now he worked in a dead end job and had no one to really confide in and no hobbies - though he played darts in the pub - that truly interested him. Thoughts of stalking and taking and molesting another child increasingly dominated his life.

Robert Black was thirty-five by the time he committed his first known murder - but police believe he may have murdered earlier and may be responsible for many more murders than the three that he was ultimately charged with. The case is interesting because his adult sex crimes were eerily similar to the sex crimes he'd committed as a child.

Robert Black was driving near the English village of Coldstream in 1982 when he saw an eleven-year-old girl, Susan Maxwell, walking home from a tennis club. He did what he'd done as a teenager with a victim - took her away from the scene to a place where he could control her, in this instance his van.

He has never talked about exactly what he did to Susan or exactly how he killed her, but when her decomposed body was found a fortnight later her panties had been removed. He went on to kill five-year-old Caroline Hogg from Portobello in 1983 and when her body was eventually found it was nude.

Three years passed, then in 1986 he abducted ten-year-old Sarah Harper, molesting her repeatedly then placing her - alive but probably unconscious - into a river. When her corpse was found it had been undressed and then reclothed.

It's believed that he gagged and bound each victim and that they were kept alive for some time as he drove around the country, stopping to abuse them whenever the desire overtook him. Repeated sexual assaults were the motive and he didn't really care whether they lived or died.

He was caught whilst abducting six-year-old Mandy Wilson after an alert neighbour saw him pull the child into his van. By the time police waved down the vehicle he'd already briefly assaulted her. He was given a life sentence in 1994 that will keep him behind bars until he is at least eighty-two.

As it's virtually unknown for a paedophile sex killer to avoid killing for three years, it's likely that he is responsible for other missing children's untimely deaths between that of Caroline Hogg and Sarah Harper. We know that he tried to abduct Teresa Thornhill but though she looked childish she was actually fifteen and was able to lash out at him and attract attention. His younger victims were not so fortunate and were unable to get away. The authorities want to question him about seventeen other child murders throughout the country. After the case, a police spokesman said that Robert Black had been so abused throughout his childhood that there was no humanity left behind his eyes.

## 20
# BLAME IT ON THE PONY EXPRESS
## The Scapegoats

Numerous case histories show that it's the violence meted out to children that spurs them on to kill. Paul Mones has said that though the police are good at protecting banks from being robbed, 'they do an absolutely abysmal job of shielding children from the criminal excesses of their parents.' Psychologist Dorothy Rowe has also noted that police tend to side with the parent unless the case involves sexual abuse. Yet many adults refuse to recognise the connection between their hitting and ridiculing children and these children going on to hurt them back or harm someone else. Instead, society's scapegoats include:

**Violent videos**

Millions of children watch television dramas and videos with a partially violent theme - so if they were the *sole* cause of inciting murder, we'd have a juvenile killing epidemic. Instead, the number of children in Britain who kill each year is in the low double figures. Clearly, there are other factors at work.

It's possible that a child who is already disturbed may be more affected by televised violence than a child from a stable home. It's certainly true that the loved child will have access to a wider range of sensory input. He's hugged and taken places and read stories - whereas the neglected child is left for hours in front of the TV. Gavin de Becker, a world renowned expert in predicting violence, has said that though violent content matters, the main harm comes through what the excess TV-watching replaces. That is, the child is overdosing on celluloid images instead of enjoying interaction with others.

A fatherless boy who lacks a male figure (such as a kindly uncle) in his life, may look to television to provide him with role models. Unfortunately he's then faced with numerous violent or verbally aggressive macho men.

Once again, the negative social factors come first. If conditions are sufficiently bad they can turn the child into a budding psychopath - and as psychopaths always seek out excitement, they're going to watch the most violent programmes available and will feel no empathy with the victims of such storylines.

Some psychologists believe that psychopaths (people who only care about themselves and have no conscience) are born rather than made but when fledgling psychopaths were taken from their parents they usually showed improvement, suggesting that the home environment does play a critical part.

That said, there are instances of children who were so relentlessly abused and neglected by their biological parents during their first few months of life that they were incapable of bonding with caring adoptive parents. And the *adult* psychopath appears to be untreatable.

But watching a violent video doesn't turn a loved child into a psychopath. Violent parents, violent school bullies - or the occasional severe chemical imbalance or brain tumour - does that.


## Rock music

Millions of young - and some not so young - people listen to heavy metal rock, and they don't go on to kill. Yet when a teenager who happens to be a rock fan commits murder, the media often blame the music. They'll note that the suicidal or murderous victim played the same downbeat lyrics again and again. In reality, the teenager will have become depressed by his immediate environment. Thereafter he seeks out the lyrics which best suit his mood.

Young men can be rejected by society in many different ways. First, their mothers often stop hugging them when they are around twelve years old so they receive no physical affection. Boys tend not to talk intimately to each other in the way that girls do, so their emotional problems remain unshared. Alienated from their surroundings, they understandably turn to the music of alienation. It makes them feel as if someone understands.

Many of us listen to such alienated lyrics at some stage in our lives, but it doesn't turn us into miniature psychos. A happy and loved child or teenager simply doesn't commit suicide because he plays a few downbeat tunes. The children who take a life have been scarred by their life experiences, not by some angry words on a CD.

Ironically, when those who scapegoat music find that the lyrics aren't as bad as they feared, they sometimes say that the troubled teen heard *sublimi-*

*nal* messages on the record. They'll play such records backwards and try to find 'dangerous messages' in the soundtrack. It's clear that some people have overactive imaginations and too much time on their hands.

As Gavin de Becker has written - when discussing a para-suicide victim who blamed his attempt on heavy metal music - 'once he excluded family life and parenting from the enquiry, he might as well have cited anything... By pointing his finger at a rock band, James washed away all the scrutiny that might reasonably have been focused on himself, his family or even his society.'

## Secularity

Religious leaders like to suggest that our secular society is to blame for children who kill - but reality doesn't bear this out. Indeed, most of the children profiled in this book had religious families.

William Allnutt lived with a deeply devout grandfather. In jail he told his mother that it was a 'terrible thing to fall into the hands of a living God.' Wendy Gardner was frequently taken to church by her religious grandmother - and Wendy turned up at her trial wearing a crucifix and clutching rosary beads.

Luke Woodham's mother was heavily involved with the local Baptist Church and took Luke to Sunday school every week. Luke continued to attend church into his mid teens. He also had a religious friend who 'witnessed' to him (told him that there was a deity) at least twice a week. Kip Kinkel, who would embark on a similar killing spree, had a paternal grandfather who was a minister.

Mary Bell's mother, Betty, was so religious that her family expected her to become a nun. At age thirteen she suddenly surrounded her bed with rosaries and crucifixes. Later she and her clients abused Mary in a room that had crucifixes on the wall. Mary herself was always reading the Bible and owned five of them.

Jesse Pomeroy was sent to Sunday school and Johnny Garrett's mother was a Jehovah's witness. Johnny's experiences at home were so horrendous that he later invented a new Jehovah-less religion for himself. Jon Venables and Robert Thompson went to a Church Of England School - and after battering James to death, Jon told his psychologist that good children went to heaven and that bad children went to hell. Robert's mother wore denominational jewellery in the form of a five-pointed Orange Lodge star at his trial.

Cheryl Pierson spent most of her childhood with her religious mother and grew up in a house that had a prayer on the kitchen door and a picture of the Pope on the front door. Cheryl wore a cross to her trial and told people that she believed her mother was in heaven and her father was in hell.

Sean Pica, who Cheryl hired to kill her father, also came from a religious household. His mother took him to Sunday school every week and also taught a group of children the catechism in her home. And Rob Cuccio, who acted as the go-between, had a mother, father and siblings who were all heavily involved with their local church.

Rod Ferrell spent much of his life with his grandparents who were Pentecostal fundamentalists. He believed in the existence of a god and in the existence of a devil.

We know that violence breeds violence yet some religious schools still physically punish children. Patricia Knox, author of *Troubled Children*, noted that 'I am surprised and dismayed... that Church schools are amongst those least inclined to abandon corporal punishment.' She noted that being beaten didn't just traumatise the injured child, it also caused neurosis in the classmates that had to witness it.

Paul Mones, writing of how the general public can be alert for signs of child abuse, has written that 'It is especially important to be aware of these men and women who pride themselves on being stern disciplinarians - parents who boast that they will go to any lengths to install moral, religious or other values in their children.'

## Pornography

Exposure to adult pornography is often given by anti-porn groups as a cause of sex crime. But many studies refute this - and those that do show a link have often been criticised for their methodologies. Several, such as Tjaden's *Pornography And Sex Education* (published in the *Journal Of Sex Research* in 1988) and Padgett & Brislin-Slutz's *Pornography, Erotica And Attitudes Towards Women* (published in the same journal in 1989) have shown that young men benefit from viewing porn as they use it as a sex education aid.

In 1973, Kant & Goldstein conducted a study which involved three groups of men - occasional users of porn, regular users and men convicted of sexual offences ranging from paedophilia to rape. They found that the sex offenders had seen *less* porn when growing up than the non-offenders had - and that they continued to see less porn as adults. (*Pornography And Sexual Deviance: A Report Of The Legal And Behavioural* University of California Press.)

It's certainly true that boys who rape and kill have often been made to feel guilty about their sexuality. Ed Kemper was so cruelly mocked by his alcoholic mother that it distorted his entire view of womanhood. By ten he was cutting the heads off his sister's dolls - and also burying cats alive. At fifteen he shot his grandfather and grandmother dead then stabbed her corpse repeatedly. Afterwards he told authorities that he wished he'd undressed her to see what she looked like.

Repressing or mocking a child's normal sexual development simply doesn't make that development stop - instead, it's like holding a beachball firmly under water. When you eventually let go, the beachball races to the surface again.

Authoritarian parents often try to control their teenage children's sexuality, perhaps believing that this will make the child a 'better' person - but sexual dysfunction clinics are filled with flashers, Peeping Toms and obscene phone callers who come from repressive backgrounds like this.

Sexual therapist Roy Eskapa has written of how one boy was found masturbating into a pair of his female cousin's panties. Most of us would just have pretended not to notice, but as a punishment his mother made him dress up as a girl and put on makeup. Then she let his cousin treat him in the exact same way - but when the cousin noticed that the boy had an erection she hit it. This aroused him further and he became a transvestite who eventually sought therapy. (Most transvestites are harmless - but it has to be noted that some of society's most vicious rapists and killers have also been found to cross-dress.)

Sexual curiosity in young people is a normal part of life yet some parents expect their children to remain asexual until their eighteenth birthday. Some puritans even object to their children being given sex education in school. Ironically, it's not the young person with a relaxed attitude to sex who becomes the sexual offender - it's the child who was taught that sexual exploration is dirty and wrong.

## Hyperactivity

Nowadays when a child is having difficulty concentrating in school, he's often diagnosed as having Attention Deficit Hyperactivity Disorder and given powerful mind-altering drugs. Kip Kinkel was given Ritalin for supposed hyperactivity and Prozac for clinical depression. (For information on the violence these drugs can provoke, please see the chapter on kip kinkel.) And Jon Venables was diagnosed as hyperactive though he doesn't appear to have been prescribed any drugs.

It's argued that there's something wrong with these children's brains and that they are liable to develop into delinquents - but despite extensive research, no organic disorder has been found.

Clinical psychologist Dr David Keirsey has worked with delinquent boys and has been a professor of behavioural science. He's also the best-selling author of the book *Please Understand Me*. His paper, *The Great A.D.D. Hoax*, points out that children who were once merely considered to be 'bundles of energy' are now negatively labelled as 'hyperactive.' And children who were once seen as 'daydreamers' are now designated as suffering from 'attention deficit disorder.' He's rightly horrified that these vague diagnoses are allowing medics to 'invade children's brains' with 'brain disabling drugs.'

David Keirsey has been working with children since 1950 and has noted that the ones who had difficulty concentrating in class simply weren't interested in the subject matter. There was nothing wrong with their brain function as they could concentrate perfectly well on subjects that interested them. He found that the boys wrongly diagnosed as having attention deficit disorder were boys who were 'concrete, impulsive players'. In other words they were very practical in their interests and abilities. (Persistent truant Robert Thompson had very little interest in his schoolwork - but he loved taking electrical gadgets apart to see how they worked. Similarly, Kip Kinkel scored badly in written work but was sufficiently scientifically knowledgeable that by the age of twelve he was able to make bombs.)

Keirsey points out that school children are told to stay still, keep quiet and get to work - and that the supposed attention deficit disorder child manages to do the first two things but doesn't do the third as he can't engage with the material. The problem then is that the curriculum is wrong for that particular child's mindset. There's nothing wrong with his mind.

## Vampirism

An interest in vampirism is often scapegoated when children kill. Rod Ferrell is often given as an example of a vampire cult killer. He battered a friend's parents to death and was completely remorseless. Watching him stick his tongue out at the camera again and again it's hard to imagine a more irritating, immature jerk.

But Ferrell didn't just form a cult and change from a regular nice guy. Instead, his childhood was so unnurturing that he was desperate to latch on to anything that would give him a sense of identity. A court-appointed official even said that Ferrell's family was the most dysfunctional he'd ever seen.

Society often blames such occult practices when children kill - but, in truth, a youth's interest in vampirism is no more outlandish than his mother's calls to a psychic hotline. They are all just belief systems that humans have invented to give themselves the illusion of control over their fate.

Unfortunately studies have shown that many people hold onto their beliefs even when overwhelming evidence contradicts this, so an adult who wanted to blame vampire books for various murders would simply filter out all the studies which link violent children with violent parenting.

Vampire-lovers can probably be classed as immature - but dressing as a Goth and reading about supposed life after death doesn't make children turn to murder. It's usually an abusive background that causes people to kill.

## Single parent families

Politicians and newspapers which have a political axe to grind always make much of the fact that child killers like Robert Thompson come from single parent families. But when Robert's parents were together he merely had two violent parents rather than one.

And many of the children profiled lived with both their parents. Cheryl Pierson's mother and father stayed together until her mother's death from kidney disease - and her boyfriend, Rob Cuccio, who helped mastermind James Pierson's murder was from a stable two parent family. Shirley Wolf's parents were still together years after she went to prison. And, though Billy Bell was not Mary Bell's biological father, he lived with Mary and her mother for many years.

The Bells had a very odd marriage - but Kip Kinkel's parents were devoted to each other. Kip admitted that he'd killed his mother because he couldn't bear to see the pain and disappointment on her face when she saw that he'd killed his highly critical dad.

Children are, of course, affected by their parent's divorce - but it's the constant arguing accompanying the split that often does the most damage. Sean Pica's mother fought constantly with Sean's dad even after he'd left her and remarried. (Sean's father wasn't one of the bad guys. Though he'd found it impossible to stay in the marriage, he returned to it from a sense of duty when his oldest child was very ill.) Mary Anne Woodham screamed at her husband in front of the children then blamed little Luke when her spouse left the family for good.

Children need to know that they are loved by their parents. They also need a sense of stability. The profiled children with married parents didn't have this because at least one of the parents was physically, sexually or emotionally abusive. The children with the single mother - such as Cindy Collier - also didn't feel safe because she introduced numerous violent boyfriends to the home.

## Defective genes

A percentage of the population believes that some children are simply born uncaring and that as a result they can easily turn into mini-killers. But the facts suggest otherwise.

William Allnutt missed his mother so much (and became so ill) when he was at boarding school that he was sent home to her. In prison, he was more concerned about her feelings than he was his own. Cheryl Pierson often went to her father's room to shield her terminally ill mother from his violence and sexual demands. Peter Dinsdale left children's homes again and again in the hope that this visit with his mother would turn out to be a loving one and little Sean Sellers cried every time his mother went away.

Even after they've murdered, many of these children remain attached to their abusive or inadequate parents. Shirley Wolf lay across her father at visiting times - and was desolate, years later, when he stopped answering her letters from prison. And one of the few times that Rod Ferrell got tearful was in court when his mother cried.

Sometimes the child is still desperate to believe that at least one parent is good. This tends to mean that the child still believes that she herself is bad and it makes it difficult for her (or him) to move on emotionally. Cindy Collier at first made little progress in prison therapy as she refused to see that her mother had failed her by leaving her with numerous violent boyfriends and by not reacting when Cindy was raped again and again by a relative.

It's clear, then, that these children start off feeling love - yet geneticists try to tell us that these juveniles who go on to kill are simply born bad. They blame nature rather than nurturing - or rather the lack of nurturing.

Whilst it's true that one child may be born with more timidity or verve than his siblings, we can see again and again that it's the environment that determines how these qualities are moulded. When young troublemakers are placed in a caring, positive-parenting style environment they improve. Dr Dorothy Lewis, who assesses teenage prisoners on Death Row, has said that even at this stage she sees a softening in some of them, as they've been around kind and intelligence adults for the first time in their hate-filled lives.

That said, it would be wrong to suggest that a few acts of kindness can undo the years of damage and neglect. Sean Sellers killed a shop clerk who'd spent the last hour happily chatting to him. And Cindy Collier and Shirley Wolf murdered a lady who'd let them in to her house for a drink and to use the phone. Luke Woodward shot a girl who had hugged him and other pupils frequently at school. He later apologised to the girl's family in court, but obviously this did nothing to take away their pain.

Society erroneously gives the impression that these children are simply born bad. One book on the subject explains in depth about how often these children are violently parented - but the publishers put the words 'bad seeds' on the front cover so the casual observer in a bookstore comes away with the impression that these youngsters sprung malevolent from the womb. Another book gave the impression that these were children from good homes (including some of the children who were profiled here!) who mysteriously went awry due to some inner demon, whereas more research would have shown that these children were relentlessly mocked and struck. The following chapter identifies some of these myth-makers and looks at how insidiously they work.

# 21

# RIDERS ON THE STORM
## The Myth-Makers

Numerous individuals and groups contribute to the myth that children who kill have chosen to go bad or were born bad. Some will do so out of ignorance, others because it's easier to blame the child than to change society. This author identified the myth-makers below whilst researching this book:

### The child's adult relatives

When a child kills his or her violent parent, the family tends to close ranks. Relatives praise the abusive parent and either deny that abuse took place or strongly minimise it, sometimes because they feel guilty at their own failure to intervene.

These families tend to have many dysfunctional members who assume that the way they were raised was normal therefore they put all of the pathology onto the juvenile who kills. Psychologist Dorothy Rowe has written that adults can 'inflict the same pain, humiliation and fear that had been inflicted on them.'

Many of these adults were too immature and damaged to raise a child, but they procreated regardless then blamed the child for all their woes.

One parent (most often the mother) often also looks the other way when their spouse rapes their daughter. This topic was raised in an edition of the *Kilroy* talk show where the topic was *Sexual Abuse Within The Family*. One woman explained that when she was six she'd told her mother that her father was interfering with her. Sadly, the mother's response was never to speak to the child directly again, only talking to her through her sisters. The family chose not to believe that this little girl was being molested - but the authorities eventually let her wear a wire and they were able to hear the abuse for themselves.

Another situation where adults had failed to protect a child was revealed in an episode of *Correspondent* which looked at paedophile priests. One boy who had been inappropriately touched by a certain priest knew that the man was coming to his aunt and uncle's house where he was staying. The boy begged them not to let him be taken anywhere by the priest and the relatives agreed. But as the priest was leaving the house he asked to take the child with him to show him the new church organ. The aunt said 'Yes, of course, Father' because she'd been raised to have respect for priests. The child was then taken away and abused by the man who was unrepentant about the child's anguish and made it clear to the boy that he'd do this to other boys.

Again and again there were reports made to the local Bishop about this particular priest but he was just moved from one parish to the next where he continued to rape male children. Some adults in the community simply refused to believe that a priest would do such things - but in reality there are so many clergy abusing children that there have been special sexual offender courses set up to treat them. And if they are married clergy the course leaders can co-counsel their families.

This particular priest continued to deny any wrongdoing but one boy used a hidden camera to videotape what was happening. Thereafter the priest was finally charged. Whilst on bail this paedophile committed suicide. Sadly, several of the youths he'd spent time alone with also committed suicide.

It took many years for this man's paedophiliac activities to *officially* come to light - yet dozens of his parishioners suspected he was harming the community's children. Those adults who did react seem only to have informed someone in the church's hierarchy. It appears that no one went to the police.

If one of this man's victims had snapped and killed him, it's a safe bet that child would have been classified as bad and the priest as good.


## The child's siblings

The child who kills often has siblings who turn against them. Cheryl Pierson and Wendy Gardner both had younger sisters who took the side of their dead relatives in court. The prosecution suggested this meant that Cheryl and Wendy were just 'born bad' as their siblings said they had no problem with the dead relative. But a closer look at the facts doesn't bear this out.

Witnesses had seen Cheryl's sister being slapped across the face and mocked by her father - and Cheryl's brother was so tired of being hit and

236

ridiculed that he left home at the earliest opportunity. Neighbours had tried to keep the children away from the man.

Cheryl's sister had said that any sexual contact between Cheryl and her dad was Cheryl's fault as she was 'always laying all over him.' The younger child understandably didn't know that this was learned behaviour, that incest victims are coached into being sexual by their abusers in order to avoid further punishment.

Wendy Gardner's sister also said that her guardian had treated them well - but in court, when questioned, she admitted to being beaten with a paddle and a fly swat. Neighbours had heard screams and someone had contacted the social services. Both Wendy's sister and Cheryl's sister were now staying with relatives of the deceased, something that must also have helped shape their view of things.

It's also evident that a controlling parent or guardian often doesn't act so controllingly towards a younger child as the younger child has fewer places to go and thus fewer chances to anger the parent. Wendy and Cheryl were both teenagers desperately trying to find love with their new boyfriends, something that neither Wendy's grandmother (who had called the police and asked them to stop the teenagers caressing each other) or Cheryl's incredibly jealous father could tolerate.

The other strong difference between the older sister who snapped and the younger one was that the older girls had started menstruating. Menstruation puts a strain on over eighty percent of even the most balanced women - for a physically and emotionally abused young girl, the additional stress must be nearly intolerable. Stress strongly exacerbates premenstrual syndrome and it's known that it can also change the length of the cycle. This was likely in Cindy Collier's case for at one stage she bled for almost three weeks and had agonising cramps.


## Not-so-true crime writers

Some crime writers - perhaps pandering to public option - further misrepresent the cruelty that these children endured before they fought back and killed. They get round the parental violence by saying that the child was difficult so the parents 'had to beat' him or her frequently. They also treat the child's natural attempt to evade further assaults by running away as another form of pathology.

Encyclopaedia-style works about children who kill often don't mention the circumstances leading up to the murders at all, so that the casual reader is left with the impression that these children were simply born bad and chose to be exceptionally violent. The reality is very different.

## People with negative mindsets

We seem to live in a culture that expects the worst from our children. Parents assume that the terrible two's (when two-year-olds have endless temper tantrums) are an inevitability. But educationalist Patricia Knox has noted that these frustrated outbursts are often due to an active, inquisitive two-year-old being confined to the house with little to do and no other children to interact with and a parent who is busy with other chores.

There's also a common misconception that if you don't hit a child it will cause chaos. But Claire Rayner said in an episode of the BBC programme *Question Time* that she had never hit her children as she recognised this to be a form of bullying - yet her children always knew right from wrong and were very well behaved. (This author's interview with Claire Rayner appears later in this book.) Educational writer and psychologist Penelope Leach said the same thing at a *Children Are Unbeatable* seminar held in London in January 2002. She was never hit as a child so had never hit her own offspring.

Psychologist and writer Dorothy Rowe, speaking at the same seminar, said that her friends had brought their children up without hitting them. These children had grown into the most confident, caring and hardworking adults that she knew and had a strong sense of who they were.

Contrast that with the numerous troubled abusive adults and abused children detailed in this book, and it's easy to see that violence doesn't work.

School teachers can also add to this culture of negativity by suggesting that pupils are becoming more disruptive than in previous years. In truth, children with problems are sometimes expelled nowadays whereas they'd have previously been seen - and hopefully helped - by a child psychologist.

America is equally guilty of misrepresenting its young as Mike Males, author of *Framing Youth* pointed out in an informative internet article called *Why Demonize A Healthy Teen Culture?* He stated that 'Ignoring clear statistics and research, authorities seem to lie in wait for suburban youth killings, months and thousands of miles apart, to validate a false hypothesis of generational disease, even as they ignore the more compelling evidence of deteriorating adult behaviour.' He notes that adults killing kids is far more common than kids killing kids. Other American writers have also remarked on this trend, pointing out that four-million American children are seriously hurt by their parents every year.

## Popular television: a licence to hit

Many TV programmes add to the notion that hitting children is a normal part of life. Characters in soap operas often threaten to clip their children around the ear - in other words, to hit them about the head, something that the medical profession recognises as very dangerous. Violent criminals usually have neurological damage caused by blows to the head. These are known as the 'soft signs' of abuse. Even more alarmingly, threatening to clip a child around the ear is designed to raise a laugh in working class comedies.

In other instances, misinformation about child rearing is given by one character and not corrected by another. For example, a character in an episode of *Coronation Street*, aired in January 2002, said 'In my day you picked a baby up once every four hours for feeding and changing and let it cry the rest of the time.'

The viewer is left with the impression that this behaviour will toughen the baby up - but educational writer Patricia Knox noted in her book *Troubled Children* that low-weight babies who were subjected to this routine in hospital often failed to bond properly with their mothers. The babies weren't fed when they cried for food then were woken when they finally fell asleep. They were too small and confused to feed sufficiently in these circumstances so remained hungry and distressed. The vital mother-baby bond didn't form and these babies had numerous problems as they matured.

Such lack of bonding - especially if combined with a later lack of care - can even cause serious pathology. Co-ed killer Ted Bundy and child-killer Ian Brady were both left alone for long periods during their first few weeks of life. Bundy's religious mother was ashamed of his illegitimacy and initially left him at the orphanage. Brady's mother bravely ignored the stigma of having a baby out of wedlock but had to go out to work in the evenings, leaving him with whoever she could find. Both men matured into dangerous psychopaths who killed many times.

One of the female serial killers that this author profiled in *Women Who Kill* - Gwen Graham - had been left to cry by her mother who wrongly believed that cradling a crying baby spoiled it. Gwen soon showed the signs of an unbonded baby, refusing to look at her mother when she entered the room. This lack of bonding was reinforced by physical abuse from both parents and Gwen eventually went on to kill. There's an unfounded notion that too much love spoils a baby - but it is hate that ruins human beings. A child who feels loved has the confidence to increasingly explore and enjoy his or her world.

Another opportunity to tell it like it is was lost during an episode of the *Richard And Judy* show aired in February 2002. A man whose son had just been jailed for torturing pensioners appeared on the programme. Whilst introducing him, the presenters said he believed his son was simply born bad.

But during the short discussion which followed the father said that he believed in corporal punishment and would hit his children on the backs of their legs. Now, our prisons are full of violent adults who were subjected to corporal punishment as children but neither of the presenters picked up on this fact. Instead, they asked the man if his son had been in any way unusual as a child. The father replied 'Well, he'd always lie. I'd tell him I'm going to slap you for what you just did but I'll slap you harder if you lie to me and he always lied.'

No one pointed out that of course a child will lie to avoid being physically hurt and humiliated. An adult in the same position would do the exact same thing. The man said that he also believed in capital punishment and that his son now deserved to hang. Shortly afterwards the interview ended with one of the presenters murmuring sympathetically 'I feel sorry for you.'

Such programmes offer an opportunity to inform the general public. Instead, they simply bolster the status quo. Sadly, our formal educational system can equally fail children in various ways.


**The educational system**

Children who are being poorly parented are understandably unable to concentrate in the classroom so they are labelled as suffering from attention deficit disorder and may be punished with powerful drugs. The influential and rich drugs lobby gives the impression that such tablets are a cure for all ills but in truth, all drugs have side effects.

An abused child is liable to play truant from school in order to have a few hours refuge from the demands of authoritative adults. Jesse Pomeroy, William Allnutt, Robert Thompson, Rod Ferrell, Wendy Gardner, James Evans and Johnny Garrett fall into this category. Again, these truants are simply penalised and there's little effort made to understand the reasons for the truancy. Educationalist writer Patricia Knox tells of distressed school-phobic children being told by judges that they'd have to go to jail if they didn't return to class.


## Anyone who downplays bullying

A child who is being bullied at home will go to school with violence on his or her mind. Some of these children become bullies - Jesse Pomeroy, Cindy Collier, Jon Venables and Johnny Garrett fit into this category. Others will remain victims - Shirley Wolf was taunted because she smelt bad. Wendy Gardner was called a tart by less promiscuous classmates. And Kip Kinkel was so remorselessly picked upon that he wrote in his diary that he was ready to kill another boy. (This is not to imply that all bullying victims are being brutalised at home. Children who are in any way different can be picked upon with bullies honing in on a victim's clothing, weight, height, hair colour, intellect and so on.)

Bullying causes numerous problems for the victim. A victimised child may become school-phobic, develop an eating disorder, have nightmares and start to do badly in their schoolwork. It's regrettably common - when four thousand children were polled in the mid eighties, 68% of them reported being bullied at some time.

Bullies also have many problems. Kidscape, the charity which specialises in alleviating bullying, has said that most bullies are 'afraid, jealous, envious, cruel, angry, insecure and unhappy.' This may be due to family problems, loneliness or other frustrations. Clearly, there are no winners when bullying occurs.

Yet many parents and teachers continue to downplay the misery that such behaviour causes, saying that they went through it themselves so today's children will just have to live with it. But as Michelle Elliot of Kidscape has pointed out, we used to stuff children up chimneys and down mines then we realised that this was wrong and stopped doing it. We can stop school bullying too.

Some teachers and parents erroneously try to change the personality of the victimised child rather than confront the bully - but children are often bullied for their special qualities. These qualities are the very ones which society will value in later life. Many of today's most successful adults - including Harrison Ford, Tom Cruise and Ranulph Fiennes - have stated that they were bullied when young.

A bullied child may only confide in a parent when they've run out of coping strategies of their own so it's unhelpful if the parent simply says 'just stand up for yourself.' Kidscape offers various helpful leaflets for both parents and children and further details appear in the Useful Addresses section of this book. Briefly, the child can be helped by being reassured that he or she is loved, supported and not to blame for the bullying. Parents should also praise their child and help them to develop social skills, perhaps by finding a hobby that they really enjoy. The school should play its part in stamping out this misery so Kidscape offers training programmes which help schools implement an anti-bullying policy.

Bullying can be serious. If a larger adult ran up to you in the street, tore your clothes and yelled offensive comments about your size, you'd have recourse to the police and your victimiser would hopefully be facing an assault charge. Yet if a child is picked on in the exact same way by another child, a large sector of the community will ignore the terrified victim's plight.


**Newspaper reports**

Certain sectors of the press demonise children who kill. Ten-year-old Robert Thompson was described by one reporter as a hard-staring mini Charles Manson. In reality, he liked to sit on his mother's knee, still sucked his thumb and had an asthma attack after being sentenced. Eleven-year-old Mary Bell was also made out to be cold and compassionless when in truth she was childishly confused and alternated between asking if she could go home and expecting the state to hang her like they did in cowboy films.

The press suggests to the public that such children will always be dangerous - yet the *early* intervention of caring adults suggests otherwise. Mary Bell, who killed two toddlers, hasn't committed any acts of violence since being removed from her violent and sexually abusive household. It's over twenty years since she was released from prison. Previous newspaper reports about her beating a goldfish to death turned out to be completely fabricated by parties interested in earning money from the press.

The tabloids did the same thing when Robert Thompson was due for release, claiming that he'd tried to choke another inmate. It was yet another attempt to blacken the name of a child who has apparently made enormous progress since being removed from his dysfunctional home at age ten. And Wendy Gardner, whose grandmother described her as a whorish wild child, has been described as a model prisoner.

Criminologists and others who understand media speak can read between the lines - but members of the public who have little knowledge about crime tend to believe what they are reading. Yet many policemen will tell you that if a journalist can't get them to give genuinely sensational detail they will simply invent sensational quotes.

Newspapers tend to give stories about children who have killed a 'child born bad, parents good' slant. As such, a journalist may write that a family was 'loving but strict' for which read 'cold and demanding.' For 'tightknit' read 'emotionally suffocating.' For 'disciplinarian' read 'controlling and cruel.'

Gavin de Becker has noted that people who know that a child is being abused don't usually talk to the press. As a result, journalists end up talking to neighbours who hardly knew the family. That neighbour then innocently says that they seemed like a good family, that there was nothing wrong.

This author found similar myths about the parenting of female serial killers. They'd endured relentless violence yet certain sectors of the media suggested that their childhoods were normal. And a newspaper initially described Rose West - who ferociously beat and sexually abused her off-spring - as a strict but loving mum.


## The legal system

Most of the children profiled in this book had good legal representation but this isn't always the case. Dorothy Lewis, who evaluates teenagers on Death Row, has found that lawyers aren't particularly interested in young clients. They tend to take the case at face value and don't delve deeply into the child's background to find out exactly what he or she endured. Dr Lewis writes that 'many of these families would rather see their children put to death than reveal what had happened behind the closed doors of childhood.' She also found that 'many of the adolescents themselves preferred death to exposing their abusive parents.' There have even been instances of lawyers being belatedly sent information about the child's numerous hospital visits for suspicious injuries, information that the lawyer didn't use to force an appeal.

Clinical psychologist Lenore E Walker has also noted this trend and writes in the Foreword to *The Kids Next Door* that 'attorneys make deals that benefit themselves rather than their young clients, that judges play at being mental health professionals, picking and choosing whom to believe without the information needed to make informed judgements, and that doctors untrained in the dynamics of family violence commit gross errors that might be considered malpractice if their clients were not so young and vulnerable and rendered invisible.'

Such damaged children fare little better when it comes to the jury. Paul Mones has found that 'the jurors will react first as parents, second as the children they once were, and third as the impartial decision-makers they take an oath to be.'

Judges often compound the child's distress by labelling them as bad and evil. Patrick Wilson, a respected schoolteacher and author of a book called *Children Who Kill* published in 1973 (out of print but available from libraries) wrote 'If any criminal has an option on our usefully applied pity, it must be the child who kills.' Yet thirty years later there is still little sympathy or understanding from the judiciary. As former UN Secretary General, Peres de Cuellar said 'You measure the justice of a society by how it treats its children.'

# 22
# SHE'S SO COLD
## Telling It Like It Is

As the profiles in this book delineate, the children who killed were mostly children who'd been almost killed themselves by adults. Often the abusive adult was their primary carer - so they were struck, mocked and neglected by the people they trusted most. Dr Roy Eskapa, a sex therapist, has written that 'Almost every violent prisoner investigated turns out to have been subjected to severe corporal punishment during childhood' and 'when children are subjected to corporal punishment, they learn that violence is the norm.'

And in an American conference about violence in schools, psychologist Frank Zenere said that the factors included 'child abuse, ineffective parenting, violence in the home, poverty, prejudice, substance abuse and easy access to guns.'

A recent article on compassion by Julia Goodwin, the editor of a parenting magazine, confirmed that 'children aren't born bad - in fact, experts say we're all born with a tendency to be kind. Witness the toddler who, in an effort to alleviate another child's distress, will offer up their teddy to be cuddled.'

Dan Korem has studied children who commit ostensibly random acts of violence. He found that the family profile included divorce, separation, physical abuse, sexual abuse or a severely dysfunctional parent. (Korem and other such experts are briefly overviewed in Jon Bellini's excellent study of child killer Luke Woodham, *Child's Prey*.)


**Not so grand grandparents**

This abuse - be it sexual, emotional or physical - usually goes back several generations for such cruelty is learned behaviour. The hunted becomes the hunter, with a man or woman who has been abused or unnurtured as a child going on to perpetrate very similar abuses on his own offspring. Ironically, when these parents desert the child, it's often given to grandparents whose parenting methods left their own children with low self-esteem. William Allnutt, Rod Ferrell, Wendy Gardner and Johnny Garrett all fit into this category.

Older parents, who understandably have lower energy levels, can also pose a problem to their children if they see normal activity as hyperactivity and seek to curtail it, as happened with late baby Kip Kinkel. Older parents (and very young immature ones) can also have unrealistic expectations of what a child can offer them. Luke Woodham's mother demanded that her sons get A's at school then come straight home and offer her adult conversation. She even insisted on driving Luke the one mile journey to his school, refused to let him go to school dances and accompanied him on his pitifully few dates. Such parents presumably believed that they wanted children - but they refuse to let them be childlike.

This author once spoke to a children's charity worker who said the worst case of abuse she'd seen involved a professional woman who had waited until her late thirties before having her first child. She expected a textbook child and was soon complaining to neighbours that the baby 'wasn't playing properly' with its toys. By the time the child was a toddler she was so disturbed by its normal toddler-like playing that she shut it in a playpen and went out for the day. She did this every day until neighbours complained to the authorities and the horrendously neglected child was taken away.

## Traumatised brains

Some of these neglected and traumatised children's brains will develop differently to the brains of children raised in loving families. A Royal Society Of Medicine conference showed images of the brains of Romanian orphans who hadn't enjoyed normal adult-child playtimes or been shown love. The frontal-temporal areas of the children's brains were noticeably underdeveloped. As this area is responsible for regulating the emotions, these children showed abnormal emotional responses to everyday stimuli.

Professor Perry of the Child Trauma Academy in Houston commented on such brain abnormality in an article on the subject in *The Observer Magazine* (20th January 2002) and explained that 'Adverse experiences influence the mature brain, but in the developing brain they actually play a role in organising the neural system.' The Professor added that such understimulated children 'can have profound social problems, but are often very bright.'

The article also noted that the children who are understimulated by the parent are also often overstimulated by stress. (For example, if the parents are ignoring the child but hitting each other.) The article said that as a result of such ongoing fear, the children often had increased muscle tone, extreme sleep disturbances and abnormal heart regulation. Child psychiatrist Dr Dora Black added that this constant hyper-arousal was so unbearable that many of the sufferers turned to drink or drugs.

Dr Black said that, though later stimulation can improve the child's brain, prevention is better than cure and children should be removed from a toxic environment as soon as possible. Professor Perry added 'In order to solve the problems of violence, we need to change our childrearing practices. If not addressed, maltreatment in early life increases risk for substance abuse, mental health problems, school failure and criminality.'

## Generations of abuse

Most of the parents in this book will understandably be viewed by the reader as hate figures – but if this author had profiled *their* childhoods there would be equal sympathy for them. Thomas Pomeroy was battered by his father – and went on to batter his sons Jesse and Charles. James Pierson was slapped across the face so often by his parents that his friends were desperate to get him out of the house. When James became a father he would slap his three children across the face and was proud of his youngest daughter because she refused to cry.

Lou Wolf's early life was marred by a violent father who sexually abused Lou's sister, by an alcoholic stepfather and by a priest who took nude pictures of him whilst he was in care. In turn, Lou beat his own children, sexually abused his daughter Shirley and took explicit photos of her when she was small.

Ann and Robert Thompson senior had endured violent childhoods - and passed this violence on to their children. Johnny Garrett's mother Charlotte was so multiply-abused that she was in and out of psychiatric care. By marrying one violent man after another, she recreated this sexual, emotional and physically abusive hell for Johnny until his mind fractured and he too ended up mentally ill.

Betty Bell was frequently spanked by her mother and was terrified of her. By five she had developed eating disorders and her mother would also spank her for not eating. Upset after her father's death at age fourteen, she started staying out late and her mother gave her further hidings. An uncle also hit her

247

for stealing a purse from another relative. At fifteen she took an overdose of her mother's tranquillisers and almost died.

These individuals parented as they were parented and were unable to look clearly at the damage they were doing. As psychologist Dorothy Rowe has written 'until we meet the important needs we bring into adulthood from childhood we are not ready to take on the responsibilities of bringing up a child.'

## Zero tolerance

Psychologists such as Alice Miller have been writing for decades about the harm done by such so-called legitimate childhood punishment. Her book *Banished Knowledge: Facing Childhood Injuries* has received worldwide recognition. Other psychologists such as Gitta Sereny have made it clear that all children are born good and that 'the offending child is a symbol of family - and more than that, of societal - breakdown.'

In 1999 E Thompson overviewed 88 studies which showed that physical punishment led to less compliance in children aged two to six. It caused increased aggression in the child, an aggression which remained when that child grew up. The smacked children had less ability to empathise with others and had more mental health problems than children who weren't hit. They grew into adults who were more likely to hit their spouse and who had an increased probability of antisocial and criminal behaviour in adulthood.

Criminologist Lonnie Athens has written about why our value system wrongly believes that hitting is good and not hitting is bad. He says it stems from more warlike times when people believed that they had to toughen children up for when they went into battle. Ironically, corporal punishment in the home today continues to make children more warrior-like so that the violence goes on.

## Games adults play

It should be clear to the open minded reader by now that adults hitting children is both wrong and damaging. Yet many of the people who champion or tolerate such violence against minors are the first to mock eroticised corporal punishment between consenting adults.

In reality, they are entirely different. The adult who hits a child does so to cause pain and distress, whereas the dominant adult who hits a willing submissive adult does so to invoke pleasure. The first is an abuse of power whereas the second is a consensual power exchange.

In his book *Radical Desire* which looks at fetishism, bondage and domination, author Mark Ramsden explains that 'like most people with this sexuality, I have experienced much anguish along the way; partly because of the constraints imposed by the Christian religion and partly because of the myths propagated by the therapy industry.' He adds that 'Many otherwise liberal people still confuse S/M play with abuse. It is actually a reaction to abuse, an attempt to heal a deep wound.'

Many frequently-punished children end up with a sado-masochistic adult sexuality. No one knows exactly why this is, but perhaps children try to make sense of corporal punishment from supposedly caring parents by convincing themselves that this is a form of love. After all, they are frequently being told that it's for their own good. Or maybe the beatings just happen to occur at the same time as the libido is awakening so that sexual stimulus and blows become confused.

Whatever the reason, the punished child grows into an adult who has erotic fantasies involving discipline. For the first time ever, he or she can take a hated act and turn it into something where the ultimate result - in the form of an orgasm - is good. It's incredibly ironic that the adults who failed the child when he or she was being beaten now try to punish it again for its adult sexuality, calling it deviant or sick.

In truth, intelligent adult players in the BDSM (bondage, domination and sado-masochism) scene often go to great lengths to ensure that the only pain they offer is erotic. And anecdotal evidence suggests that these adults view spanking as an erotic act so they don't hit their kids.

Consensual sado-masochism is a world away from criminal sadistic acts where one person terrorises the other and causes intense fear and unendurable pain.

Ironically, many unthinking adults will criticise the man or woman who canes their partner for joint sexual release. Yet these same adults will champion an adult caning a helpless child.

## A voice of reason

Broadcaster and writer Claire Rayner OBE has fought energetically for an end to such violence towards children. She also has a long term interest in crime and has written many crime novels. This author interviewed her on 24th January 2002 whilst researching *Children Who Kill*.

Claire said that she'd first become interested in the subject when she was a child. 'I saw the way that adults lied and behaved towards children.' In 1939, at the age of eight, she became a wartime evacuee and had a very unhappy time.

When she grew up she became a nurse at the Royal Northern Hospital in London then studied midwifery at Guy's Hospital. She later became a Sister in the Paediatrics Department of the Whittington Hospital. Throughout her nursing career, she was appalled to see some of the nurses smacking sick children and she saw other children brought in with injuries caused by their parents. One night two little girls from different families were brought in dead, both killed by parental punishments that had gone too far.

Claire started to appear on radio programmes suggesting that parents shouldn't hit their children but in those days almost everyone regarded her viewpoint as stupid. The general public and the media believed that if children weren't beaten they would simply go wild.

But slowly the broadsheets started to come round to her way of thinking bolstered by the number of studies showing that it is children who are hit who have problems, not children from violence-free homes.

During these years she became well respected for her medical advice and published bestselling books on everything from sex education for children to home nursing. Everyone could see that her advice on a broad range of issues worked - yet many people still ignored her recommendations to stop hitting juveniles.

Asked why a significant percentage of the public is still in favour of smacking kids, Claire says it's because it's what they're used to so they think it's normal. So what would she say to those people who suggest that they were hit as children but that it didn't do them any harm? 'I'd tell them that you can't know how much harm has been done to you,' she says simply, adding that you can often see by such adult's aggressiveness or depression that they have been damaged by their early experiences.

In 1996 she was given an OBE for her services to women's issues and to health issues. In truth, she has done equally valid work to protect children. Yet it's still an uphill struggle with one child per week in Britain dying at its parent's hands.

Claire has never struck her own children, so they in turn have never struck their children. Asked which parenting guide she'd recommend she says *The No Smacking Guide To Good Behaviour* by Penelope Leach.


## No smacking

Penelope Leach is a childcare expert and research psychologist, the author of several bestselling parenting books and the writer of the aforementioned no smacking leaflet. The leaflet explains that 'giving up smacking altogether doesn't mean going soft on discipline' and 'children don't get spoiled because parents are gentle and try to treat them as people.' The leaflet stresses the importance of praising a child's good behaviour rather than ignoring the child until it does something bad. (For details of how to obtain this free leaflet please see the Appendix at the end of this book.)

Penelope spoke at the *Children Are Unbeatable* conference in January 2002, noting that child-beating was rooted in the historical belief that children were the property of the father and his to do with as he wished. In other words, children were originally domestic slaves.

She noted that today our government protects a wife from her husband, but not a child from its parent. Our most vulnerable citizens have the least protection under the law.

She's found that adults who were hit as children try to hide behind the mantra of protection, namely the belief that 'it didn't do me any harm.' This comes about because children blame themselves for the violence rather than blaming their parents. It is easier - in the short term - to deny the emotional hurt caused by these blows.

Penelope said that being struck was not a trivial matter and that it affected the hurt children strongly, though not in the way that its parents desired. In other words, a naughty child that was smacked became naughtier. She'd found that the more educated the parent, the less likely he or she was to hit.

Penelope has found that some parents try to minimise the amount of physical pain they cause their children whereas in the USA and France parents thought they had a moral justification for hurting their young. Indeed, Arizona and Arkansas recently passed laws strengthening the parental right to hit a child.

## Positive parenting

But more and more people are turning to positive parenting. In 2001, the Open School Network – in partnership with Save The Children – produced a video called We Can Work It Out, subtitled *Parenting With Confidence*. The video is a before and after look at children who were parented with criticism then parented with praise.

During the criticism-based parenting, the children behaved exactly as the adults did. That is, if the parent shouted then the child shouted. If the parent pointed aggressively then the child pointed aggressively. The segment was called *Copy Cats* and explained how 'much of our own behaviour determines the behaviour of our children.'

The parents then went on a parenting course and began to praise the good things that their children did rather than concentrating on the negative. The result was happier parents and more responsive children. Even parents with autistic children were helped as clinicians showed how to make a bedroom a pleasant place for an autistic child who had previously been very distressed when left in his room.

The video showed that children mainly felt fear when a parent was angry and that the child learned little or nothing from the verbal or physical assault. But when parents acknowledged their children's good behaviour - even the little things - the entire family became happier.

Parents on such positive parenting courses find that they get results when they are loving and give praise - not when they shout and criticise and hit.

## A planet without pain

Slowly, the world is becoming aware that corporal punishment by parents promotes violence and constitutes an assault. Sweden was one of the first to ban smacking, doing so in 1979. They've subsequently seen impressive reductions in youth convictions for theft and for alcohol abuse. At the moment, over fifty children a year die in Britain at their parent's hands and more than three-thousand children a year die in America at their parent's hands - but Sweden has only had one such death in the past seven years.

In 1983 Finland followed, as did Norway in 1987 and Austria in 1989. The nineties saw further strides towards abolition with Cyprus banning all corporal punishment in 1994, Latvia in 1998 and Croatia in 1999. Germany followed in 2000, for their research showed a clear link between hitting a child (which included even light smacking) and later adult violence. Italy, South Africa and Belgium have also made anti-corporal punishment statements that have yet to be confirmed in legislation. Sadly, both America and Britain still take a punitive stance.

Gavin de Becker, the survivor of a violent home, went on to establish a forty-six member agency which specialises in predicting violence. He has written that it is crucial that we stop mistreating children and view them 'not as temporary visitors who will someday grow into citizens, but as fully fledged, fully contributing, fully entitled members of our society just as they are right now.'

Murray Strauss, an expert on family violence has said 'I want to see a national effort to help people avoid using physical punishment... 99% of the physical punishment that goes on, parents don't want to hit their kids. They just feel it's necessary for the child's own good.' He adds that most of these parents haven't even considered alternative methodologies.

Strauss explains that when Sweden introduced a complete ban on smacking in 1979, three quarters of the population were against it. Nowadays, three quarters of Sweden's population are in favour of the ban.


## Moving on

But we don't have to wait for a change in the law before we create a non violent future. Adults who dare to recognise how their parents damaged them can avoid making the same mistakes.

Dorothy Rowe has written that though we may not be able to forgive such parents we can pity them 'just as we can pity the child we once were, and so remember our past with sadness and mourning. Those of us who suffered in childhood, and most of us did, can never again live in total bliss, but it is better to live freely with sadness than to trap ourselves in denial and depression.'

Sadly, at the moment such depression is rife. More than seven thousand people in the UK commit suicide each year. That is, someone kills themselves every seventy-nine minutes. And one in four people will be deemed mentally ill at any one time. Depression is now so common that it often goes unremarked and we are becoming a Prozac nation. The UK anti-depressant market is valued at 600 million pounds, the second largest in the world. It's no accident that both child abuse and subsequent adult depression are on the rise.

Paul Mones dedicates his book *When A Child Kills* 'to all the children who suffer silently at the hands of their parents.' He especially thanks those children he interviewed who have to read his words from the confines of their dimly lit cells.

Most of these children will eventually be freed and have their first chance of happiness - assuming they aren't killed by enraged members of the public. Ironically these members of the public will make no connection between their own humiliating childhoods and their current aggressive stance. So misery is passed on from generation to generation, for as the philosopher Santayana said 'those who cannot remember the past are condemned to repeat it.'

# APPENDIX: USEFUL INFORMATION

## Helpful organisations
Childline - a 24 hour free helpline that any child in distress can call.
Tel: 0800 1111

National Society For The Prevention Of Cruelty To Children - a 24 hour free helpline that anyone who fears a child is being hurt can call. Tel: 0800 800 500

Children Are Unbeatable, 77 Holloway Road, London, N7 8JZ - an alliance of organisations and individuals seeking legal reform to give children the same protection as adults under the law on assault. They also promote positive, non-violent discipline. For a membership form, send an SAE marked 'Please Send Membership Details.'

## Free leaflets
EPOCH, 77 Holloway Road, London, N7 8JZ. For a free copy of the leaflet *The Anti-Smacking Guide To Good Behaviour* by Penelope Leach, send an SAE marked 'Penelope Leach Leaflet.'

Kidscape, 2 Grosvenor Gardens, London, SW1W 0DH. For a free copy of the leaflet *Why My Child?* which helps parents deal with the sexual abuse of their child, send a large SAE marked 'Why My Child?'

## Recommended reading
*Banished Knowledge: Facing Childhood Injury* by Alice Miller (Virago, 1990)
*The Successful Self* by Dorothy Rowe (Harper Collins, 1993)
*Toxic Parents* by Dr Susan Forward (Bantam Press, 1990)
*The Gift Of Fear* by Gavin de Becker (Bloomsbury, 1997)

# SELECT BIBLIOGRAPHY

Bell, David *Murder Casebook: Staffordshire & The Black Country* Countryside Books, 1996

Bellini, Jon *Child's Prey* Pinnacle Books, 2001

Britton, Paul *The Jigsaw Man* Corgi Books, 1998

Carnes, Patrick *Out Of The Shadows: Understanding Sexual Addiction* CompCare Publishers, 1983

de Becker, Gavin *The Gift Of Fear* Bloomsbury, 1997

DeFelice, Jim *Kill Grandma For Me* Pinnacle Books, 1998

Elliott, Michelle (edited) *Female Sexual Abuse Of Children: The Ultimate Taboo* Longman, 1993

Eskapa, Roy *Bizarre Sex* Parrallel Books, 1995

Frasier, David K *Murder Cases Of The Twentieth Century* Macfarland, 1996

Gekoski, Anna *Murder By Numbers* Andre Deutsch, 1999

Hale, Don *Town Without Pity* Century, 2002

Hare, Robert *Without Conscience* Warner Books, 1994

Harrower, Julie *Applying Psychology To Crime* Hodder & Stoughton, 1998

Holt, John *How Children Fail* Penguin Books, 1964

Jackson, David *Destroying The Baby In Themselves* Mushroom Publications, 1995

Jacobs, David (edited) *Sex Sadists* Pinnacle Books, 2000

Jacobs, David (edited) *Too Young To Die* Pinnacle Books, 2001

Jones, Frank *Murderous Innocents* Headline, 1994

Kingsbury, Karen *Missy's Murder* Dell Publishing, 1991

Knox, Patricia *Troubled Children: A Fresh Look At School Phobia* The Self Publishing Association, 1990

Lane, Brian *The 1995 Murder Yearbook* Headline, 1994

Lasseter, Don (updated by) *Killer Kids* Pinnacle Books, 1998

Lewis, Dorothy Otnow *Guilty By Reason Of Insanity* Arrow Books, 1999

Leyton, Elliott *Sole Survivor* John Blake Publishing, 2001

Markman, Ronald & Bosco, Dominick *Alone With The Devil* Futura, 1991

Miller, Hugh *Unquiet Minds* Headline, 1995

Mones, Paul *When A Child Kills: Abused Children Who Kill Their Parents* Pocket Books, 1991

Morris, Greggory W *The Kids Next Door* William Morrow & Co, 1985

Morrison, Blake *As If* Granta Books, 1998

Newton, Michael *Killer Kids* Loompanics Unlimited, 2000

Pantziarka, Pan *Lone Wolf: True Stories Of Spree Killers* Virgin Publishing, 2000

Ramsden, Mark & Randall, Housk *Radical Desire* Serpent's Tail, 2000

Reel, Guy & Perrusquia, Mark & Sullivan, Bartholomew *The Blood Of Innocents* Pinnacle Books, 1995

Rowe, Dorothy *The Successful Self* Harper Collins, 1993

Sagar, Ron *Hull, Hell And Fire: The Extraordinary Story Of Bruce Lee* Highgate Publications (Beverley), 1999

Sereny, Gitta *The Invisible Children: Child Prostitution In America, Germany And Britain* Andre Deutsch, 1984

Sereny, Gitta *Cries Unheard: The Story Of Mary Bell* Macmillan, 1998

Sereny, Gitta *The Case Of Mary Bell* Pimlico, 1995

Schechter, Harold *Fiend* Pocket Books, 2000

Smith, David James *The Sleep Of Reason* Century, 1994

Thomas, Mark *Every Mother's Nightmare* Pan Books, 1993

Tutt, Norman (edited) *Violence* HMSO, 1976

Ward, Bernie *Families Who Kill* Pinnacle Books, 1993

Wilson, Colin *A Plague Of Murder* Robinson, 1995

Wilson, Patrick *Children Who Kill* Michael Joseph, 1973

## Magazines, reports and leaflets

*Be A Great Mum* column in *Best*, 19th March 2002. Article by Julia Goodwin on how to encourage children's compassion.

*Child Abuse* leaflet Kidscape.

*It Is Our World Too! A report on the lives of disabled children.* For the UN General Assembly Special Session On Children. By Gerison Lansdown New York, September 2001.

*Insider* magazine vol 2 no 5 *Pets In Prison*. Article by Peter J Lewis.

*Master Detective*, February 2002. Article *Teenage Rage* by Micky Cohen.

*Observer Magazine*, 20th January 2002. Feature *Back To The Beginning* by Jo Carlowe.

*Prevent Bullying: A Parents Guide* leaflet Kidscape.

*Protect Children From Paedophiles* leaflet Kidscape

*Stop Bullying* leaflet Kidscape.
*You Can Beat Bullying* leaflet Kidscape.


## Webography

*Children Are Unbeatable* www.childrenareunbeatable.org.uk
*The True Crime Library* http://crimelibrary.com


## Filmography

*The James Bulger Story* Broadcast in Britain on Channel Five 2000.

*A Killer Among Friends* Bonnie Raskins Production in association with Green Epstein. Broadcast courtesy of Lorimar Television.

*The Kids That Kill: The Killer At Thurston High* Broadcast in Britain on Channel Four 2000. WGBH/Frontline Co-production with The Kirk Documentary Group.

*Manhunt: Catching A Child Killer* Broadcast in Britain on ITV 2001. Ray Fitzwalter Associates.

*Paedophile Priests* Correspondent. Broadcast BBC2 17th March 2002.

*Sexual Abuse Within The Family* Kilroy talk show. Broadcast BBC1 March 2002.

*Unforgiven: The Boys Who Murdered James Bulger* Despatches investigation for Channel 4. Broadcast 2000.

*We Can Work It Out: Parenting With Confidence* An Open School Network Production in association with Save The Children. Produced 2001.

# INDEX

murder, attempted 17, 18, 24, 87, 143, 169, 175, 220, 221, 222, 223
murder, statistics 15, 18, 19, 239

Nelme, Samuel 34-35
NSPCC 207

oral sex, forced 32, 117, 123, 155, 162, 201, 202, 223
organised killer 27, 193

PACE 183
paedophiles 81, 99, 123, 199, 200, 203, 205, 223, 225, 230, 235, 236
Pantziarka, Pan 167, 258
para-suicide 94-95, 228
parentally-encouraged killer 177-179
Patient's Pets 206
patricide 139, 166, 207
Perry, Michael 175
Pica, Benjamin 42, 43
Pica, JoAnn 38-43, 45, 46
Pica, Joe 42
Pica, Sean 37, 42-47
Pica, Vincent 42
Pierson, Cathleen 37-41, 45
Pierson, Cheryl 37-47, 229, 232, 233, 236, 237
Pierson, James 37-41, 43-46, 232, 247
Pierson, Jimmy 37, 39, 45
Pierson, JoAnn 38-41
Pomeroy, Charles 21, 23, 25, 26, 27, 29
Pomeroy, Jesse 21-32, 175, 207, 228, 241
Pomeroy, Ruth 21, 25, 27, 30
Pomeroy, Thomas 21, 22, 25, 247
pornography, adult 229-230
pornography, child 85, 86, 162, 223
Prozac 137, 143, 231, 254
prostitution 48, 122, 125, 127, 129, 144, 166, 205, 221
psychopaths 25, 64, 129, 152, 194, 196, 197, 204, 215, 227, 240
pulp fiction 29